PRESBYTERIAN

NATIONAL UNION CONVENTION,

HELD IN THE

CITY OF PHILADELPHIA,

NOVEMBER 6TH, 1867.

(MINUTES AND PHONOGRAPHIC REPORT.)

For they shall see eye to eye, when the Lord shall bring again Zion. Isaiah lii. 8.

That they all may be one; as thou Father art in me, and I in thee, that they also may be one in us; that the world may believe that thou hast sent me. John xvii. 21.

PHILADELPHIA:
JAS. B. RODGERS, PRINTER, 52 & 54 NORTH SIXTH STREET.
1868.

NOTE.

In sending forth this document to the public a few remarks of an explanatory and apologetic character may be proper:

First, The delay in its publication has been mainly due to the fact that the Phonographic Reporters were unable at once to transcribe their work for the printer.

Second, There were three such Reporters reporting the proceedings during as many different stages of the sessions of the Convention; hence any apparent diversity in the character of the Reporters may be accounted for.

Third, The reports of speeches and prayers would doubtless have been more to the satisfaction of the respective authors, if, before being sent to Press, they could have been submitted to them for revision. But in the nature of the case—the range of speakers embracing perhaps fifty persons, scattered over an area of two thousand miles,—this was found, without great difficulty and delay, to be impossible.

Fourth, In a few instances the names of the speakers were not at the time obtained either by the Secretaries or the Reporters, and it was found impossible from memory to supply them. Speeches and prayers in such cases are ascribed to "A Delegate."

Fifth, Great difficulty has been experienced in revising and correcting the Roll. During the sessions of the Convention, owing to the shortness of the time, and the press of devotion and business, it was found impossible to do this: and after the adjournment the work was assigned to a competent committee, consisting of one from each branch of the church represented, in connection with the Secretary on the ground, who, it is believed, have made the Roll as nearly perfect as was possible under the circumstances. Still there may be errors which will be observed by persons immediately concerned.

Finally, It has been no small work in the brief time allowed, and with pressing pulpit and pastoral duties on hand, to prepare this document for publication. The work has mainly devolved upon the junior and resident Secretary, in connection with the Rev. Dr. Grier, editor of the Presbyterian; Rev. W. W. Barr of the United Presbyterian Church; and Prof. B. F. Kendall of the New School Branch. It is now sent forth to the churches in accordance with the order of the Convention itself, and with the prayer and hope that its circulation may do something toward perpetuating and even increasing the blessed spirit of Christian unity, the exhibition of which, in what was, perhaps, one of the most remarkable gatherings of the disciples of Jesus since the day of Pentecost, was so marked and glorious: and in this way contribute to the bringing on of that blessed consummation for which the Convention labored and prayed.

WILLIAM T. EVA, Jun. Sec'y.

PRESBYTERIAN

NATIONAL UNION CONVENTION.

THIS Convention originated in a proposal made in the Synod of the Reformed Presbyterian Church, at its meeting in the city of New York, in May, 1867, by George H. Stuart, Esq., an Elder in that body; in reference to which, the following resolutions were adopted:

Whereas, The interests of the cause of Christ require us, at this time, to inaugurate measures to heal Zion's breaches and to bring into one the divided portions of the Presbyterian family; therefore,

Resolved, That this Synod recommend to the several Presbyterian judicatories, now met or soon to meet, to unite with us in calling a General Convention of the Presbyterian Churches of the United States, to meet in the city of Philadelphia, on the second Wednesday of September next, or at such time and place as may be agreed upon, for prayer and conference in regard to the terms of union and communion among the various branches of the Presbyterian family.

Resolved, That we recommend that the said Convention shall consist of a minister and a ruling elder from each Presbytery.

Resolved, That certified copies of this action be immediately communicated, by the Clerk of the Synod, to the bodies included in this call.

Resolved, That each body represented in said Convention shall, without respect to number of delegates, be entitled to an equal vote on all questions submitted for decision.

Resolved, That the delegates appointed by the Presbyteries of this Church be required to report to this Synod for its action at its next meeting, the result reached by the Convention.

Resolved, That Rev. J. N. Mc Leod, D.D., Rev. T. W. J. Wylie, D.D., and Geo. H. Stuart, Esq., be and they are hereby appointed a Committee of Arrangement and Correspondence in regard to such Convention.

The time for the meeting of the Convention was afterwards changed by the Committee to the 6th of November.

In the month of September, on the 24th day, in response to a circular letter issued by the Committee, a number of Ministers and Elders of the different branches of the Presbyterian Church, met in the city of Philadelphia to make arrangements for the assembling of the Convention. At this meeting the following Address was adopted and ordered to be published, signed by the Chairman and Secretary, in the different Presbyterian religious newspapers:

TO THE PRESBYTERIES OF THE UNITED STATES.

Fathers and Brethren—Allow us respectfully to call your attention to the invitation addressed to all the churches of the Presbyterian order, to assemble in convention in the city of Philadelphia, on the first Wednesday of November next, "for prayer and conference to promote union and communion among the various branches of the Presbyterian family." That all these now divided departments of the Church of Christ *should* be one, is universally admitted; that they *will* be one, cannot be doubted. It is proposed to ascertain if the time has *now* come when they *can be* one; and if so, to take measures to accomplish this grand result. The present condition of our country, with slavery abolished and peace restored, now more than ever *united* in all its parts—the movements of a similar kind in the lands of our fathers—the urgent necessity there is for a combination of resources and energies, in order to supply the spiritual wants of the destitute at home, and to extend the Gospel among the heathen—and, especially, the evident influences of the Divine Spirit leading the people of God earnestly to desire and pray for the re-union of all who love the Saviour and seek for the redemption of our world—all these considerations lead us to hope that "the time to favor Zion" in this regard, "yea the set time, is come."

Will you, dear brethren, give your co-operation by appointing a minister and ruling elder to attend this meeting?

We are, dear brethren, your friends and fellow-servants in the love of the great God our Saviour.

ALEXANDER REED, *Chairman.*
WILLIAM T. EVA, *Secretary.*

The *place* appointed for the meeting of the Convention, was the First Reformed Presbyterian Church, Philadelphia. And the Pastors of the churches of the several branches of the Presbyterian family to be represented in the Convention, were required to make it a subject of special public prayer on the Sabbath preceding its assembling. It was also asked that there should "be much and earnest prayer in the closet, at the family altar, the social meeting, and the public congregation, on behalf of this first convocation of Churches of a common ancestry and of the same ecclesiastical order." Beside which, a general Union Prayer Meeting was appointed for the evening previous—Tuesday, the 5th inst., in the church at Philadelphia, to be continued on Wednesday morning at 10 o'clock.

At the Tuesday evening meeting, the Pastor of the church, Rev. T. W. J. Wylie, D.D. presided; and it was an occasion of such interest, that it was resolved to hold an *Elders'* prayer-meeting at 9 o'clock, the next morning. The general prayer-meeting continued, was also held at 10 o'clock, led by the Rev. B. W. Chidlaw of Cincinnati, Ohio.

The Convention was called for 11 o'clock, A. M., and when the hour arrived a large number of delegates and others, were found, "with one accord in one place," beseeching a blessing from on high to rest upon those who should come together, and upon their deliberations and acts.

First Reformed Presbyterian Church, Philadelphia.
Wednesday, November 6th, 1867, 11½ *A. M.*

The Convention was called to order by the Rev. W. W. Barr of the United Presbyterian Church, on whose motion George H. Stuart, Esq., was elected temporary Chairman.

On taking the chair, the Chairman announced that the first business in order was the appointment of a temporary secretary, when, on motion of Rev. Wm. T. Eva, the Rev. G. D. Archibald, D.D., of the Old School branch of the Church, was chosen to that office.

The Chairman called upon the Rev. David Blair, of the United Presbyterian Church, the oldest minister present, who opened the Convention with prayer.

The 100th Psalm, L. M.

All people that on earth do dwell, etc.

was announced and sung by the Convention, standing.

The Chairman then read the 4th chapter of the Epistle to the Ephesians, and addressed the Convention in these words:—

Fathers and Brethren—Members of the same household of faith, and heirs to the same blessed inheritance, in the name of our once crucified and now ascended Redeemer, we hail your gathering to-day as the harbinger of better and brighter days for our now divided Zion, and for the cause of Christ in this land and in the world. This is the first general Convocation of Presbyterian churches in America. We hail your appearing in the midst of us; we believe every delegate has come up in the spirit of fervent love to Christ; and that you believe in the Unity of the Church, and have been praying for its manifestation in your closets, at your family altars, in the fellowship meetings, as well as in your great congregational gatherings. We rejoice in your meeting together in Philadelphia, and in the name of all the Presbyterian Churches here, we welcome you to this city of Brotherly Love—to our homes, to our hearts, to our heart of hearts, to our churches and our pulpits—and gladly hail you as brethren and fellow-servants of Christ.

It may not be out of place briefly to sketch the origin of this Convention. I have been, as I suppose many here have been, long praying and hoping for such a Convention. At the last meeting of the General Synod of the Reformed Presbyterian Church, held in New York in May last, I felt constrained from a high sense of duty to propose a preamble and a series of resolutions, which, after some slight modifications, were adopted as follows:—

Mr. Stuart here read the resolutions, found on page 5.

It was at first intended that the Convention should meet in September, but many important considerations led to its change to this day. The great object of our assembling is to give opportunity for prayer and conference in regard to the organic union of the whole Presbyterian family in the land. Oh, Dear Brethren! that we could realize the full value of prayer! It seems to me that Payson caught a glimpse of the value of prayer, which we need, when, as he stood near the kingdom of glory he exclaimed, "If I were permitted to return to earth again I should spend half my life in prayer." If this spirit of prayer be here, our conference will be sweet, and pleasant, and useful. Let us remember the purpose for which we are convened; we do not come to set up our denominational banners, or to gather around the standard of any one church; we come rather to unfurl the banner of King Jesus, to gather around the standard of the cross.

Union is the order of the day among the nations of the world. Union is the great object for which we have been contending in our own land, and our efforts for which, God has so wondrously crowned with success. I never knew the value of union among the followers of Christ, until I stood upon our recent battle fields and heard men from different sections of Christ's Church speaking of Jesus and his salvation, and singing the songs of Zion, with those who were standing in their grave-clothes. Satan is, Brethren, marshalling his forces; Christ, the great King and Head of the Church, is calling us to come together; a voice comes to us from the colonies of the mother country where union has been already accomplished. It comes also from the Presbyterian Churches of Scotland and England, where they are happily and hopefully seeking a union of their divided forces. It comes, too, from the graves of Thomas Brainerd and John M. Krebbs, the respected Chairmen of the Committees of the Old and New School Churches on Union, now joined together in glory.

The eyes of the Church are upon us. A cry comes to us from earth's perishing millions to close up our ranks, and to go forward to the conquest of the world for our blessed Immanuel. I hope that the spirit which has pervaded the prayer-meetings of last evening and this morning, may guide all our deliberations. I use not the words of man but of Holy Scripture, in invoking upon you the blessing of God, praying "that "Christ may dwell in your hearts by faith, that ye, being rooted and "grounded in love, may be able to comprehend with all saints what "is the breadth, and length, and depth, and height, and to know the "love of Christ, which passeth knowledge, that ye may be filled with "all the fulness of God. Now unto him that is able to do exceeding "abundantly above all that we ask or think, according to the power "that worketh in us, unto him be glory in the Church by Christ Jesus, "throughout all ages, world without end. Amen."

The Chair is now ready for business.

On motion of Rev. J. Howard Suydam of the Reformed Protestant Dutch Church, a Committee on Credentials, consisting of one minister and one elder from each branch of the Church represented in the Convention, was appointed, as follows:—

Reformed Dutch,	Rev. J. H. Suydam,
	Elder James Peters.
Pres., New School,	Rev. J. Fewsmith, D.D.,
	Elder Jas. B. Pinneo.

Reformed Pres.,	Rev. Jno. N. McLeod, D.D.
	Elder William Blair.
Pres., Old School,	Rev. Cyrus Dickson, D.D.,
	Elder William Rankin, Jr.
United Pres.,	Rev. A. G. Wallace,
	Elder R. C. Stewart.
Cumberland Pres.,	Rev. A. B. Miller,
	Elder Robert Carr.

The Rev. John N. McLeod, D.D., Reformed Presbyterian, remarked that it might at some point during the Convention be of importance to have read the official record of the proceedings of the late Reformed General Synod, so far as they related to the call for this meeting under which the Convention were now acting; and stated that, as Clerk of that Synod, he had in his possession, and here, the original documents pertaining to the call.

Rev. George Duffield, Jr., New School, moved the appointment of a Committee to consist of one minister and one elder from each branch, to nominate officers for the permanent organization of the Convention, except the President, which being adopted, he moved that George H. Stuart, Esq., be elected permanent President, which was carried by acclamation. Rev. G. Archibald, D.D., was also in the same way elected permanent Secretary.

The Committee was appointed, consisting of the following persons:—

New School,	Rev. George Duffield, Jr.,
	Elder George W. Beale.
Old School,	Rev. S. L. Yerkes, D.D.,
	Elder Robert Carter.
United Pres.,	Rev. Matthew Clarke,
	Elder William Getty.
Reformed Pres.,	Rev. Samuel Young,
	Elder J. C. McMillan.
Reformed Prot., Dutch,	Rev. J. W. Schenck,
	Elder James Peters, M.D.
Cumberland Pres.,	Rev. J. N. Edmiston,
	Elder Robert Carr.

On motion of Rev. Jno. Eagleson, D.D., Old School, it was

Resolved, That all persons who furnish the Committee on Credentials, with satisfactory evidence of their having been regularly appointed, shall be entitled to seats as delegates, and that the Committee be so instructed.

Rev. W. T. Eva, on behalf of the Committee of Arrangements, recommended, which was adopted, that the hours of meeting and adjournment of the Convention in its daily sessions, be fixed as follows:—Meet at 9 o'clock, A. M., and adjourn at 12, M.; meet at 3 o'clock, P.M., and adjourn at 5, P.M.; meet at 7½ o'clock, P.M., and adjourn by motion; and that the first hour of each morning session be spent in devotional exercises.

Adjourned until 3 o'clock, P.M.

Concluded with prayer by Rev. Robert J. Breckinridge, D.D.

Wednesday, November 6th, 3 o'clock, P.M.

The Convention was called to order by the President.

Prayer was offered by the Rev. Edwin F. Hatfield, D.D., N. S.

The minutes of the morning session were read and approved.

The Committee on the Nomination of Permanent officers of the Convention reported, recommending the following, which was adopted:

President, George H. Stuart, Esq., as already elected.

Vice Presidents,

Old School,	Rev. Charles C. Beatty, D.D., L L.D.
New School,	Rev. Samuel W. Fisher, D.D., L.L.D.
Reformed Pres.,	Rev. Jno. N. McLeod, D.D.
United Pres.,	Rev. Wm. Davidson, D.D.
Reformed Prot., Dutch,	Rev. J. H. Suydam,
Cumberland Pres.,	Rev. David Cooper, D.D.

Secretaries,

Old School,	Rev G. D. Archibald, D. D., as already elected,
United Pres.,	Rev. R. D. Harper, D.D.
New School,	Rev. Wm. T. Eva.

The Chairman of the Committee, Rev. George Duffield, Jr., also asked for instructions as to whether they should report the names of a Permanent Business Committee. The Rev. D. V. McLean, D.D., Old School, moved that they be instructed to report such a committee, consisting of one minister and one elder from each branch represented in the Convention.

Rev. Dr. Breckinridge, (Old School,) opposed the appointment of a Business Committee as likely to tie the hands of the Convention. He preferred that every member of the body should have freedom in offering suggestions. He would inquire what purpose was to be subserved by this committee.

REV. MR. DUFFIELD.—The Doctor himself is nominated as one of the members.

DR. BRECKINRIDGE seemed to regard this assertion as an insult, and alluded to the previous speaker as "that young man."

REV. DR. MUSGRAVE, (O. S.,) opposed the resolution. He desired to know whether members of the body would be permitted to submit independent resolutions to the house, and whether such resolutions would be considered independent of the action of the Business Committee concerning them.

DR. McLEAN stated that he made the motion to facilitate the business of the house. Every member, in his opinion, had a right to introduce business for the consideration of the Convention.

The resolution was adopted, and the committee was reported and appointed, as follows:

United Pres.,	Rev. A. G. Wallace,
	Elder R. C. Stewart.
Old School,	Rev. Robert J. Breckinridge, D.D.,
	Elder Hon. Chas. D. Drake.
New School,	Rev. Henry B. Smith, D.D.,
	Elder Hon. Henry W. Williams, LL.D.
Ref'd Prot., Dutch,	Rev. J. M. Schenck,
	Elder Joseph Campbell.
Reformed Pres.,	Rev. Wm. S. Bratton,
	Elder Wm. Blair, M.D.
Cumberland Pres.,	Rev. A. B. Miller, D.D.,
	Elder Robert Carr.

REV. J. H. SUYDAM, from the Committee on Credentials, presented the following report:

That they have examined the credentials put into their hands, and heard the statements of gentlemen not bearing credentials but who say they are appointed either by the Presbytery or Synod to which they belong; and have arranged their names in alphabetical order, with the denominational name, and the Presbytery or Classis to which they are attached, set over against them.

They have in every case enrolled the principal delegates, and if their alternates are present it is suggested that they answer in the name of the principal, and report themselves to the Secretaries.

There are a few exceptional cases which your committee refer to the Convention for action: One that of Rev. J. H. Huntingdon of California, who has been requested to sit as a delegate by some of the brethren of his Presbytery, although not regularly appointed. Another is that of Elder A. Bierce, Esq., who is appointed by the church to which he belongs. Another still, is that of Rev. D. V. McLean, D.D., of the Presbytery of Monmouth, who states, that the Presbytery authorizes any one of their body who may be present to sit, as their representative, although a regular delegate had been appointed.

Your committee recommend that those gentlemen be admitted to seats, and if there are any others present whose circumstances are similar to these, that they also be considered delegates, and be requested to hand their names to the Secretaries.

Respectfully Submitted,

J. HOWARD SUYDAM.

Rev. W. S. Bratton, (Reformed Presbyterian,) said: I have something to offer as a substitute for the report:—

That inasmuch as the Convention in its organization has departed from the plan proposed by the last Synod of the Reformed Presbyterian Church; therefore,

Resolved, That the Convention be regarded as the Convention of the day.

Mr. President, I believe this is a necessity, and that we cannot carry out the full design of the Synod of the Reformed Presbyterian Church, and the spirit of the members of that Synod, otherwise. I feel that in justice to the Synod of the Reformed Presbyterian Church, something like that should be adopted. It would be more speedy; it would be better for all concerned; it would be better for all the churches represented, to step aside from the plan of the General Convention, and simply make it the Convention for the day. Already our churches have departed from the general design. The Old-school Presbyterian Church has appointed delegates by Presbyteries, and from some Presbyteries more than the number originally contemplated. I think that justice to the Reformed Presbyterian Church, and the good and welfare of the Convention, require that we should take some such course as this.

The President:—The call of the Convention simply *recommended* the appointment of a minister and a ruling elder from each Presbytery. What is the pleasure of the Convention in reference to the resolution just offered? If the Chair is asked for his opinion, it seems to be entirely uncalled for. Whether they came by ones or threes, by rail or steamboat, it seems they came together to pray over this question of union.

Rev. J. M. Morton, (R. P.) Is this an amendment to the report?

Rev. Mr. Bratton:—It is a substitute for the report of the Committee.

Rev. Mr. Morton:—Now, do we understand that can be made as a substitute for the report, or not?

The President:—The Chair decides it cannot; it is entirely foreign. It will have to be offered subsequently.

The report of the Committee was adopted.

The Committee also reported the roll of names of members of the Convention, which, as afterwards corrected and completed, was ordered to be recorded, as follows:

OLD SCHOOL PRESBYTERIAN CHURCH.

NAME.	PRESBYTERY.	POST OFFICE.	STATE.
Rev. James Allison,	Allegheny City,	Pittsburgh,	Pa.
" G. D. Archibald, D.D.,	New York 1st,	New York,	N. Y.
Elder E. C. Bridgeman,	" "	"	N. Y.
" David N. Byram,	Monmouth,	Red Bank,	N. J.
Rev. F. W. Brauns,	West Jersey,	Salem,	"
" F. R. Brace,	"	Blackwoodtown,	"
" H. N. Brinsmade,	Passaic,	Newark,	"
" James M. Burchfield,	Allegheny City,		Pa.
" John M. Barnett,	Red Stone,	Mount Pleasant,	"
" W. Y. Brown,	Huntingdon,	Port Royal,	"
" Jacob Belville,	Luzerne,	Mauch Chunk,	"
" Robert A. Brown,	Donegal,	Columbia,	"
Elder F. G. Bailey,	Ohio,	Pittsburgh,	"
Rev. L. G. Bell,	Southern Iowa,	Monmouth,	Ill.
" R. J. Breckinridge, D.D.	Kentucky,	Danville,	Ky.
" C. C. Beatty, D.D., LL.D.	Steubenville,	Steubenville,	Ohio.
Elder D. N. Bryan,	Monmouth,		N. J.
" James Blake,	Indianapolis,		Ind.
" E. R. Bower,	Miami,	Oxford,	Pa.
Rev. E. D. Bryan,	Newton,		N. J.
" A. M. Beveridge,	Troy,	Lansingburg,	N. Y.
Elder Robert Carter,	New York 3rd,	New York,	"
Rev. Charles W. Cooper,	Long Island,	Babylon,	L. I.
" Charles C. Corss,	Synod of N. Jersey,	East Smithfield,	N. J.
" Wm. C. Cattell, D.D.,	Philadelphia 2nd,	Philada.	Pa.
" Thomas Creigh, D.D.	Carlisle,	Mercersburg,	"
Hon. Judge Collins,	Luzerne,	Wilkesbarre,	"
Elder Cornelius Collins,	Donegal,	Middle Octorara,	"
Rev. L. W. Chapman,	Whitewater,	Richmond,	Ind.
" J. N. Candee, D.D.,	Warren,	Galesburg,	Ill.
Elder D. M. Chapin,	Ogdensburg,	Ogdensburg,	N. Y.
" A. E. Chamberlain,	Cincinnati,	Cincinnati,	Ohio.
Rev. R. Davidson, D.D.,	Long Island,	Huntingdon,	L. I.
" Robert P. Dubois,	New Castle,	New London.	Pa.
" Alex. Donaldson, D.D.,	Saltsburg,	Eldersridge,	"
" Cyrus Dickson, D.D.,	Baltimore,	Baltimore,	Md.
Elder Robert Cornelius,	Philada. 2nd,	Philadelphia,	Pa.
" L. J. Drake,	Sydney,	W. Liberty,	Ohio.
" James W. Dale, D.D.,	Philadelphia,	Media.	Pa.
" S. C. Day,	New Albany,	New Albany,	Ind.
Hon. Chas D. Drake,	St. Louis,	Washington, D.C.	Mo.
Elder W. P. Erney,	Raritan,	Frenchtown,	N. J.
Rev. J. S. Elder,	Clarion,	Limestone,	"
" Jonathan Edwards, D.D.,	Ohio,	Canonsburg,	Pa.
" Otho Evans,	Miami,	Franklin,	Ohio.
Elder Wm. Eaglesfield,	Crawfordsville,	Terre Haute,	Ind.
Rev. Ebenezer Erskine,	Rock River,	Chicago,	Ill.
" John Eagleson, D.D.,	Upper Buffalo,	Upper Buffalo,	Pa.
Hon. Wm. M. Francis,	Beaver,	New Wilmington,	Pa.
Daniel N. Freeland,	Hudson,	Monroe,	N. Y.
Elder Joseph Fithian, M.D.,	West Jersey,	Woodbury,	N. J.

NAME.	PRESBYTERY.	POST OFFICE.	STATE.
Elder Winthrop S. Gilman,	New York 1st,	New York,	N. Y.
Rev. M. S. Goodale, D.D.,	Albany,	Amsterdam,	"
Chancellor H. W. Green,	New Brunswick,		N. J.
Rev. P. H. Golliday,	Oxford,	Harrison,	Ohio.
J. M. Glover,	Sidney,	West Liberty,	"
Rev. S. C. Hepburn,	Hudson, (alt.)	Goshen,	N. Y.
Elder John M. Harper,	Philadelphia,	Philadelphia	Pa.
Rev. Isaac N. Hays,	Carlisle,	Middlespring,	"
" George Hill,	Blairsville,	Blairsville,	"
" J. Addison Henry,	Central Philada.,	West Philada.,	"
Elder Joseph Harvey,	" "	Philadelphia,	"
Rev. W. H. Hornblower,	Passaic,	Patterson,	N. J.
Prof. F. W. Hastings,	"	"	"
Rev. Charles Hodge, D.D.	New Brunswick,	Princeton,	"
" Wm. E. Hunt,	Zanesville,	Coshocton,	Ohio.
" R. Irwin, Junior,	Crawfordsville,	Waveland,	Ind.
" J. Jones,	Genesee River,	Genesee,	N. Y.
" John L. Janeway, D.D.,	Raritan,	Flemington,	N. J.
" D. Junkin, D.D.,	Beaver,	Newcastle,	Pa.
Elder David Johnson,	Steubenville,	Richmond,	Ohio.
" Joseph K. Johnson,	Zanesville,	Zanesville,	"
Rev. Everard Kempshall,	Elizabethtown,	Elizabeth,	N. J.
" Luther Littell,	Hudson,	Mount Hope,	N. Y.
" Aaron L. Lindsley,	Connecticut,	South Salem,	"
Elder James M. Lasher,	Albany,	Schenectady,	"
Samuel Linn,	Huntingdon,		Pa.
Rev. R. W. Landis, D.D.,	Kentucky,	Danville,	Ky.
" S. C. Logan,	Lake,	Pittsburg,	Pa.
Elder W. C. Lawson,	Northumberland,		"
Rev. L. Merrill Miller, D.D.	Ogdensburg,	Ogdensburg,	N. Y.
" Thomas Murphy,	Philadelphia 2nd,	Frankford,	Pa.
" George S. Mott.	Newton,	Newton,	N. J.
" D. V. McLean, D.D.	Monmouth,	Red Bank,	"
Elder Wm. W. Marsh,	Newton,	Hackettstown,	"
Rev. Thomas McAuley,	"	"	"
" Samuel Miller,	Burlington,	Mount Holly,	"
Col. Wm. R. Murphy,	"	"	"
Rev. S. C. McCune,	Huntingdon,	McVeytown,	Pa.
" George Marshall, D.D.,	Ohio,	Upper St. Clair,	"
Elder James Macfarlane,	Synod of N. Jersey,	Tonawanda,	"
Rev. G. W. Musgrave, D.D.,	Central Philada..	Philadelphia,	"
" Samuel Mahaffey,	St. Clairsville,	Washington,	Ohio,
" Algernon McMaster,	New Lisbon,	Poland,	"
" J. G. Monfort, D.D.,	Cincinnati,	Cincinnati,	"
" W. C. McCune,	"	"	"
Elder J. W. Monfort,	Indianapolis,		Ind.
" M. Mulford,	Passaic,		N. J.
Rev. O. H. Miller,	Redstone,	West Newton,	Pa.
" Geo. M. McLean, M.D.,		New Brunswick,	N. J.
" Joseph Nesbitt,	Northumberland,	Lockhaven,	Pa.
" J. L. Nevins,	Ningpo,	China.	
" S. J. Nichols, D.D.,	St. Louis,	St. Louis,	Mo.
Elder David Olyphant,	Synod of N. Jersey,	Morristown,	N. J.
Rev. Wilson Phraner,	New York 2nd,	Sing Sing,	N. Y.
" John T. Pomeroy,	New Castle,	Parkersburg,	Pa.
Elder John Palmer,	Connecticut,		Conn.
" N. Grier Parke,	Luzerne,	Pittston,	Pa.
Hon. Cyrus L. Pershing,	Blairsville,	Johnstown,	"

NAME.	PRESBYTERY.	POST OFFICE.	STATE.
Rev. D. W. Patterson,	Donegal,	Lancaster,	Pa.
" Jno. H. Pratt,	Hocking,	Athens,	Ohio.
" M. A. Parkinson,	Steubenville,	Bloomingdale,	"
" Wm. Jeffrey Park,	Wooster,	Fredericksburg,	"
" Alexander Rankin,	Buffalo City,	Black Rock,	N. Y.
Elder Wm. Rankin, Junior,	Passaic,	Newark,	N. J.
Rev. J. D. Randolph,	Raritan,	Frenchtown,	"
" E. H. Reinhart,	Elizabethtown,	Elizabethport,	"
Elder Wm. G. Reed,	Carlisle,	Chambersburg,	Pa.
Rev. R. H. Richardson, D.D.	Londonderry,	Newburyport,	Mass.
" Addison K. Strong.	Mohawk,	Syracuse,	N. Y.
" A. W. Sproull,	Philadelphia,	Chester,	Pa.
" J. M. Stevenson, D.D.,	New York 1st,	New York,	N. Y.
Elder John Stewart,	" "	"	"
Rev. Morris C. Sutphen,	" 2nd,	"	"
" Wm. D. Snodgrass, D.D.,	Hudson,	Goshen,	"
" Daniel Stuart, D.D.,	Albany,	Johnston,	"
" Joseph G. Symmes,	Synod of N. Jersey,	Cranberry.	N. J.
" Wm. E. Schenck, D.D.,	Philadelphia,	Philadelphia,	Pa.
Elder John Sutton,	Saltsburgh,	Indiana,	"
" A. K. Strong,	Luzerne,	Pittstown,	"
" Robert Sloan,		Buffalo,	"
Rev. Sylvester F. Scovel,	Ohio,	Pittsburgh,	"
Elder A. Sterling, Junior,	Baltimore,	Baltimore,	Md.
Rev. Samuel Steele, D.D.,	Chillicothe,	Hillsborough,	Ohio.
Elder Josiah Scott,	Oxford,	Hamilton,	"
Rev. Alexander Scott,	Richland,	Savannah,	"
Elder J. A. Scott,	Maumee,	Toledo,	"
Rev. Robert F. Sample,	St. Paul,	St. Anthony,	Min.
" J. P. Safford, D.D.,	New Albany,	New Albany,	Ind.
Elder J. W. Scott,	West Lexington,		Pa.
Rev. S. S. Sheddon, D.D.,	Elizabeth,	Rahway,	N. J.
" J. W. Torrence,	Beaver,	Clark,	Pa.
" H. A. True,	Marion,	Marion,	Ohio.
" Adam Torrence,	Blairsville,	New Alexandria,	Pa.
Elder G. B. Temple,	West Lexington,	" "	"
" G. L. Taney,	New Brunswick,		N. J.
Rev. Justus T. Umsted,	New Castle,	Cochranville,	Pa.
Elder Ashbel Welsh,	Raritan,		N. J.
Rev. Jos. K. Wright,	North River,	New Hamburg,	N. Y.
" D. J. Waller,	Northumberland,	Bloomsburg,	Pa.
Elder George F. Wiggan,	Luzerne,	Mahanoy City,	"
Rev. R. H. Williams,	Baltimore,	Frederick,	Md.
" John Woods,	Sidney,	Urbana,	Ohio.
" J. Warren, D.D.,	Illinois,	Salem,	Ill.
" S. H. Weller.	Rock River,	Rockville,	"
Elder Columbus Williams,	Cincinnati,	Cincinnati,	Ohio.
Rev. F. B. Wheeler,	Red River.		
Elder H. J. Williams,	Philada. 2nd,	Chestnut Hill,	Pa.
Rev. T. Wilson,	Monmouth,	Shrewsbury,	N. J.
Elder O. E. Weir,	New York,		N. Y.
Rev. Stephen Yerkes, D.D.,	Kentucky,	Danville,	Ky.

SOUTHERN PRESBYTERIAN CHURCH.

Rev. A. D. Hepburn,	Orange,		N. C.

NEW SCHOOL PRESBYTERIAN CHURCH.

NAME.	PRESBYTERY.	POST OFFICE.	STATE.
Rev. Richard Allen, D.D.	Philadelphia 4th,	Philadelphia,	Pa.
" Robert R. Booth, D.D.,	New York 3rd,	New York,	N Y.
Elder George W. Beale,	" "	"	"
Rev. Elias L. Boing.	Genesee Valley,	Angelica,	"
" J. G. Butler, D.D.,	Philadelphia 3rd,	Philadelphia,	Pa.
Elder George V. Bently,	Montrose,	Montrose,	"
Rev. Daniel E. Bierce,	Ripley,	Troy,	Ohio.
" James H. Burns,	Ottowa,	Granville,	Ill.
" S. W. Crittenden,	Philadelphia 3rd,	Philadelphia,	Pa.
" Benj. W. Chidlaw,	Hamilton,	Cleves,	Ohio.
" John Covert,		Chicago,	Ill.
Elder E. D. Cleaver,	Wilmington,	Delaware City,	Del.
" J. H. Catlin,	Schuyler,	Augusta,	Ill.
Rev. J. G. Craighead,	New York 3rd,	New York,	N. Y.
" Charles H. De Long,	Delaware,	Deposit,	"
" George Duffield, Junior,	Knox,	Galesburg,	Ill.
" Charles S. Dunning,	Montrose,	Honesdale,	Pa.
" Albert Erdman,	Utica,	Clinton,	N. Y.
" W. T. Eva,	Philadelphia 4th,	Philadelphia,	Pa.
Elder D. P. Evans.	Ripley,	Troy.	Ohio.
" Wm. C. Foote.	New York 3rd,	New York,	N. Y.
Rev. S. W. Fisher, D.D.,	Utica,	Utica,	"
" J. Fewsmith, D.D.,	Newark,	Newark,	N. J.
Elder Wm. Finn,	Hudson,	Florida.	"
" John C. Farr,	Philadelphia 4th,	Philadelphia.	Pa.
Rev. Ezra H. Gillett, D.D.,	New York 4th,	New York,	N. Y.
Dr. J. C. Gallup,	Utica,	Clinton,	"
Rev. E. F. Hatfield, D.D.,	New York 3rd,	New York,	"
Elder John B. Hall,	Harrisburgh,	Wiliiamsport,	Pa.
Rev. E. L. Hurd,	Schuyler,	Augusta,	Ill.
" H. S. Huntington,	San Jose,		Ca.
" Y. Hickey,	Catskill,		N. Y.
Elder Henry Ide,	Brooklyn,	Brooklyn,	"
" Wm. H. Jessup,	Montrose,	Montrose,	Pa.
Rev. O. M. Johnson,	Hudson,	New Hampton,	"
" John L. Jones,	Chenango,	Guilford Centre,	"
" John M. Johnson,	Rockaway,	Hanover,	N. J.
Elder Benjamin Kendall,	Philadelphia 3rd,	Philadelphia,	Pa.
" Wm. F. Lee,	New York 4th,	New York,	N. Y.
" John Loch,	Philadelphia 4th,	Philadelphia,	Pa.
Rev. Geo. E. W. Leonard,	Cedar Rapids,	Cedar Rapids,	Iowa.
" Joseph M. McNulty,	Hudson,	Montgomery,	N. Y.
Elder George W. Moulton,	Watertown,	Watertown,	"
" Edward Miller,	Philadelphia 3rd,	Philadelphia,	Pa.
Rev. Jacob G. Miller,	Montrose,	Montrose,	"
" S. W. Pratt,	St. Lawrence,	Livonia,	N. Y.
Elder James B. Pinneo,	Newark,	Newark,	N. J.
Rev. John Patton, D.D.,	Wilmington,	Middleton,	Del.
" J. J. Porter, D.D.,	Watertown,	Watertown,	N. Y.
Elder Jesse Roe,	Hudson,	Chester,	"
Rev. Samuel N. Robinson,	Otsego,	Springfield,	"
B. W. Raymond,	Chicago,	Chicago,	Ill.
Rev. H. B. Smith, D.D.,	New York 4th,	New York,	N. Y.

NAME.	PRESBYTERY.	POST OFFICE.	STATE.
Rev. Edward Stratton,	Long Island,	Greenpoint,	L. I.
" J. F. Stearns, D.D.,	Newark,	Newark,	N. J.
" Samuel Sawyer,	Synod of Tennessee,		Tenn.
Elder Wm. G. Taylor,	Utica,	Utica,	N. Y.
" Oliver F. Wood,	New York 4th,	New York,	"
" S. D. Ward,	Montrose,		Pa.
Rev. C. P. Wing, D.D.,	Harrisburg,	Carlisle,	"
" John Ward,	North River,	La Grange,	N. Y.
" John E. Werth,	St. Louis,	St. Louis,	Mo.
" W. T. Wylie,	Pittsburgh.	New Castle,	Pa.
Hon. H. W. Williams, LL.D.,	"	Pittsburgh,	"

UNITED PRESBYTERIAN CHURCH.

NAME.	PRESBYTERY.	POST OFFICE.	STATE
Rev. W. W. Barr,	Synod of N. York,	Philadelphia,	Pa.
Elder Wm. E. Brown.			
Rev. Matthew Clarke,	2nd Synod West,	Laporte,	Ind.
" Wm. Davidson, D.D.,	" "	Hamilton,	Ohio.
Elder Wm. Getty,	Synod of N. York,	Philadelphia,	Pa.
Rev. R. D. Harper, D.D.,	Xenia,	Xenia,	Ohio.
J. B. Knox,	2nd Synod West,	Clifton,	"
Rev. N. C. McDill,	" "	Richland, Rush Co.	Ind.
" David McDill,	" "	Cherry Fork,	Ohio.
" J. Y. Scouller,	" "	Fair Haven,	"
Elder R. C. Stewart,	" "	Hamilton,	"
Rev. A. G. Wallace,	Synod of Pittsburg,	Stuartsville,	Pa.

REFORMED PRESBYTERIAN CHURCH.

NAME.	PRESBYTERY.	POST OFFICE.	STATE.
Elder W. W. Blair,	Western,	Princeton,	Ind.
Rev. W. S. Bratton,	"	Coulterville.	
" S. W. Crawford, D.D.,	"	Chambersburg,	Pa.
" J. Y. Morton,	Ohio,	Cedarville,	Ohio.
James C. McMillan,	"	Xenia,	"
Rev. John McMillan,	Pittsburgh,	Allegheny,	Pa.
" John N. McLeod, D.D.,	New York,	New York,	N. Y.
Elder George H. Stuart,	Philadelphia,	Philadelphia,	Pa.
" Thomas Smith,	Pittsburgh,		"
" James Stewart,	Northern,	New York.	
Rev. T. W. J. Wylie, D.D.,	Philadelphia,	Philadelphia,	Pa.
" Samuel Young,	Chicago,	Bloom,	Ill.

REFORMED PROTESTANT DUTCH CHURCH.

NAME.	PRESBYTERY.	POST OFFICE.	STATE.
Elder Joseph Campbell,	Classis Philada.,	Philadelphia,	Pa.
" D. S. S. Jones, M.D.,	"	"	"
" James Peters,	"	"	"
Rev. J. W. Schenck,	"	"	"
" J. H. Suydam,	"	"	"

CUMBERLAND PRESBYTERIAN CHURCH.

NAME.	PRESBYTERY.	POST OFFICE.	STATE.
Rev. D. Cooper,	Pennsylvania,		Pa.
Elder Robert Carr,	Penna. Synod,		"
" Oliver Cromlow,	"		"
Rev. J. N. Edmiston,	Pennsylvania,	Waynesburg,	"
" A. B. Miller, D.D.,	Penna. Synod,		"
Elder Chas. R. B. Morris,	"		"

The Rev. John Hall, D.D., late of Dublin, Ireland, now of New York, being present, was invited to sit as a corresponding member.

REV. MR. BRATTON, (R. P.):—I now offer this resolution:

That in as much as the Convention, in its organization, has departed from the plan proposed by the last Synod of the Reformed Presbyterian Church; therefore,

Resolved, That the Convention be regarded as the Convention of the day.

I will say, in a few words, the reason why I offer this resolution. It seems to me the Convention would be less trammelled by its adoption, and that the members of the Reformed Presbyterian Church will not be treated with disrespect. There may be some important questions brought up here, that may or may not, I cannot tell, affect, to some extent, the bodies represented in this Convention. The plan admits this: That, as the questions would be discussed and voted upon, that would, in some degree, change the various bodies represented. We are called upon, in one part of the plan proposed by the Reformed Presbyterian Church, to say that votes should be taken by denominations. How shall we adhere to that? That is a question that will come up. I think it is a necessity that the Convention be simply considered as an informal Convention, and not bound to act in the plan originally constituted by the Reformed Presbyterian Church in drawing out this plan.

On motion of Elder A. E. Chamberlain, Old School, the resolution was deferred for the present.

HON. J. W. FRANCIS, (Old School):—Mr. Chairman, what rules have you to guide you in your deliberations?

The PRESIDENT:—I am governed by the rules of common sense. I am aware, sir, you have been Speaker of the Senate, and I shall always defer to you with great pleasure.

The following was offered by Rev. John Eagleson, D.D., Old School:

Resolved, That a committee of one Minister and one Elder from each body represented in the Convention, be appointed to prepare and report a *Basis of Union*, to be submitted for consideration and adoption by the various branches of the Presbyterian Church.

Rev. Dr. Breckinridge said: Mr. Chairman, I wish to make a casual remark. How are you to appoint a small committee of the most competent men in the house? What can we do by that? I mean, what selection, with a hope of doing good, can you make? If you have a committee of two persons from one denomination, and so many for each of the others, in all probability you thereby cut yourselves off from some of the most proper persons in the house. The Old School Presbyterian Church, as I suppose, is the largest denomination of Presbyterians in the world. Here are sitting, also, the New School, and the Cumberland brethren, which are, in the main, offshoots from the Old School Presbyterian Church. I am perfectly willing to give to the United Presbyterian Church the responsibility of calling this Convention; but are we to be willing to let the smallest denomination in the house present to us a form of agreement, thinking they could do it better than we could do it ourselves? I object to all that view of the subject. I will say if the brother now will agree to withdraw his motion, I will give way; if not, I must say a few more words.

Dr. Eagleson:—I have not the power to withdraw the resolution after it is discussed.

Dr. Breckinridge:—I must say, then, a few more words.

The President:—Come on the platform. We have a platform strong enough to hold the whole Presbyterian Church.

Dr. Breckinridge here came upon the platform:—I do not mean to say much, but that which I think ought properly to be considered. Well, sir, what I was going to say was, that I think it would be utterly impossible for this Convention, or any other that can assemble, to do anything that will presently induce the organic union of any two, much less of the whole five or six bodies here met together. Sir, I never intended to introduce that subject here; but it has been introduced here already several times; and the Lord has been told, two or three times, He must do this thing. In my judgment, He does not intend to do this. I say that organization you will never see. Sir, I seldom prophesy. I told you this a year ago, and I tell you now. I hope you may live a thousand years, and live to be satisfied there is no possibility of getting all these bodies into an organic union now. You have no call in that direction; you can do nothing except cast a moral influence upon the public. We are not authorized to do it. There is not a single denomination represented here whose people would be bound. In the Old School, to which I belong, we have not a particle of power except over our own members. The understanding is, they are to observe, they are to inquire; the understanding is, they have no power to come to conclusions which shall bind them. This is an advisory body. It is perfectly obvious you cannot now proceed, at this present time, to make this present body the means of organizing all the bodies represented here into one body. If that is the case, it would be wise in us to lay that view of the subject to one side. It is a thing which must be settled between each denomination. You have settled it, and are here as a new church—the United Presbyterian Church. It must be done in that way if any organic union is effected. That is, it must be two denominations uniting together; five cannot come together in a union of that sort.

What can we do in the position of the parties? It strikes me there are two things that may be advantageous. One is, that you get this

Committee of the very ablest men. I do not pretend to say from where they shall come. In reference to our Committee on Correspondence with the committee from the other branch, while I love and honor most of the brethren upon our side, I know very few of the others. Among those gentlemen of the Old School Committee, while they are known for the highest form of excellence, yet it is notorious there was not a single man that was known as a learned theologian. (Cries of "Order," and disapprobation.) If it is not the pleasure of the gentlemen in this house that I shall say anything further, I will stop. I am responsible for what I say to God and to man; but I mean it in kindness. If any gentleman takes offence at what I say, he knows where I live. I mean to say, that there are, in the bounds of the Presbyterian Church on our side, some of the most learned men.

A DELEGATE:—Mr. Chairman, I rise to a point of order. Is it proper that the qualifications of the members of that Committee should be questioned?

THE PRESIDENT:—Any difficulties, Dr. Breckinridge, in your own church, had better be settled at home.

DR. BRECKINRIDGE:—I am at home.

THE PRESIDENT:—With all deference to Dr. Breckinridge, I must enforce this point of order. I speak not for myself, but for others.

DR. BRECKINRIDGE:—I speak for myself. If this Convention has come here for the purpose—

THE PRESIDENT:—The Chair will not allow this; though he has as much respect as any one for Dr. Robert J. Breckinridge. We are here, to-day, to see wherein we differ; we are here for prayer and conference. No man in the house has, for a single moment, any idea that we have any ecclesiastical unity in the Church. We are here to see how near we are to each other. Brother Breckinridge will take a seat here.

DR. BRECKINRIDGE:—No, sir. If I am not permitted to stand here and speak my views, I will not sit here. I made no personal allusions that were offensive.

A MEMBER:—I move that Dr. Breckinridge be allowed to go on, as a representative of the Old School Presbyterian Church. [Cries of "No! No!"]

THE PRESIDENT:—It is not competent for this house to decide whether there were learned theologians, or not, on the Committee. Dr. Breckinridge will go on with his remarks.

DR. BRECKINRIDGE:—I did not come here to be lectured by the Moderator. My opinion is we have changed the whole tone of this assembly, by making a layman president of it. Such a thing was never before heard of. If this body is to be governed by intrigue, the curse of God will rest upon it. [Amid loud expressions of disapprobation, Dr. Breckinridge retired from the platform.]

A DELEGATE, said:—I second that motion to appoint a Committee to form a basis of union. It strikes me as very important there should be such a Committee. We do not assume that the thing is settled and impossible; we should never have come here, if we supposed any such thing. It is not settled that it cannot be done. It is by no means certain that a union can be made; but this, sir, is one step. No one supposes you, Mr. Chairman, to state that there is any authority here that binds any one. We are here to throw out a matter that will receive the serious consideration of gentlemen from the common branches of our family, and let it go for what it is worth. It is to be a starting point. If they can agree on anything, let us have it, and talk about it; and that will bring us to the point we desire.

Rev. Alex. Donaldson, D.D., (Old School):—I wish to say a very few words. I greatly regret that this motion is brought at so early a period. If it had been in the loving spirit of the Master, it is very probable that our hearts and minds—our hearts first, and our minds afterwards—would be prepared for it after a while; but if it is pressed forward now, it will produce feelings that will disturb the spirit that must prevail in this assembly. I hope the house will vote it down now; and if we get a good spirit, after talking a day or two, it will come in good time.

Rev. Geo. Marshall, D.D., (Old School):—I am very sorry that there has been any unhappy state of feeling. I wish to say, we have come here, as I understand, for two objects. The first is, to pray together, as representatives from the great Presbyterian families of the United States. The great God give us light, and give us righteous hearts, that we may view and consult in His providence of what He would have us to do in His Church! That is one of the first things. The next is, to try and deliberate, and see wherein we agree, and wherein we differ; and with regard to our particular differences, whether there is such agreement that we could come together; or whether there are such mighty mountains as cannot be overcome, and we must stand apart as we have done in days past. Now, as I understand this matter, it was not to force matters, but to bring the paper before the house as a matter of business; and comparing notes, and looking at it in all its aspects, to lead us to say, in view of the paper the Committee should present, whether we would yet differ. Now, we might go on for a whole month without coming to anything, perhaps, if it had not been introduced.

Our object is two-fold. One is, to pray together; the other is, to deliberate together. We came here to see whether in these days, when God in His providence, seems to be leading His Church to union—in view of the fact that the infidels of all lands are uniting their forces to oppress the Church—we could unite. All that we want is, to compare notes; and that is, I think, the object of this paper here. My good friends, I do not agree that it is in the light of forestalling; but I want something to bring out the points on which we could unite, and then we will see the points precisely on which we stand.

Rev. Wilson Phraner (Old School):—As this question has come up in a very early stage of our proceedings, perhaps before we are ready for it; and with some little acquaintance with the object of this question, we are in danger of becoming confused in the order of our business, I, therefore, move the reference of the paper to the Business Committee, that it may come before this house at the proper time. That it, after a view of all the circumstances of the case, may bring the matter before the Convention, if, in its judgment, the purpose be proper. I, therefore, move the reference of this paper to the Committee on Business.

Elder A. E. Chamberlain (Old School):—I hope this will not pass, as the object appears particularly to be to forestall our actions. If I understand the purpose of this paper, it is simply to digest the sentiments expressed here in this Convention; that the Committee may bring in a paper that will embody the sentiments of all the members. It seems, of all times, this is the very time for the Committee to be appointed, while we know nothing about the persons to be selected on the Committee. It seems to me, before we close this discussion, this Committee should be appointed, to bring in their report before the close of the Convention.

Rev. Dr. Musgrave (Old School):—I am opposed to the motion of reference; because I am in favor of the motion as at first submitted, and for this reason: I think the sooner we have such a Committee appointed, the more time it will have to mature its sentiments; and we, in the meantime, can go on with our prayers, and our conference, and get our hearts as soft and warm as possible; so that, when that Committee reports, we shall be ready to act. I have a word to say in regard to the general object of that motion. I commonly agree with my venerable brother,—I cannot call him father; for he and I were, forty years ago, together in public matters. I generally agree with him in Church politics; but I regret the course he pursued on this occasion, and yet was sorry he was not allowed to proceed. I believe the Convention would have been instructed, if they had allowed the venerable brother to proceed.

Sir, I do not believe that it is impracticable for us to agree upon a basis of union—

A Delegate:—Organic union.

Dr. Musgrave:—Yes, sir; I mean, just as I say, an *organic* union is the union for the Convention to consider. In a new spirit of love, of faith, we are one, I think; and therefore, when I speak of a basis of union, I mean *organic* union. Now, sir, I am an Old School man; I have been so from my youth up, and I think, consistently, sir. And I rejoiced, sir, to be present here, to-day; because I felt I was in a body of sound Calvinists—of sound Presbyterians. I promptly agreed with my friend here, because I saw this motion was in the right direction; and I see no reason, no substantial reason, why the different branches of the Presbyterian family should not be united organically.

Now, with reference to the union with the New School; while I am utterly dissatisfied with the terms proposed, still I do not despair of our getting even an organic union upon a Scriptural basis, upon the basis of standards, necessarily the Scriptures, according to the Westminster Confession. If we could get that, I would rejoice with all my heart, and thank God for that union. Well, sir, here we are surrounded by sects—by denominations. I dislike to use the word myself, as the Papists, aggregated, make so much out of it. Still, we cannot well make ourselves understood, without employing certain language. We are here surrounded by *churches*, I will say—that is the better, the Scriptural word—who do not differ from us in any matter that is essential. I do not mean, now, essential to Christianity; but I mean with reference to our Calvinism, and our Presbyterianism. Why, sir, what keeps us apart? What are these little insignificant points? Insignificant, as they strike me; but I do not mean to be disrespectful when I say so; and I hope none of my brethren will take offence at language of that character. They seem to me to be so utterly insignificant. We all belong to Westminster Presbyteries. The United Presbyterians, the Covenanters, the Secession Churches, are thoroughly sound in their Calvinism and Presbyterianism.

What keeps us apart? Cannot we form a basis of organic union, when we have the same Confession, the same organization, the same Church homilies? What is the inference? Why, sir, the wonder to me is, we should be so long separated; that is my astonishment. It may be because I was not educated in one of those branches, that I do not appreciate those minor points; but they seem to me, looking upon them as a Presbyterian, as utterly insufficient to keep us apart. Well now, as to my New School brethren, I will never consent, as one man, to an organic union that will not secure and give us the Scriptures and the Westminster Confession; and will not render it more certain that if any man shall teach or publish errors really inconsistent with the Reformed doctrines, that such a man can be disciplined for his error. I will never consent to any other than such an organic union. But my hope is, there are so many really orthodox, sound men in that denomination, that even that Church, will agree, as a Church, to such a basis of union as will secure permanent peace, and unity, and soundness in the faith. Why, sir, if they are orthodox, as they say they are, if they are sound Presbyterians, as they profess to be, then it is to their interest, as well as to the interest of Old School men, to find such a basis of union, as will secure purity, and permanent unity, and peace in the Church of God. I do not despair of that.

Now, sir, I think it might help even that if we here—a Convention of these various Presbyterian branches—could agree upon some basis of union. Why, sir, long ago we might have had such a moral union as to secure the practical result. I never felt so happy in all my life, as I did this morning, not saying much, while the brethren were delivering their excellent speeches, and while listening to the unctious prayers that were offered up to the great Head of the Church. Oh, it was a happy hour spent here! I hope to God, that in my declining age, I may yet live to see the time when the whole Presbyterian Church shall be one body. [Applause.] Not a latitudinarian body, but a sound Calvinistic, Presbyterian body. Why cannot it be, when men all over the land profess this oneness of faith, and of the Spirit? What is to hinder us, under the mighty influence of the Spirit of God, and His holy providence; and in answer to the prayers of millions, what is to prevent it? I do not see that it is impracticable. With not only my profound respect, but also my deep love for that good brother, and for his fidelity in his post, I must differ from him on that point.

Now, sir, I am opposed to the reference. I think we are ready for the appointment of such a Committee. Why, sir, if it is so difficult a subject, then they need the more time to mature something; and it is not too early this afternoon, I presume, to attend to a subject of such importance. It is not a moment too early to appoint such a Committee. And can it be so difficult, after all, to propose a common standard which we all accept, which we all revere? Why, it seems to me, if we just simply take those standards as the basis of union, and insist upon a sound Scriptural interpretation, all difficulty will vanish. I do not know but that I ought to add to this my earnest prayer to God, if it please Him, that I may live to see all these churches one. I confess to you that my heart is expanding hopefully. I always loved the Presbyterians in all these churches, and because they are Presbyterians; and the more orthodox, the more—if I may use such a hyperbolical expression—the more orthodox and Presbyterian they are, the more I love them. When I looked around, and heard men from different branches of the Church expressing precisely my views, and all advocating union upon the basis of our public standard, I said, Thank God! I hope the day is now at hand when that common platform will be the ground upon which we will all unite. Let us have the Committee, and give them time to make their report. ("Question," "Question.")

REV. MR. BRATTON, (R. P.):—Mr. President, I rise to a point of order. You see the necessity now of the resolution offered a little while ago. There is the rule of the Reformed Presbyterian Church, that on important questions like this we are to act by bodies, by denominations; and by refusing to adopt my resolution, we are acting simply on the call of the Reformed Presbyterian Church. The point of order is, we are acting too fast.

THE PRESIDENT:—The brother must excuse me for saying, that, while I continue in this chair, I know of no Reformed Presbyterians, nor of any churches; but only brother Presbyterians in Christ. While I continue to preside here, my aim will be to glorify God, and keep you in amity and love as fellow Presbyterians. If the Convention sustains me, I will continue in the chair. I love all my brethren.

MR. BRATTON:—How shall this vote be taken?

THE PRESIDENT:—By *viva voce.*

MR. BRATTON:—We are acting by the call of the Reformed Presbyterian Church.

The Chair overruled the point of order. An appeal was taken from the decision of the Chair, which was seconded, pending the consideration of which the motion of reference to the Business Committee was withdrawn.

The motion of reference was renewed by a delegate, and lost. The original motion of Dr. Eagleson was then almost unanimously adopted, and the Chair authorized to appoint the Committee.

MR. BRATTON:—I appeal from the decision of the Chair in the manner of taking the vote.

THE PRESIDENT:—There is nothing before the House now. I had previously announced the vote, and it was owing to the neglect of yourself to speak louder that I did not catch your appeal in time for consideration.

MR. BRATTON:—Now, sir, there is something at stake, and I wish the Convention to understand it. I saw this difficulty when I offered this hastily drawn up resolution a while ago. I thought that these important votes would be taken by the Convention *viva voce,* as you took this vote now; and I offered this resolution in good faith, to relieve this Convention from the trammels put upon it by the action of the Reformed Presbyterian Church. I offered this resolution to free this Convention from these trammels; and I thought that the Convention should have passed that resolution. Now, I do say, before this Convention, that we have ignored the principles upon which the Convention was called together.

I suppose a great many do not understand the position in which I am placed. I have to go back to my Synod, and report to that Synod of the Reformed Presbyterian Church, how we acted on the call given by them; if I did not protest against this action, they would hold me accountable. That is the reason why I make these remarks.

THE PRESIDENT:—All our votes this day have been taken in the same way. According to the view of our brother, all our votes should be taken by churches, which would consume too much time. We are not acting, as yet, on any important question. The idea is, that when we come to consider the basis of union, we should adopt it by votes of the separate churches.

REV. DR. H. B. SMITH, (New School):—Mr. Moderator, it seems to me, as far as I can understand, that Mr. Bratton is clearly right in presenting the resolution as he did, before our taking any important vote. We did come together under the call of the Reformed Presbyterian Church, which contained certain conditions, in which it was supposed we would abide when we came together. We are now, partly from the necessity of the case, acting outside of these conditions; because the Convention is so much larger in representation than was anticipated. We came together under that call; and until we can, in some way, remove these conditions, we are bound to conform to them. I therefore move you, that the resolution offered by Mr. Bratton be taken up, and now considered; namely, that in the further proceedings of the Convention, we act without reference to the conditions contained in the call of the Reformed Presbyterian Church.

REV. DR. CHAS. C. BEATTY, (Old School):—The question is, that it be taken from the table, and now considered. I fully agree with the views of Dr. Smith. I think that Mr. Bratton is correct, and that the Convention is not now in a position to vote in this matter according to the original call. I think, as he does himself, his resolution was drawn up hastily; perhaps not precisely in the form that might be given, if he had had a little more time. I hope it will be drawn in such a form that we may resolve ourselves into a convention of these churches without these limitations. That is the object, I presume, of Mr. Bratton's resolution. If that be the object, I fully concur with it, as I do not want to complicate him with his church, or embarrass the Convention in its proceedings.

REV. DR. GILLETT, (New School):—It seems that we are convened at the call of the Reformed Presbyterian body; that the documents connected with, and explanatory of that call, have been laid on the table, and we have declined to read them. We are acting in ignorance of the intent with which they call us together. Is it courteous to a considerable branch of our body that we should let these be unread; and while called together by them, to take up an object not contemplated in the call?

REV. DR. T. W. J. WYLIE, (Reformed Presbyterian):—In the form in which that resolution has been presented by Mr. Bratton, I think it is not suitable to be adopted here; this would appear, I think, if it was read. It would be better, I think, if Mr. Bratton, according to the suggestion of Dr. Beatty, should revise it himself. One word may be permitted in reference to the merits of the case. It should be understood that the action of the Synod of the Reformed Presbyterian Church was simply to recommend certain things; and thus they referred not merely to taking the vote by different denominations—the delegations from each denomination counting as a unit—but also as to the way in which the delegates should be appointed. The General Assembly of the United Presbyterian Church appointed by synods, others by presbyteries, and others upon another division. It is in regard to that matter, as in regard to taking votes; it may be by denominations, and, as well by *viva voce.*

Sir, I think it is not the design at all of the Reformed Presbyterian Church to trammel this Convention. We are perfectly free; and we should feel that we are so. We might act, simply by individually giving up the recommendation of the General Synod of the Reformed Presbyterian Church. As one of the delegates of this Synod, I am free to say we do not ask this—I speak simply for myself—and that we are content that all the brethren who come here together, however they have received their appointment, should be members of the Convention, and act as they think proper. All the Synod of the Reformed Presbyterian Church has done is, it has recommended such a Convention as we have now organized. I think, therefore, there is no need whatever for our acting on this matter. I have no objection, Mr. President, to suppose that we ignore all that has been done, as that resolution of Mr. Bratton contemplates, and as he states, that we consider this the Convention of the day.

Sir, when our delegates go back to their respective bodies, they will not appear as representatives from the Convention recommended by the Reformed Presbyterian Church, for it would be immediately said, this Convention is not the Convention which the Reformed Presbyterian Church recommends. When the delegates go back to their respective bodies, they go back as delegates of their own church; and thus we are quite at a loss to see what could be our objections. I merely take the liberty of saying the Reformed Presbyterian Church called the Convention, leaving the matter of the appointment of delegates to the different bodies, and leaving the question of taking the votes to the Convention.

A Delegate:—I hope we will not vote for this, Mr. President. It seems to me we ought to hear again these resolutions which the Chairman read in his opening remarks. Has this Convention been organized on a different basis? That is a question of fact, which those resolutions which you read will state.

The resolutions of the General Synod of the Reformed Presbyterian Church on which the Convention was convened, were read.

The President.—This is all *recommendatory.* This Synod would not, of course, instruct you how to do your business; it might as well instruct you as to the mode of union. These recommendations you can adopt, or not.

Rev. Mr. Temples, (Old School):—Mr. Moderator, allow me a single suggestion in regard to this matter. Do not our good brethren of the Reformed Church differ among themselves as to what they want us to do in this matter? Dr. Wylie makes one statement, which seems to meet with the almost unanimous approval of this body. Now, if these brethren will confer together and bring in a paper upon which we can agree, it would be well; for we do not exactly understand what is meant by the resolution offered by Mr. Bratton. If these brethren of the Reformed Church, who have so kindly and courteously invited us, will only consult together after adjournment, and bring in some paper conjointly, we can get out of this trouble.

Rev. Mr. Morton, (Reformed Presbyterian):—I was a member of the committee that drafted and presented these resolutions to the Reformed Presbyterian Synod. I was a member of the Synod that issued this invitation, or call for this Convention. I know that that call would not have been issued by that Synod had it not been for that resolution. We are a small body; and we knew that without some such resolution as that, when we met here we would be swallowed up, we would be overwhelmed; and without such a resolution, the call would not have been issued by that Synod.

Rev. Dr. John N. McLeod, (Reformed Presbyterian):—I was very solicitous this morning to have these documents brought before this highly respectable body; because I was convinced before they had made any considerable progress in their deliberations, they would meet with these very difficulties which now seem to impede their path. These documents, had they been read, would have given information to this Convention of which they have not as yet become possessed. They would show very distinctly, as they mutually explain themselves, what was the object which the Reformed Presbyterian Church had in view in inviting this Convention; and what was the mode by which they hoped to secure its accomplishment. Now, Sir, I think yet, that twenty minutes—perhaps, fifteen would do—of the time of the Convention could not be better spent than in hearing these documents, and judging of them for themselves. It is certainly true that this highly respectable body is not the body that was convened by the invitation of the Reformed Presbyterian Church. There are but three distinct principles which we regarded as of importance, and by which it was our endeavor to guard our own cause, while we presented the present matter generally to the deliberations of the Presbyterian Churches, that call having been taken off the platform on which it was intended to stand originally. If these documents were read, it would be shown that under the three different principles presented there, this Convention has already deviated from the course that the Reformed Presbyterian Synod indicates. I think that if the documents were read, they would be sufficiently intelligible of themselves; and would furnish a different view of things from what is presented in the original paper from my excellent friend, Mr. George H. Stuart, which was no doubt the occasion of the calling of the Convention. The Synod did not adopt this paper as it stood; they simply received it for consideration, and referred it to a committee composed of delegates from each of the Presbyteries, along with all other papers that would be brought up during those sessions for the consideration of the Synod. After due consideration, the short report which was adopted, was brought in. Now, there will be found, if these are examined, to be a very considerable difference between the original proposition of Mr. Stuart and the one adopted by the Synod. This Convention of Presbyterian Churches to-day assembled here, is on the basis of Mr. Stuart's paper; but that is far off, in my judgment, from the papers adopted by the Synod. The papers adopted by the Synod formed part of the invitation sent by the Synod to the various Presbyterian bodies invited to come into this Convention; and they have sent their answers.

REV. DR. MARSHALL (Old School):—We have fixed our time of adjournment at 5 o'clock.

DR. MCLEOD:—I can finish in a moment. If the Convention would determine to hear the papers, my object could be accomplished, without detaining you by any long explanation. If they are not inclined to do so, but are inclined to move on in the line in which they are now moving, so let it be. I will act as a member of the General Convention; but I will not consider myself as acting as in the Convention called by the Reformed Presbyterian Church. I move that the papers be read, that the previous motion may be settled

THE PRESIDENT:—Are you prepared to decide the question upon the motion of Rev. Dr. Smith, or shall we adjourn?

A DELEGATE:—Were those papers referred to published with the call of the Convention?

DR. MCLEOD:—Some of them were.

A DELEGATE:—Mr. Chairman, we cannot go behind the published proceedings of the call for this Convention by the Reformed Presbyterian Church. I move that we now adjourn.

The Convention was adjourned by prayer by Rev. Dr. Davidson.

November 6th, 7½ o'clock, P. M.

The Convention met pursuant to adjournment, the President in the chair, and was opened with singing the 133d Psalm, and prayer by Rev. Samuel Steele, D.D.

Minutes of the afternoon session were read and approved.

The Committee on Credentials presented an Additional Report, which was adopted, as follows:

The Churches of St. Anne and of St. John the Baptist, Kankakee, Illinois, have appointed the Rev. Charles Chiniquy, their pastor, to represent them in this Convention. Mr. Chiniquy and these churches are attached to the Synod of Canada, a body outside of the limits of the United States. The Committee, therefore, recommend that the name of Mr. Chiniquy be not enrolled as a delegate, but that he be invited to sit as a corresponding member.

THE PRESIDENT:—When we adjourned, the motion of Dr. Henry B. Smith, of New York, to take up the consideration of the resolution postponed, offered by Mr. Bratton, of Illinois, was before the house.

REV. DR. MCLEOD (Reformed Presbyterian):—I understood, Mr. President, that after the adjournment, the Convention would hear the documents referred to in the morning session. I have now produced them.

THE PRESIDENT:—There was no motion on the subject; there was nothing done by the Convention. The Chair suggests that the Doctor can read them as part of his speech.

REV. DR. C. P. WING (New School), said:—I would like to inquire as a matter of order, Mr. Chairman, as to what force are the resolutions of the Reformed Synod? These were documents never published; and while the Reformed Synod gave the invitation to all the denominations meeting here, yet these papers had no influence in bringing the members together, and, therefore, they can have no influence now.

Dr. McLeod:—I would say the documents were mainly published; there is only one that has not been extensively published. Perhaps, also, that has been published, although I have not seen it.

Dr. Wing:—It strikes me the remark of Dr. Marsh is very appropriate here. I do not see what we have to do with the private record of the proceedings of that Synod, which brought not a single member here; so far as we know, not a single member from any presbytery in the land, came with any reference to the documents now proposed to be read. In addition to the remark of Dr. Marsh, it would seem that if we go behind the published proceedings of that Synod on which we proposed to come, we shall trammel ourselves exceedingly, if we propose to be in the least influenced by it; and although I feel great respect to that Synod, and am exceedingly desirous to give all deference to them—for they struck the chord that vibrated in every heart throughout our land, and unquestionably has influenced those in hearing to-day—at the same time, I prefer very much indeed that we be left to all the freedom which that published summons gives. I do not desire that we should be cramped in any degree whatsoever, by the proceedings which lie behind the published records. For if we go back of the published proceedings, we shall be bound by the proceedings of that Synod; and that Synod, I presume, has no desire to govern this Convention. With reference to one action of that Synod—which has a bearing on this Convention so far as relates to the action of the Convention by denominations, or by branches—it would seem to me that we can comply with that part of the resolution. In deference to the remarks made by some members, it strikes me we are bound by that action. We came on that published action of the Synod, and that resolution which has reference to our action as denominations, is binding on this Convention. It was the understanding on which I came here. It was the understanding on which all the members of this Convention came; and it would seem to me, according to the various remarks made, we are bound by that action.

Dr. S. W. Fisher (New School):—Mr. President, it seems to me, we can dispose of this matter, and at the same time act in good faith towards this Synod. I came here, as I suppose others did, in view of this document as published. I do not wish to go behind the published documents. There is only one point in that, in which fault is found; that respects voting in certain cases by churches. I propose a resolution like this, if it would satisfy the Synod:

Resolved, That in all cases involving direct action on any terms of the basis of union, the vote of the Convention shall be taken by churches; in all other cases in the usual manner, unless a majority of the Convention shall determine otherwise.

That, I believe, settles that question, and is very fair and full. I merely read this in reference to meeting this difficulty of Mr. Bratton's.

The resolution of Mr. Bratton was then by vote taken up from the table.

Dr. Fisher:—I offer this as an amendment.

Mr. Bratton.—What part of the original motion does it amend ?

The President:—It strikes out all the original motion, and leaves the Preamble.

Dr. Fisher:—In the cases contemplated by this Synod, it was feaɹed that when some basis of union was proposed, they being a small Synod, would be overwhelmed by the larger number in this Convention; and the design was to have them have, therefore, an equal vote with each of the other churches in this Convention. So, I understand the recommendation, as given by that Synod; and with it I am willing to comply. It seems to me, that whatever amendment may make this more satisfactory to this body, is preferable; and I will accept any modification which seems better fitted.

Rev. W. W. Barr, (United Presbyterian):—There is another church besides the Reformed Synod, and that is the United Presbyterian Church, which appointed two delegates from each Synod at the General Assembly; and the reason they appointed such a small delegation was owing to this resolution, coming from the Reformed Synod. It was understood there would be a vote by the bodies, and that each body would have an equal vote; and therefore it was not judged necessary that a larger number should be present. That Church acted with that distinct understanding. If you pass this resolution, you depart from the view the United Presbyterian Church had; and, therefore, rule out of this Convention the United Presbyterian Church. They came here with that distinct understanding; that, although in such small numbers, yet they would have the right to vote as a body. There were but four appointed, and there are but four on the floor of the Convention; the passage of that resolution would leave them helpless in such a case.

Rev. Dr. McMillan, (Reformed Presbyterian):—I think Dr. Fisher's resolution meets the case, and will satisfy all the branches.

Rev. Dr. Fisher:—I move the resolution as a substitute for the whole of the previous resolution, including the preamble.

Rev. Dr. Musgrave, (Old School):—I heartily approve of that substitute; but I think it would be very impolitic in us to adopt that preamble. What would it be, strictly interpreted? Why, we say to the people that we have departed from the original call. If that substitute is adopted, do we not comply literally with the call of the Convention? and if so, had we not better simply adopt that as a substitute, without the preamble?

The substitute was unanimously adopted.

The President announced, that after much anxious thought, and earnest prayer for Divine guidance, he had concluded to appoint the following gentlemen as the committee to prepare and report a Basis of Union, according to the Resolution adopted in the afternoon session.

Old School,	Rev. John Eagleson, D.D.
	Elder A. E. Chamberlain.

New School,	Rev. Samuel W. Fisher, D.D., LL.D.
	Elder Hon. H. W. Williams, LL.D.
United Presbyterian,	Rev. J. Y. Scouller, D.D.
	Elder William Getty.
Reformed Pres.,	Rev. T. W. J. Wylie, D.D.
	Elder Jas. C. McMillan.
Ref. Protestant Dutch,	Rev. J. W. Schenck.
	Elder James Peters.
Cumberland Pres.,	Rev. A. B. Miller, D.D.
	Elder Robert Carr.

REV. DR. MARSHALL, (Old School):—Mr. President, it occurred to me it would be proper to fix on some time to have a conference of the Convention touching the subject of union, in order that the committee might ascertain what was the prevailing view of the body. I am hardly prepared to make the motion; but I venture to move that it be the first order for to-morrow morning, after the religious services, to have a conference of the Convention upon this subject.

ELDER W. W. MARSH:—I wish to make a remark. How long are we to sit here? I move to have that conference this evening; we cannot sit here all this week. I offer it as an amendment.

The motion, as amended, was adopted.

THE PRESIDENT:—We are ready now, brethren, to commence this conference. I hope some one here is full of the Spirit. I presume the object of the motion is, that the brothers from the various Presbyteries should give free expression to their feelings on the subject of union, and in reference to the basis of union.

It was on motion resolved that the speeches should be limited to five minutes each.

REV. MR. BLAIR, (United Presbyterian Church):—I think, sir, the matter is plain before us. The question is, the union of the churches of Presbyterians. The basis on which they are to unite is always the first thing to come up. The basis of doctrine, I say, should be the Westminster Confession of Faith, and the Catechism. They have been always considered as sufficient by all the churches. We have all agreed upon that; there is no difference now. We are all agreed upon that matter now; we are all loyal; we are all in favor of such a basis of union of the Synods of the United States. Well then, that matter being settled, that being always the standard of doctrine, the Confession of Faith and Catechism, then we are all united. We settle upon the questions which were always considered sufficiently broad for all the ages since they were formed. Then comes up the question about the form of government. We are all Presbyterians. We are not to be Independents, nor to be on the non-presbytery system; but we are Presbyterians. That matter, then, is settled. Well then, we have the question of Psalmody. Well, all that we want on that head may cover the whole question. We may all sing the genealogy and we all sing it.

"God, born at Bethlehem, of the tribe of Judah, of the family of David, of Mary, the virgin." Well, it extends thus far, and then we propose the question to our Presbyterian brethren, Old School and New School, will you be satisfied with that? We will give you the Book of Psalms; we will let you take the Book of Psalms according to the interpretation of Dr. Alexander and Dr. Plummer. Dr. Plummer has given us a record of every man who has written a line on the Psalm Book, and he has given the true meanings. Presbyterians ought all to be uniform. We will take the Psalm Book and sing it, or we will read it, or we will pray over it; or will we still vary over it? I have now done, sir.

Rev. Dr. L. M. Miller, (Old School):—Some of us would not be sorry, sir, if union would take place to-night. We think it would depend entirely upon the basis. Many of you may remember the name of Judge Fine, of excellent memory, of the Presbyterian Church, Old School. Several years ago, on a conference with that good brother, this subject of the re-union of the two churches, the Old and the New Schools, came up in our Presbytery. After talking over it for a little time, our Presbytery proposed to meet with a New School body, then forming a part of the Church which they represented in the eastern part of the county. On that invitation we came together. We prayed over this matter, and we talked it over; then we passed a series of resolutions conjointly, and afterwards separately. Those resolutions some of you have read. From that day to this, the same mind has pervaded those two bodies. During the past summer, on the invitation of the New School body, another conference was held. The results have been stronger than those which prevailed before, and all for the best; and it was the sentiment of that body that however much some might require another basis than that, it was unnecessary while the Committee of Conference of the two bodies were satisfied with that. They were, however, anxious that there should be unanimity; and if another basis should be presented which should meet the wishes of all, they desired such. Now, in our part of the State, we have looked each other in the face; we have exchanged pulpits, not only in the two great branches, the new and old, but with our brethren of other parts of the Church; as far as I am able to judge of their orthodoxy by their platform which they present to me, we can cordially adopt their sentiments. We have no objection to their singing the Psalms of David when they please. We will sing them when we understand them, and our hearts will go with them; but it seems to me that we should recognize the influences of union which are brought to bear in our part of the Church. I do not know how it prevails in Philadelphia unless I judge of it from this congregation. I do not know how it prevails South; but I know that in the northern part of our State, in the western part of New York, there is a cordiality and an exhibition of orthodoxy on both sides of the Church which will in no way be impeded, and can in no way retard this movement. We invite each other to exchange pulpits, from the one extreme on the western border of the State to the other; and we find that they all present the same views, and have the same fraternal desire to have enlarged and made more specific the common basis on which all can agree, and thus definitely to invite the hearts of the people to the hearts and sentiments of the leaders. In that direction, however, this assembly might decide to wait at the present day and hour, is the wish and desire of that part of the Church I represent; for I came here to represent, as another brother by my side, the Synod of Buffalo, as well as my own Presbytery. I am instructed to present their desires. We are one in heart, desire, and aim.

Why, look at the sermons preached during the meetings of the General Assembly. When they talk of the Great Presbyterian Church, what do they say? They do not speak of twenty-five hundred ministers that belong to the Old School; they sum all up, and say, What a magnificent Church represented by all these Synods. Why should not fellow-Presbyterians, accustomed to the same church organization, be united, and have the same government to represent them all? We are ready at the North; perhaps more ready than other parts of the Church. We have looked each other in the face, and our hearts have flown together, and we are ready to strike hands together as one body, and work for the cause of Christ. I sincerely and heartily rejoice in the call for this Convention.

Rev. G. E. W. Leonard, (New School):—I fully endorse what the brother has stated; but in the North West we have a still stronger desire for union. I have mingled extensively with brethren, especially laymen, in Iowa, and I have not found a man of any church among the laymen—and few among the ministers—but who is desirous of Union. Our Church is slimly represented here, because the churches are scattered, and the ministers have small salaries; perhaps, I am the only one. We need union for many purposes. Ecclesiastically, we have not a literary institution of any magnitude, connected with any branch of the Presbyterian Church; and there are, no doubt, two hundred of our Presbyterians, whose children are going to Catholic schools, because we are behind in the department of education. We need a Union in order that the different forces of the various Presbyteries may be united to complete and endow, with a little assistance from the wealthy churches of the East, an institution of learning. We need it on this ground, further, because we have such a great rush of immigration, not only from the different Eastern States, but from Europe. The Atheists and Catholics of Europe are coming by thousands and tens of thousands, filling up the States and Western territories. We need to be united in order that we may relieve many ministers. I have estimated, and I think I am not far from correct, that if these different bodies were united, we might release one thousand to fill the places that imperatively demand ministers now; and, perhaps, $200,000 to sustain them. The cry from the Territories and the North West States is, More men! Towns are forming along the Pacific Railroad, which is extending at the rate of three miles a day. New towns are opening; Infidels, Catholics, and Universalists, are pushing forward. Why should not we unite, brethren, as a body, and lift up our standards against the flood of iniquity that is flowing to our shores, and filling up the best parts of the country; and plant first, in advance of all others, the great church that reflects the Reformed doctrines in all their purity? I am in favor of Union for these reasons, and others I might state if the time permitted. I represent the New School Presbyterian Church.

Rev. Dr. C. P. Wing, (New School):—Mr. Chairman, I feel hardly to belong to the Old or New School Presbyterian Church. I come from a portion of the Church which has been, to some extent, the battle ground between different portions of the Presbyterian Church—(Louder). (I will be loud enough in a short time.) And if there is any part of the Church in which there may, perhaps, be expected some misunderstanding, or some fear, it may be found, probably, in that region of the country. It is entirely useless for us to conceal from ourselves, that there are some very material difficulties in the way of union; although I have yet to see the first man in connection with the body to which I belong, or in connection with the Old School Presbyterian Church, who is not in favor of union. I have found a very large portion, in both branches of the Church, who are greatly in fear, and whose hopes are sadly dampened, in view of the extreme difficulties which are in the way. I, myself, do not feel quite as sensitive to these fears; and one thing, it seems to me, has greatly relieved these fears, which I, in connection with many of the brethren, have entertained. Some considerable number of Presbyteries in our region of the country have expressed the difficulties in the way of reconciliation. They have told us what they demand from other portions of the Presbyterian Church. The various Presbyteries in the interior of Pennsylvania have expressed themselves on this point in clear and very explicit terms. I know not a single instance in which these Presbyteries have expressed themselves in which they have not been cordially met. They have found difficulties in relation to ecclesiastical connections; they have found difficulties in relation to doctrine; they have found difficulties in relation to theological seminaries. We acknowledge these difficulties, and yet we believe that there are some influences which have taken place, and been presented in those resolutions, that have cleared the way to a very great extent. One thing, which at first seemed to be very much in the way of union, in that region, and in other portions of the country, in my estimation, has turned out, under the good providence of God, to produce a state of things highly favorable. We all know that different Presbyteries, and some periodicals, have presented their objections to the union of two branches of the Presbyterian Church. They have presented them in very strong terms; somewhat too strong for the feelings of some individuals among us. But, very fortunately, another portion of the Presbyterian Church has replied to these. Whilst one portion come out and say, we demand certain explanations on these points, and we require you to come up to certain terms, the other portion of the church, and their periodicals, adopt the terms and say, we are not only up to that platform, but we always have been there. (Applause). We were always precisely on the ground demanded of us. When they say to us, and in various of the periodicals demand we should entertain certain doctrines, and express ourselves as entertaining those doctrines, I am quite prepared to prove we have always stood there, and always intend to be there; and so far as relates to the demands of theological seminaries, and ecclesiastical government, we will do all in our power to produce the result desired. (Applause). After this, it would seem to me, the necessary thing demanded on both sides is confidence. They tell us what is necessary; the other portion says, we come up precisely to these terms. After that we need no other basis; we stand, sir, clearly on the subject of union.

Rev. Dr. Marshall (Old School):—I come, sir, from that region of the country called the backbone of the Old School Church, in Ohio, west of Pittsburg. We, sir, since this matter of union has been broached, have felt a great deal of interest in that part of the church, especially amongst the laity, amongst the elders and private members of the church, and those especially, sir, who are pre-eminent for piety. There is a great interest, sometimes, I would say an absorbing interest at this present time in reference to this matter of union. It is, let me say, sir, the prayer, the earnest prayer of God's people, that He will, in His righteous providence, speedily bring about this union. Now, sir, we are here, a Convention; and why are we here as a Convention? Is this a Convention, called and directed to meet by man? I think not, sir; I think the hand of God is in this matter. I think, sir, the signs of the times are showing us that we are approaching that point when the Son of God, says, Unite your ranks; stand up as a united phalanx against the powers of darkness. I think that is what the Lord Jesus Christ says to denominations at this time. Now, we have here five or six different branches of the Presbyterian Church represented. Wherein do we differ? If we cannot reach an organic union, cannot we reach a higher, a more active co-operative union? I am not without hope that in regard to the differences with one of these denominations, the time is near when we can reach this organic union.

When I was a young man, I was active in the early controversies of our church. I remember, in the first Assembly I attended, in this city, there was there a brother, highly esteemed, full of ardor like myself, earnest, pious, holy. He was chairman of another branch of the church; he has now gone home to heaven. I refer to Dr. Brainerd. When I look back, I see and acknowledge there was a great deal of self then; we had not the spirit of the Lord Jesus Christ resting in our hearts, as we ought to have had it. The more now I look at the matter, at the condition of our land, and at the world, the more anxious I am that we should have union between these bodies.

In regard to some here, I can conceive of no difficulty to union. In regard to the Covenanter brethren and the United Presbyterian brethren, what are the influences that can keep us apart? It is the matter of psalmody and communion. Now, I cannot conceive that in this contest, principles like these should keep apart Presbyterian brethren. In regard to our New School brethren, I am charitable enough to believe that the great body of the New School Presbyterian people are as sound in the faith—and I have read a great deal and made inquiry—as sound in the principles of the faith as I am; and I glory in standing upon the platform of Presbyterian principles embodied in the Confession of Faith, and shall so stand until I die. [Applause.] I believe, sir, they are heart and soul with us. I believe God is now saying, unite your ranks and come together.

Let us show to the world that the Presbyterian Church is a unit; that we love Christ, and the souls of men; and that we are so anxious to build up the kingdom of God in the world, that we will not let these small matters that have kept us apart, and caused us to spend our strength in strife among ourselves, any longer hinder our union. We shall show the world we are so anxious for Christ and the salvation of men, that we shall go heart and soul in this great work of uniting these ranks, and taking up the the Cross of Christ, put to flight our enemies.

Rev. Dr. McGill (United Presbyterian): Mr. President, I presume we are all in favor of union. In fact, I would almost pity the man who is not in favor of the union of these churches; not only of Presbyterian Churches, but all the churches of Christ. The present divided state of the Church is certainly unnatural. We should do everything we can do, consistently with our views of the teachings of the Word of God, to unite not only the Presbyterian, but all the Churches of Christ in the land. But while this is so, Mr. Chairman, it is well that we should look at our differences, speak about them, and talk about them. That is the very thing now that we propose to do; to propose terms of union, and see if we are all agreed to unite together, without further difficulty or consideration. If there are differences among us, we can determine whether or not those differences are sufficient to keep us apart.

Now, we have been told again and again, on the floor of the Convention, that those differences should not keep us apart. One brother, or rather father, says, these were fine threads. Well, that is so in the opinion of many; but then they seemed to others not to be fine threads. The very father who used this expression, said if he could only get an honest subscription from the New School brethren to the Confession of Faith, he was willing to unite with them. This is the way in which we are all inclined to regard these matters. These differences are small, if, indeed, our brethren will only come on our platform. We think if these differences keep them off our platform, they are only small differences; they should get over these difficulties and come to us at once.

Now, I would say, Mr. Chairman, that I, perhaps, would go much further than the great majority of ministers and people of the United Presbyterian Church in favor of Union. I could exercise forbearance to a much greater extent than some of my brethren, perhaps, could to those differences that are now supposed to keep apart the Presbyterian Church. But, then, Mr. Chairman, it is a fact that we, of the United Presbyterian Church in general, do hold some views that are not held by other Presbyterian branches. It is also true that Old School Presbyterians in general have some views that are not held by other branches of the Presbyterian Church. Now, to talk about the desirableness of union may have a good effect upon us; but still, the thing to be determined now is, on what terms shall we unite. Will we sing the Psalms of Scripture, learned in some faithful version; or shall we sing, in preference, other parts of the word of God; or shall we sing hymns written by Dr. Watts and other men? What shall we do? Will the brethren who are in favor of singing the hymns of Watts and Cowper agree to a good version of the one hundred and fifty psalms, as united brethren, to be used by the United Presbyterian Church? I use that term to apply to all branches. These are questions to be considered. Let us bear in mind that different persons hold different views on these points. The United Presbyterians hold the view that nothing but the Psalms should be used in the worship of God. I would go much further than my brethren, and most of the ministers in that church; but these brethren are conscientious. They are not bigoted; they have examined the subject, as they think, carefully, and they hold their views earnestly.

The question is, can we, consistently with our views of duty, unite with the other branches of the Presbyterian Church, whose congregations and ministers practice as they think fit in regard to this question?

It is well to understand one another. It is well the Old and New School Presbyterians should understand one another. The Old School

Presbyterians make an honest confession on this floor, of the Westminster Confession of Faith. If the New School brethren are not in favor of such a subscription as the Old School demand, then there is a difference of opinion which ought to be settled in some way. Let us understand one another, and talk about these matters; let us talk about them fairly. There are some differences among us. How are we to get together, holding these differences? It is said there is nothing to keep us apart; but as a general thing that language means, come over to us; come to our platform. These differences are nothing at all, just come to us. That is about the meaning of all those declarations. I would about as lief the brethren would plainly say, your differences are not of importance; come at once and join our Church.

REV. JOHN McMILLAN, (Reformed Presbyterian):—After these things have been looked at—you are all willing certainly that we should look at them—I do not conceive that there are inseparable barriers in the way of union. I do not suppose that all those fine things that are said by the Old and New School brethren here to-night, should be confined to themselves. I love to hear these brethren talk together as they do; and standing looking on, I cannot see why they should not unite, even before to-morrow, if the Lord will, and they are as willing as He. I do not feel like being left out of this union. I belong to the least of all these tribes that are here to-night. I feel that the Lord Jesus Christ is looking down upon all the members from this body who have met together; and that He does not judge of any one branch of the Presbyterian Church that it is altogether free of sin, in regard to this divided state of the Church. I cannot believe that all the sin of the divided Church lies at the door from any one branch of it; or any two branches of it. I believe that if we felt as Christ certainly feels, that the little finger in our bodies is a member with which, if pricked, or burnt, or injured, all the other members sympathize, that our hearts would be fraternally united. I cannot but feel that there is sin enough at the door of all our churches to bring us all down to the dust; but we are looking continually, as we are in our human nature disposed to look, away off from ourselves at some others, rather than turning our looks in upon ourselves. We must be willing, as we are here to-night in this house of prayer, as we have come up from the wide quarters of this land, to meet each other in a spirit of prayer; we must be willing to get down, each for himself and each for his own church, in the dust of humiliation, and pray to God for light, and look to Christ for His love to flow through all our hearts—through my heart more than it does. I do believe if we thus come before the Lord in all devotion—if we do not all feel to-night that we are all formed as notes of music are for one another—that thus will be upon us the religious spirit, which is the proper spirit we must cherish; which is the spirit, if I know my heart, I am willing to cherish. In that spirit we are each to pray to God to dwell with us and guide us, and teach us the way for us that we may have a better union than we have ever had in the Church, a sweeter union than we have had in the Church yet. May God grant it, and help us to see it.

THE PRESIDENT:—We are getting nearer to the Throne of Grace to-night. Let us go now, each of us to the Throne of Grace, and be led in prayer by the Rev. Dr. Hodge, of Princeton.

At the conclusion of prayer by Dr. Hodge, beseeching the Spirit of grace and truth to guide and direct the proceedings of the Convention, the 13th and 14th stanzas of the 102d Psalm were sung by the congregation.

Rev. Dr. H. B. Smith, of New York, offered a prayer, especially asking the blessing of God upon the meeting of the Evangelical Episcopalians in session in the Church of the Epiphany, in reciprocation of their fraternal prayers for the Divine guidance of the Presbyterian Convention.

Rev. Dr. Sheddon (Old School):—Mr. President, we are all agreed there are difficulties in the way of union; and the question occurs, is our desire for it so great as to make us willing to melt down and fuse away those difficulties? We all feel, no doubt, that great expense attends our separate organizations; that it exists in the churches and in the boards; and that in various ways our union would save men and money. I believe there is one general feeling represented here, to stand firmly and decidedly upon one basis of doctrine. And saving the essentials, can we so fuse, or so arrange touching some of the non-essentials, that we can gain numbers, take from the world some of its strongest weapons, in our disagreement and our want of Christian purposes? Now, sir, touching these, I hold that there is such a strong pressure upon us, that we ought certainly in regard to some of those peculiarities to yield. I believe, Mr. President, that there were some bloody losses in the days of the war, because of jealousies and ambitions between divisions. When there is one Christian War, let all these cease, and let us form one grand phalanx.

If some prefer to sing the old psalms of David, let them sing them; let us sing what we please.

If some are disposed to say, we cannot give that general invitation at our Communion table, and we will withhold it; let us extend it. Now, sir, I hold that of those non-essentials, there is not one but can be so modified or changed, that each may engage in his own peculiarity, and yet all be one body. Why, sir, before this, and in my young days, although it is some time back, I have heard the old psalms in Presbyterian Churches; and if I go into such a church, and they say that is the psalmody—well, I can sing it. I can sing it for the name and for the sake of the great cause. It is desirable that we should forget those few separating difficulties, and yet give them each and all much that is their choice and their education. I have known some families separated, and I have known some families brought back to their own homes, in spite of much that was dreaded and derided in the household; but God sent them back to their own homes again, forgetting and forsaking the things that drove them forth. If some of these, our children, will again come back and say, Come, let us join together on the same common ground; will we not meet them? But, oh, as brethren, New School brethren, Reformed Presbyterian brethren, one and all, is there such a difference between us that we cannot before the world show that co-operation? If we cannot do that, cannot we put in our platform non-interference? Let us then agree that non-interference is our first duty.

REV. W. W. BARR (United Presbyterian):—The purpose of this meeting is to ascertain our sentiments in regard to this subject of union. I have in my hand the written sentiments which I desire to express for the action of the Committee, as I can do it more definitely in this way than in any other.

We, the ministers and elders, delegates from the various branches of the Presbyterian family in the United States, met in Convention, do declare—

1. That the Scriptures of the Old and New Testaments are the inspired word of God, and the only rule of faith and practice.

2. In the present divided state of the Church, and in the existing condition of things in the world, a Creed or Confession of Faith is necessary, in order that it may be known what we believe the Scriptures do teach.

3. A Creed or Confession is the Creed of the Church adopting it; and the Church consists of ministers, elders, deacons, and members.

4. We believe that the Augustinian, Reformed or Calvinistic system of doctrine, as it is definitely embodied and stated in the Westminster Confession of Faith, and accompanying Catechisms, exhibits clearly the great doctrines of the word of God.

5. The Presbyterian Form of Government is according to the Scriptures and the modes of worship adopted by our Presbyterian fathers, and still generally practiced by their descendants, should be continued in opposition to all Ritualistic innovations.

6. The Psalms of the Bible were authorized by God Himself to be used in His worship, and this authority has never been revoked, and no unquestionable command at least has been given to make or sing any others. These Psalms, moreover, by the concurrent testimony of the most learned and pious men of ancient and modern times, are admirably suited to the giving of praise to God, and the expression of every feeling and pious sentiment of the Christian heart. They are, besides, in no sense denominational, but constitute in the language of the pious Herder, "The Hymn-book for all ages." They are the only *union* Psalms or hymns in existence, and therefore should be restored to their place in the Church, and chanted appropriately in the prose version, or sung in the best metrical translations now in existence, or that can be made by the combined scholarship and poetical talent that the Church can command.

7. The Church is a covenanted body, and it is her duty to recognize her covenant relation to God, and at suitable times to unite and combine in a public recognition and declaration of the covenant obligations that bind her to her covenant Head.

8. The law of God is the supreme rule of duty for men in their civil, as well as in their natural and religious relations; and the Lord Jesus Christ as mediator, is king of nations, and should be recognized and acknowledged as such by civil governments in their fundamental law.

9. Communion implies agreement and visible union, and therefore it is inconsistent in the Church, and destructive of her proper discipline, to admit to her fellowship in sealing ordinances those who do not declare their agreement with her profession and practice, or whom she would not admit to her fellowship upon examination and profession of their faith.

10. The union of the branches of the Presbyterian family is eminently desirable, if it can be effected without compromise or sacrifice of truth; and they should be united thus, in order that the Saviour's prayer to the Father may be answered, and that the united Church might, with superior power and energy, send the gospel to every creature in this land, and as speedily as possible throughout the world.

REV. MR. BARR:—Mr. Chairman, these are sentiments coming from myself. I believe, however, they are the sentiments of a very large portion, of a majority of the church with which I am connected. They are sentiments on which we can unite without giving up any principle that would violate our convictions. If we want union, we can come to these principles.

On motion, the paper was referred to the Committee on the Basis.

ELDER GEORGE H. STUART, requesting the Rev. Dr. Beatty to occupy the Chair, spoke as follows:—I have great faith in God's Spirit, I am going to change the speech I intended after what my brother said. As he read his speech, I hope the house will excuse me for reading mine. The difference is, he is the author of his, and I am not of mine. I hope the Convention will bear with me.

Mr. Stuart then read the following letter:

EDINBURGH, October 16th, 1867.

MY DEAR MR. STUART:—Your letter showing that the Union leaven is at active work among the brethren in America, reminded me of the words, "As a cup of cold water is to a thirsty soul, so is good news from a far country."

I am one of those who cling to the theology of our fathers, my motto being, to quote again the words of Scripture, "Thus saith the Lord, stand ye in the way, and seek and ask for the old paths, where is the good way, and walk therein, and ye shall find rest for your souls."

But while in this age of doubts and daring speculations, adhering more tenaciously than ever to the old theology, I would never place matters of inference—often remote inference, that belong only to the forms and outworks of our faith, on the same level with truths that are of clear revelation, and of saving import, yet this is the cause of more unhappy separations than error to which man is prone. The tendency of the Church, as proved by her past history, has always been to do what our Lord condemned in the Pharisees, and has described in these words, "Teaching for doctrines the commandments of men."

Here, it appears to me, has lain the difficulty in the way of Union, both in your country and in mine, and it rejoices my heart to find that our Presbyterian churches, enlightened and moved, I trust, by one divine Spirit, are becoming more alive to the duty of distinguishing between faith and forms; between what God's Spirit has revealed, and man's reason has inferred; between the doctrines of the Bible, and what I may call, without offense, "the tradition of the elders."

Do not fancy that I set little store on the views and customs of our forefathers. I cherish the memory of these men, and hold them in the highest admiration; but I cannot give you a better proof of that, than my conviction that they, had they lived in our own day, would not have allowed the differences which have too long separated our Presbyterian bodies, to separate, to divide, and weaken them. Men of great catholicity and breadth of view, who "had understanding of the times," they would have accommodated themselves to these in all matters of mere Christian expediency. They tolerated differences on minor points; they admitted certain questions to be what are called "matters of forbearance;" they regarded customs, however venerable for age, as of no imperative authority, and refused to regard anything as unchangeable and infallible but the Word of God. I am confident that union, as now proposed among the different Presbyterian bodies, would have been the counsel of all our great reformers.

There is an old Scotch song, which, describing a time when Scotland's back was at the wall, says:

"O for one hour of Wallace Wight!"

And in these days, when Ritualism and Rationalism are making such havoc in the Church of Christ, and union among his sound and faithful followers is so imperatively demanded, I am often disposed to cry, "O for one hour of Knox, or Calvin, or of some other great old champion of the faith, to heal our unhappy divisions, and gather the separate, and often rival churches, into one united and unanimous phalanx!"

I rejoice to say that the prospects of such a union here are growing brighter and brighter. The current runs with unabated, and, indeed, growing force in that direction. Yet it is not without a measure of anxiety that I, and many others, look to the march of events in America. Here, in order to obstruct the progress of this cause, some are stirring up the ashes of old controversies, and appealing to old prejudices. They may as well attempt, I believe, to arrest the rising tide as stop the contemplated union. Still the news that the good work had been consummated in America, would greatly contribute to cheer the hands of friends, and weaken the hands of the opponents of union on this side of the Atlantic. May we hear of that soon? The Lord hasten it in His own time!

Some two months ago, I attended the sittings of the Evangelical Alliance, at Amsterdam. Would that all good men in your country and mine saw things with the eyes of distinguished representatives of the foreign Evangelical Churches, whom I met there. With what astonishment did they hear of any opposition to the proposed union of our Presbyterian Churches. How little, in the eyes of these distinguished men, these impartial and unprejudiced judges, seemed the points on which the opponents of union stood. My intercourse with them but confirmed me in the opinion I enunciated so far back as the period of the disruption, and have ever since adhered to, that there is no valid excuse, or scriptural ground, for the unendowed Presbyterian Churches remaining apart.

Let us pray that God would pour out on your churches and ours, the spirit of our blessed Lord; and also of Him, the great Apostle of the Gentiles, who, liberal without being latitudinarian, tolerated much greater differences of opinion within the churches He planted than any found within those now aiming at union.

Were our Presbyterian churches, both here and in America, united together, and were such a correspondence established between them as would insure their vigorous and harmonious action, both in the old world and the new, what a power for good were this? We would go down on the ranks of heathenism, priestcraft, error and oppression, "terrible as an army with banners."

Besides binding our churches, we should, as every good man will wish, bind the two countries more closely together, rendering nugatory all the attempts of wicked men to sow discord between us, and alienate those from each other who should live in perpetual amity, and fight side by side the world's battle for gospel truth and universal liberty. Let me hear how the work goes on in your churches. May the Lord Himself preside in their assemblies, making their places at His feet glorious, and pour out on "assembled elders" such floods of light and love that they shall see eye to eye, and face to face. Ever yours, &c.,

THOMAS GUTHRIE.

REV. M. C. SUTPHEN, (Old School):—Who shall come after the king? It would be difficult for the largest platform experience to follow Thomas Guthrie seconded by George H. Stuart. You may then judge of my embarrassment. But, sir, I am a Presbyterian, and believe in the perseverance of the Saints; and having claimed the floor some time since, I will now re-assert my right. The First Napoleon sagely remarked that we should march at the head of the ideas of our age. Now, what is the great principle which gives tone and tenor to the movements of the present country? It is Union. This is manifest in the civil world. What but this inspired Prussia to that wondrous campaign which gained thirty victories in twenty days, and more effectively changed the map of Europe than all the wars of the great Bonaparte? What but this inspiration after national unity precipitated that significant conflict now raging around the walls of Rome? What but this led our country triumphantly through the fearful struggle just terminated? And this obtains in the ecclesiastical world. Reference has been made to the union of the forces of infidelity. Look also at what tremendous sacrifices of doctrine and discipline Prelacy is maintaining union! Now, if Episcopacy recognizes union as so necessary that she will compromise even her Protestantism, should we not seek it when no sacrifice of essential principle is demanded? If *Prelacy has sacrificed Christ to the unity of the Church, should we sacrifice Christ to the divisions of the Church?* O, let us march at the head of this controlling idea of our age! Let us discern the signs of the time. A basis is offered in our common Confessions. A venerable father, on behalf of the Covenanter bodies, says this is all sufficient. The claim of my own Church is simply an honest subscription thereto for the system of doctrine. Such subscription on every hand is tendered. Let us avail ourselves in time of this great irresistible principle, and not destroy ourselves by our divisions. One word more. It is written, "They that *do* his will shall know of the doctrine." Methodism even is *working* itself into orthodoxy. What we need is to advance the whole line, in order that the few minor, non-essential differences which remain may be removed.

REV. A. G. WALLACE, (United Presbyterian):—I wish to make a suggestion in regard to business; it is that the secretaries at the opening of the session to-morrow will report the number of delegates from each of the churches represented here. I think it is a matter of interest that ought to be presented to us. It may guide our minds in various points when we consider how the whole church is represented.

It having been intimated that in the meeting of the Clergy and Laity of the Protestant Episcopal Church, now convened in the Church of the Epiphany in this city, prayer had been offered for this Convention, the following resolution offered by Rev. J. M. Stevenson, D.D., Old School, was unanimously adopted:—

Resolved, That the Convention sends its cordial salutations to our brethren of the Protestant Episcopal Church, now assembled in this city, praying that grace, mercy and peace may rest upon them from God, our Father, and the Lord Jesus Christ.

The Convention was adjourned with prayer by the Rev. Dr. John Hall, of New York.

FIRST REFORMED PRESBYTERIAN CHURCH, PHILADELPHIA.
Thursday, November 7th, 1867, 9 *A. M.*

The devotional meeting was largely attended, Rev. R. D. Harper, D.D., United Presbyterian, presiding; and was opened with prayer by the Rev. Dr. Charles C. Beatty, Old School.

The first portion of the 122d Psalm was sung, and the 4th chapter of Ephesians was read.

Prayer was offered by the Rev. Samuel Miller, Old School. The latter portion of the 122d Psalm was then sung.

REV. N. G. PARKE, D.D. (Old School) said:—It was my privilege, during the past summer, to be present in the city of Edinburgh, during a meeting of the Assembly of the Scotch church—the United Presbyterian Assembly of the Scotch church; and I am able to say that if there was any subject before that meeting, it was the subject of this meeting, *i. e.* a closer union of the people of God. It was the subject of every church assembly there; it was in every sermon that was there preached; it was prominent in all the prayers; it was prominent in all the speeches that came in, in the discussions; it was prominent in the conversation; *it is the subject* that was being agitated in Scotland, everywhere; and the leading men, such as Drs. Guthrie and Buchanan,—the leading spirits in the Scotch church were, and are in favor of a closer union among the members, especially, of the Presbyterian family. And this is just the view taken of it; in not simply testifying to the advantages of a union, but they unite their hearts in spreading the Gospel throughout the world.

This thing was exceedingly interesting to my own heart. And yet, after all, there has been no more intercourse among these Presbyterian families—the Old School churches, the Reformed, and United Presbyterian churches—in my life, than there was among the Jews and Samaritans; and in view of such a meeting as we have here, in the mingling of these Christians, and the fact that God has put it into the hearts of this people, at this time, not only to pray that they may be brought closer together, and labor for it,—ought not measures, sir, to be at once taken to bring them together?

I only present this thought, prominent in my own mind, in connection with these services, and my heart's desire and prayer to God is, that we may, in these services, be brought to feel the baptism of the Holy Spirit, and to feel, in this hour, that the difficulties that have stood in our way, and kept us apart, will very readily be taken away.

The Committee to prepare a basis of union, had leave to retire to the lecture-room of the church; and, by request of the Chairman the prayers of the meeting were offered in its behalf.

Elder Robert Carter (Old School):—My heart is full this morning. I will tell you of a little incident in my own experience. When I was a child, ten years of age, I sat down in a little anti-burgher church in South Scotland, for the first time, to take up the memorials of our Redeemer's love. I remained in that connection until I left my native land and came to this country. I joined the Old School Presbyterian Church, and I had staid in connection some time when I was impressed with a desire to go back to the little valley where first I saw the light. After ten years' absence, I returned with my wife and child. I went to the little church; the Communion table was set. The old minister saw me coming back, and he grasped me in his arms, and blessed me, but was not permitted to invite me to sit down at the table. My uncle, one of the most affectionate and loving of men, doted upon me; and he was the senior elder of the church, but was not permitted to say: "Will you sit down with us to-day!" But from a little church near by, that was at variance with our little church, I am sorry to say, there came a committee, which said: "Will you join with us? You cannot sit down in your little church." No, said I, but I shall hear the Master say, "Do this in remembrance of me;" and I shall look on, and may have some of the crumbs that fall from the table; and let me say, there was not one at that table who would not have gladly welcomed me—had I been connected with the church, or otherwise; yet they were restricted by the difference of our connections. Ah! brother, that was the last time that such a scene could be enacted there, and I left them. Again, I went back, and the table was again spread, and lovingly, and affectionately they said: "Come with us to-day;" and then, I sat down at the table, and looked around. Ah! how many—how many of those with whom I had sat first, when a young lad—were gone. Nearly all were gone. Gone,—gone to that other world.

Do you wonder, friends, and brethren, that I feel now—when I see since that time that we with the Episcopalians, and all of the Presbyterian Church can sit down together—to bless God that I could sit down with my old pastor in a distant land and break the bread of the Lord's Supper? Need you wonder that I rejoice when I see brethren coming together, with their little differences melting away at the foot of Christ's cross, feeling one together; when we can look at the blessed Saviour and feel that we all are brethren; and when we all can say, brother, you can sit with me at this the Lord's table?

When I heard last night a brother read as he did, the "Basis," upon which you bore our connection, let me say that my heart was touched. Brother, we must have a great deal of forbearance. Those sweet old songs which for the first time in my life, I sang exclusively, and for the last half, scarcely sang at all, are within me yet; and I feel as though I would have all sing with me, and with one heart, and with one mind, should unite and bless God for the privilege of singing those old songs to His praise, and I can only say of those who do not feel as I do, "God forgive them for they know not what they do."

Rev. John H. Pratt, (Old School):—I wish to say, that I feel this morning as I sit here, my heart to rejoice with the things we are hearing; what I have prayed for years, and what I never expected to witness to-day, is to see these Presbyterian branches all united together, speaking the same things, and presenting their united affections to God for His blessing; and now I think there is one thing that we need. We need to be endowed with power from on high. You take two masses of silver or gold, and put them in a crucible together, and you let these masses be melted, and come to a fluid state, and the moment they touch they run together. And if God, in answer to our prayers will send us the precious baptism of the Holy Ghost, from Heaven, and humble our hearts with love to Christ, we will then flow together with new love.

We should never forget that those who learned theology from Him who "spake as never man spake," that those who spent a full theological term under His tuition, and got the truth fresh from His lips, still were not ready to fulfil the great work of going out as ambassadors for God, and winning souls to acknowledge the allegiance of our Lord Jesus Christ, until they were to tarry in Jerusalem, and be imbued with power from on high. And this is just what we need. Let us not forget that we live under the ministry of the Spirit. Let us not forget that it is peculiarly, in the province of the Spirit, to take of the things that are Christ's and reveal them unto us; that it is in the Spirit we glorify Christ—that name by which we are called.

Then I have this to say, and I do it on my own responsibility, unsolicited by any, and that responsibility rests solely upon my own shoulders. I say that while yesterday, during our various sessions, we united together in singing those psalms, grand and glorious, and gorgeous in their beauty as the temple services of old, and which never grow old, or go out of use; and while I love them, and while my heart goes out in them, and while I feel their utterances in the heart, yet I would make an amendment now, which is this: not that we sing a hymn; not that we take another book, but this: let none be compelled; as many as shall find it in their heart, let them unite in a petition to that Spirit of all power in those sweet words which we have heard so often:—

"Come Holy Spirit, heavenly Dove,
With all thy quickening powers;
Come, shed abroad a Saviour's love,
And that shall kindle ours."

I request, then, in behalf of the hearts who love that petition to the One who is the same in glory and power, that we unite in singing that one verse.

The great assemblage arose, and fulfilled the request by singing the verse with such pathos and power as can only come from hearts filled with love to their Saviour.

REV. CYRUS DICKSON, D.D., (Old School):—The brother who preceded me alluded to the primitive church in Jerusalem, and repeated the command of the Saviour, that it should remain there until imbued in the Spirit from on High! My mind turned to the smallness of that church, and the evidences of its prosperity, and its returning power. One evening I took the opportunity to cut out of a newspaper———————; before I left home—a series of statistics, one of which I shall advert to, presented, I believe, by a brother of this assembly (Dr. Smith) to a Religious Convention, held last summer. It tells us, and I have no doubt of its accuracy, that there are, in different Presbyterian organizations in this country, 5,000 churches, 6,300 ministers, and about 700,000 communicants. Then it gives the statistics of our brethren of the Reformed Dutch Church, which embraces 444 churches, with 461 ministers, and 58,000 members.

Now that primitive church had not, so far as we can tell, more than five hundred members; it may be more or less; but here, sir, we have five thousand churches, with a million communicants, and, he tells us, two, or three, or four million of children under our care; and of ministers we have six thousand five hundred, or seven thousand. Now, look at our numerical force, our size, and our magnitude, and then remember that the same power is promised to us, Mr. Moderator and brethren, as it was to that primitive church, in the words:—"Lo I am with you alway, to the end of the world;" and the promise of My Father is to you, and when ye go forth to preach My Gospel, I am with you working signs and wonders, to bring the nations to the allegiance of Christ. The Moderator of that apostolic church laid a great and gracious responsibility upon all the future part of the race! And what *do we*, standing where we are, with our immensely magnified numbers, and power, and resources? What is the responsibility under which we labor here this day? In such a vast congregation of wealth, of numbers, of influence, if we can unite to ask that Holy Spirit to descend on us, with faithful hearts, when it does descend, in all its power, it will have the influence and power to cause union, not division; not separation, but the spirit of union.

God has two ways of uniting his people. The one is Grace; the other Providence! He pours His Spirit out upon the people, and their hearts begin to melt and flow together. And if they will permit that Spirit thus to unite them, peace, quiet, and prosperity will attend them. But if they do not come thus, and put themselves under his control, then He uses the power and wisdom of His providence. And the history of God's people, in all times has been, that when they are called to unite in some great emergency, as now presses upon the Church, and they decline to obey, then He brings in the stern discipline of His providence.

When my Presbytery appointed me delegate, I remember on my way home from it, as I landed from the steamer "Baltimore," at the ancient town of Annapolis, I passed a "Smithy," or what we Scotch term a black-smith shop! And there I saw an old cart-wheel that had been running all summer, and had been brought to the shop because it was all dried and cracked; its felloes, and spokes, and hub, were gradually separated by the heat of the July and August sun; and it was all loose, crazy, inefficient, and unsafe, and the smith, after having smoothed, and fixed, and wedged the felloes, and the spokes, and the hub, took down the old tire, and after taking a little out of it, he surrounded it entirely with flames, and after it had been heated, he put it around the crazy wood-work, and poured on the water, and it began to swell, and swell, until the old hub, and the felloes, and the spokes, came tight together, with choice or without choice! (Applause).

That is what God is going to do with this great American Continent. And the Church understands what God has told us; and He is ready for it now, and the fire and the faggots are ready to heat the tire. He comes to help us to make and perpetuate a union, and He now is ready for us, and will bring us together. We should all understand that the tire has already been gotten out for the heat, and the heat for the tire! Let us understand our times! Let us remember ourselves! Let us do what we must do, in time! and when we come together in coming years, all will be quiet, peace.

We are on the eve of such disasters, if the Church of God does not understand our times, and do right, as she has never seen yet. We are just on the eve of such troubles, as we have never known, if we are regardless of our obligations and duties, and demands of the law. And because everything that has been little will grow less, and that which was big will grow bigger, for we are compelled by the power of the Providence that brings the tire upon the slack wheel to unite! The wheels of God's chariot have become loose, but God will tighten them! What we want now is that the people of God will come together and do their work! I live in what you used to call a border state; I live in the midst of the masses, and among four millions! And these poor people all need the Gospel! And I tell you, Sir, that these great Presbyterian Churches that are represented here, prayed year after year, that God might set these people free, or open the door to them, and they would avail themselves of the open door and the access afforded. And now when God has opened the door—through the calamities which attended our late struggle—we have not met the emergency. And have we not now something to do in bringing the knowledge of the Gospel to these people? I tell you, Sir, that this land will find that it has not settled that great question yet,—no nor will not have, in 10 or 20 years from now unless the enlightenment of that multitude, through the Gospel of Christ, is given. And I ask what is to be done in behalf of four millions of these people, in order that the Lord may send His gracious Spirit upon them? When they have been groping through their ignorance, feeling for those letters which could tell them of their Saviour. Among this great Presbyterian body of 5000 churches, 7000 ministers' and one million of communicants, there was scarcely a corporal's guard willing to give, and vastly less than a corporal's guard willing to go and teach them the unsearchable riches of Christ! I have nothing to say about the millions lying beyond the seas. But here are four million of people, just liberated, who are now fixing their form of life. Here are a people who are just gaining a faint glimpse of God's word and its light. They have been elevated from their degradation: and they cannot but influence our laws, forms of government, and existing institutions. And it is a duty, solemn and great, that we should seek to educate and evangelize them!

We are spending our time and means in carrying on domestic missionary work! and in communities of people, we aid to support three or four ministers, where they can only support one! Our great west clamors for men. At every little cross-road, you find more men at work than they ought to have. At some of the cross-roads you find three or four Presbyterian churches and three or four ministers are starving, and their wives and children, for want of support. At every little four-corners you will find a church that wants to be represented, and in little villages of five hundred or seven hundred, we find sometimes three or four ministers of the same denomination, who desire to be delegates. What we want is this: but one store where there are customers enough for one store! One blacksmith shop where there is work for but one blacksmith shop! One tire where there is only heat enough for one tire! One church where there are enough supporters for one church!

Let us act as wise and sensible men! Home missions cannot support men at such an extravagant rate. There are other places where help is needed,—and let them not be robbed! A Brother has prayed for the Holy Spirit as a "Spirit of light," to be poured out upon this assemblage! It is not all light, brethren, that we need! we know a thousand times more than we do. But we need the spirit of love to gain precious souls! That is what we need, my Brethren! And when you pray for the Holy Ghost—and I would not forget that He is the Spirit of all light—God grant that you may pray with hope, that He is the Spirit of all love! This is what we need, Sir! It is not knowledge that the Presbyterian Church needs, but it is love; love to reach the hearts of sinners, love to convince them of the error of their ways. Let us ask that when that Spirit comes it may enlighten the eyes and understanding, and renew our souls to receive the truth, and the love contained in it!

The Rev. Dr. D. V. McLane, Old School, then led in prayer, remembering the Committee on the "Basis of Union," and praying that such a report should be brought in, as would meet with the approbation of all the members.

After devotional exercises, the Convention proceeded to business, the President in the chair.

The minutes of last session were read and approved.

On motion of Rev. W. T. Eva, it was

Resolved, That all Ministers and Ruling Elders, in good and regular standing, connected with the different branches of the Church here represented, who may attend upon the sessions of the Convention, be invited to sit as corresponding members, and that they be requested to hand their names to the Committee on Credentials. (See Appendix V.)

Rev. E. Kempshall, D.D., (Old School), said:—Mr. President, before you proceed with the regular business, I would like to make a motion to complete the business of last evening. There was a resolution passed conveying the Christian salutations of this Convention to the Annual Meeting of the Protestant Episcopal Evangelical Societies—that is, the Assembly now in session in this city, and composed of about 450 ministers and laymen. It seems to me proper for us to appoint a Committee to convey in person that resolution to that body. The plain word from the heart, reaches to the heart; and in conversation with some of the members of that Convention this morning, I have been led to believe that if such a Committee were appointed, a corresponding Committee would be appointed in that body, returning the Christian salutation from that Convention to us. And I would move you, sir, that a Committee of five, of which the Rev. H. B. Smith shall be Chairman, be appointed to convey this resolution to that body.

President Stuart put the question, which being carried, he appointed as that Committee, the following gentlemen:

Rev. H. B. Smith, D.D., Chairman; Rev. J. M. Stevenson, D.D., and Elders, Hon. C. D. Drake, and Robert Carter.

Rev. J. G. Butler, D.D., (New School):—Mr. President, I wish on behalf of the Presbyterian Historical Society, to request the members of this Convention, after the adjournment at 12 o'clock to-day, that they assemble, compactly, at the front of the church, in order to have the instrument of the photographer applied to them. [Laughter.] The Society desire to retain a souvenir of this assemblage.

Rev. D. V. McLean, D.D., (Old School,) on the part of the Society, warmly seconded the request.

President Stuart:—Brethren, you have heard the request. You will all meet as desired, in the front of the church, to be united in one grand picture! The artist, I understand, can group three hundred in one picture, and we want to put all the good-looking men in front. [Laughter.] It is desired, by the artist, that the Chairman shall occupy the centre, and that the gray heads should gather around him as near as possible, but mixed up well in different denominations. This is an historical incident, and it will go down to posterity, in your Presbyterian Historical Society, which is gathering everything that relates to all these branches of the Church.

The President called up the unfinished business.

The Secretaries, in accordance with the resolutions adopted last evening, reported the following as the number of members of the Convention.

Whole number, 262.

Classified thus :—

From the Old School Branch,	- - - -	162
" New School do.,	- - - - -	64
" United Presbyterian do.,	- - -	12
" Reformed Presbyterian do.,	- -	12
" Reformed Protestant Dutch do.,	-	6
" Cumberland Presbyterian do.,	-	6

An invitation was received from the Board of Directors of the Union League of Philadelphia to visit the League House, at such time as may be convenient to the members of the body.

Also an invitation from the Board of the American Sunday School Union, to visit and inspect their Publishing House and Sale Rooms.

On motion both invitations were accepted, with the thanks of the Convention.

REV. DR. R. DAVIDSON, (Old School,) said :—

Mr. President: I have for a long time, greatly desired a union of all Protestantism in this country; I have thought that impracticable. I have for an equally long time desired a union of Presbyterian Christians in this country. I have thought it over a great deal, and now think and believe that it is practicable. I believe the greatest duty which rests upon me, and the first great duty for all Christians, is to secure human salvation. To help in releasing a human soul from sin, I feel to be a duty resting upon me as a man. The next greatest duty resting upon me as a minister, is to hold fast to the faith, the gospel, and to Christ. These are the two greatest first duties resting upon me as a man and minister. I believe the next greatest duty, resting upon me on this earth, is to help all I can to heal all the divisions in the Church of God, as far as may be. I believe it is practicable, if Presbyterians have a mind to work, and in a reasonable time all divisions can be healed.

Two or three plans have been suggested, more privately than publicly. One is, that at present we should seek an Evangelical alliance among Presbyterians. It has struck me, however, that when we have prayed together, and talked together, and have come to understand one another, and have come to love one another, and when the love of God is shining in our hearts, I think we can attain the conviction before we leave this Convention, that union among Presbyterians in this country is possible, and that we ought to make the effort, and it is for the purpose of giving such directions and such thoughts, that I propose to read the paper I hold in my hand; and if it meet the approval of the Convention, will request that it be referred to the Committee on the "Basis of Union:"

Whereas, The Church of Jesus Christ is, in a spiritual sense, one, purchased with His precious blood, and heir to a common inheritance of glory. *Whereas*, existing divisions in the visible church, causing strife, and apparent, or real opposition, occasion reproach, and impede the progress of truth. *Whereas*, Christ prayed for the visible oneness of his people, and the Scriptures teach us to hope and pray for it. *Whereas*, Our civil institutions and religious interests are imperiled, on the one hand by Romanism, and on the other by rationalism and infidelity. *Whereas*, The great events which are now transpiring in the world—following each other in quick succession, and the general signs of the times indicate the near approach of still greater political, moral, and religious changes, and the fulfilment of prophecy respecting the conflicts and triumphs of the Church. And, *Whereas*, In the last few years we have seen and realized the happy results of Christian union and co-operation. Therefore,

1. *Resolved*, That it is the duty of all Evangelical Christians to recognize their oneness in Christ; to cultivate fraternal sympathy, and Christian charity; to refrain from hurtful and unedifying controversy; to avoid rival and conflicting enterprises; to give their principles of agreement more, and those of difference, less prominence; to seek a closer union, and as far as practicable, to co-operate in defending and propagating our common Christianity.

2. *Resolved*, That the Westminster Standards, drawn up and adopted by the Westminster Assembly, and approved by the General Assembly of the Church of Scotland, which met in August, 1647, as these have been adopted by the Presbyterian Churches of the United States, form an adequate basis of Christian union and co-operation among all Presbyterians who receive them in their obvious sense.

3. *Resolved*, That for the purpose of promoting greater uniformity in faith and practice, and of furthering the ends specified in the first resolution, and other interests that may arise in the future, it is expedient and seasonable to form a North American Presbyterian Alliance.

4. *Resolved*, That a committee of——be appointed to draw up in due form a concise plan of said alliance, and report the same to this Convention as soon as practicable.

Rev. Alexander Donaldson, (Old School):—This meets my approbation above everything else. I was never so much gratified by any announcement, as I was, when I read in the public paper the call for this Convention by the brethren of the Reformed Presbyterian Church. I never thought in my time and day, that I should live to see that branch of the Church initiating such a movement as this. I regretted, in one aspect of the case, when the Convention was postponed from September to November, and grieved that so long a delay would occur before we could have the satisfaction of meeting together. I hoped that we might come in the Spirit of Christ, and might have our hearts warmed until they melted and flowed together. Last night it seemed as though the Spirit of Christ would come back amongst us, after the discussions of yesterday afternoon. But I had not believed that it had so fully returned as to prepare the way for this action in the appointment of a Committee on Basis. An old proverb saith, "The heart of the wise teacheth his mouth, and doeth understanding to his lips." I have felt that we were not yet in the condition to take this step. I believe if we were made to feel as tenderly as we ought to one another, that our minds would necessarily take a common direction, and believe that our harmony can only arise from such a state of feeling. Everything that tends to consolidate falls happily on my ear. Everything that tends in the slightest degree to wound the sensibilities of any brother of any branch of the Church, has fallen painfully on my ear. The idea of coming together has my warmest approbation, and is my heart's warmest aspiration. I believe that if we had spent much of the time in direct devotional exercises, such as we have had, it would have called down the Spirit from on high; that before the close, our hearts would have all been prepared to accept a basis of union.

The position now submitted, in this paper presented by the brother, seems to me to suit the time much better than anything that we have had before us yet, and I second the motion that it be referred to the committee.

Rev. Dr. Mac Masters, (Old School):—I wish simply to say, that if this Convention can heartily adopt this paper that is now before it, I think that it will accomplish far more than all that has been yet done. And I see no reason why it may not be unanimously and heartily adopted. I hope it will be referred to the Committee.

Rev. Dr. Musgrave:—I wish to inquire if the mover makes this a form of instruction for the committee. If so, I will vote against it, because I expect something more to be done. At any rate I, for one, don't feel that I should discharge my duty, without at least attempting something more. For when, in God's name, we have honestly and truly accomplished more, I feel that it will be time for us to adopt this compromise, if I may so call it. I have not the slightest objection to sending this paper to that committee for their consideration. If they, after deliberately looking at the whole subject, choose to present this as the mandate to be adopted by this Convention, let it be so. But I don't wish that committee to understand us as sending that paper to them to have them send it back to us again, as expressing our views as to what ought to be done. I therefore wish to know what is the design of this! If it is simply to enable them to consider this matter, why, I have no objection to it. I will vote for sending any proper paper or papers to this committee, to help them! Give them all the aid you can. Make suggestions if you please, but do not send this paper to them as an instruction; and have them report to us that this Convention abandons the hope of being able to present any basis upon which these churches can unite at present, and that, after all, we can only go back to our people and say that we must hope, and wait, and pray, and try to get nearer to one another in warmer hearts; and that, at some distant day, we may all come together!

Now, sir, it is my private judgment, that we are just as competent now—and the churches of this country are just as competent now to settle this question practically, as they will be five or ten years to come! I cannot see why the whole Presbyterian Church cannot be united, as we all profess to be under the same influence, believe in the same things, and agree as to government. What is to keep us apart? I do not see why sound Calvinists, and sound Presbyterians, cannot, and should not now come together upon that basis! (Applause). I believe this Convention is ready for it. I think that committee will present a safe basis. I ask, and I wish the world to understand that I am thoroughly Calvinistic, and thoroughly Presbyterian, and I will, God helping me, do nothing that will put the truth in jeopardy, but will contend for such a basis as will secure the purity, and the permanent unity of these Presbyterian churches. I believe, sir, that that can be done! And I think, too, that the hour is now upon us for it! And, moreover, I think that committee will present a proper basis, stamped with our common standards, and our common Presbyterianism, so that we can adopt it!

It does not commit the churches! Indeed, we have no authority to do that! But cannot we, as a Convention of Presbyterians, say that we think that our churches should and can be united upon such a basis? Why, sir, what is to hinder us? I must confess to you that I have been joyful all the time to hear brethren of all these churches talking the same thing, and expressing the same hearty desire for union! Where has there been an expression that would lead us to infer that this Convention was not ready for union? I have not heard a man express that—with one exception—and I do not know whether that ought to be regarded as such; because I believe if that brother—as I call him—had been allowed to proceed for a while, he would have given as his private conviction, that the union of these various branches of the church is, at present, impracticable; and I believe, from my knowledge of the man, that he would have expressed the same common feeling that we have; *i. e.*, that union, if practicable, was desired. Suppose, sir, you regard that as one exception, that was the only one that I have heard!

I never felt so happy in my life as I have been here, and under the conviction that the time has indeed come for a practical organic union of the Presbyterian Church, of this land. I am not willing to send this paper as an instruction to that Committee, to report that we are not ready! No, sir! Let it be sent to them with the express understanding that it is the expression of a respected individual member of the Convention; and is expressive of the views, perhaps, of some others in the body. It is sent to them for their consideration, but let them be untrammelled by no such half-way propositions. But, Oh, how I can thank God, if that Committee will bring us in a sound basis upon which we can unite, and if this Convention will adopt it. Why, sir, I believe such would be the moral influence of this Convention, constituted as it is, so powerful in the providence of God, and exhibiting such a spirit of love, that that influence would be so irresistible, that all Churches would be led to adopt it.

I am not so sanguine as to believe that every individnal in the land would agree to such an organic union. I think, and I am sad when I think, that probably some individual ministers and elders of churches, here and there, might stand out a while in the cold. But, sir, if we were to go into one comfortable, warm house, they would soon be glad enough to come in. [Applause and laughter.] And we would be just as glad to receive them. [Laughter.] Yes, sir! and we will keep the door open! Let us come together now, if we can, and try to get all to come in. And, if any stay out, why let it be upon their own responsibility, and not ours.

Dr. Davidson:—Mr. Chairman, I do not desire or wish to ask of this Convention any thing beyond its pleasure. I simply read the paper, leaving it with the Convention to do with it as it pleases. It is not a motion to commit with instruction, but simply to refer to the Committee on the Basis, to do with it as they wish.

(The paper was referred.)

Dr. C. C. Beatty (Old School):—I am in favor of this committal to the Committee, just as it is in hand; as a mere committal to receive and do with it as they please. That is my understanding of all such papers. And with this understanding, I will read the following paper, and move at the same time that it be referred to the Committee in the same way. I would say that this is not my own production. It has been prepared, as I understand, by some minister, or some member of the Old School Presbyterian Church. And several individuals look at it as a good thing to bring forward some such ideas before the Convention, and commit them to this Committee:—

This Convention, composed of ministers and ruling elders, representing various bodies of Christians, in the United States, all of which bear the general name of Presbyterian, and are united in the acceptance of that system of faith commonly known as Augustinian, or Calvinistic, hereby submit to their brethren in the Churches, the following propositions, in the hope that they may serve as a basis of union and Church fellowship, and that their general consideration and adoption may ultimately lead to an organic union of the various Churches of this faith and order throughout this land.

First.—We believe the word of God which is contained in the Scriptures of the Old and New Testament, to be the only rule of faith and practice.

Second.—We affirm our belief in that summary of Christian doctrine which is commonly called the Apostles' Creed, which we receive as setting forth, in brief, most important doctrines of the Gospel of Jesus Christ.

Third.—In further and more precise definition of our faith, we declare that we heartily receive and adopt the Confession of Faith of the Westminster Assembly with the accompanying catechism, as containing the system of doctrines taught in the Holy Scriptures; accepting the same in their plain and obvious meaning, and in the historic sense, given to them by the fathers in the Churches which we represent.

Fourth.—We believe in the scriptural authority of the Presbyterian form of Church government and polity, and in the rule of the churches by means of assemblies composed of ministers and ruling elders.

Fifth.—We profess our adherence to the forms of worship in use among our fathers, and thereby express our purpose to *continue* in use of the same; repudiating all ritualistic innovations as contrary to the word of God, and destructive of true devotion. In the matter of *Praise*, we judge that the Psalms of David, and other Scriptural songs inspired by the Holy Ghost, are proper to be sung by the Church in all her solemn assemblies, and we express the hope that the Psalms, as they are found in the English version of the Bible, set to such grave and simple music as may be becoming, may be used in all our churches; leaving the question whether any additional songs of praise shall be used, to the judgment of particular congregations.

Sixth.—Agreeing thus in the fundamental principles of our faith and order, this Convention respectfully submits to the various synods and assemblies of our churches, whether the time has not come when these Presbyterian churches of this land should combine in some active, Christian work,—such for example as the work of Foreign Missions—such work being regarded as the visible expression of our essential unity, and as an initial step in the process which it is hoped will gradually bring all these now divided bodies into one compact and harmonious church.

Seventh.—Since the grand object of all the denominations represented in this convention is the same, *viz.*, the entire conversion of the world to God, it is recommended that all interferences or collisions in the operations of missionary boards or other organizations, be avoided as much as possible.

Eighth.—As there is so much agreement among all the churches, here represented in all essential matters of faith, discipline and order; it is recommended that friendly and fraternal intercourse be cultivated by interchange of pulpits, by fellowship with one another in social religious meetings, and by communion with each other at the Lord's table, subject to the particular regulations of each denomination.

Now, Sir, I would just say, that while it is proper that these matters should be committed separately to the Committee without any instruction—for it is merely to lay these before them—I do hope that it will be done without further debate. That Committee is now actually engaged in this work, and in order that all these matters should come before them properly, they should have them now! This is the only reason why I press this matter just now, and hope this paper will be referred with Dr. Davidson's.

REV. SAMUEL MEHAFFEY (O. S.):—I believe as do Drs. Davidson and Musgrave, we have no power to make an organic union! Our churches have not authorized us to do this! I am pleased with Dr. Davidson's paper because it has something in prospective; it looks beyond to a conference of all branches of the church, who are empowered to make a union.

REV. DR. MARSHALL. (O. S.):—I am heartily delighted with the paper of Dr. Davidson. It did my heart good when he read it. I think, Sir, that the spirit of that paper, the spirit of the speaker, and the seconder of the paper, are such as ought to commend it to every pious heart here, and every where else, and I hope it will be referred to the committee.

REV. DR. MCILVAINE (Old School):—Mr. Chairman, I hope these papers will be referred, sir, without instruction, simply for the consideration of the Committee. I feel, sir, more than these can express. I do trust that the sense of the meeting may be, that something more may be done than is recommended by these papers. It is very true, sir, that this meeting or Convention, is not authorized, but its influence will be greater—as I think—than that of any General Assembly, of any branch of the Presbyterian Church that has ever sat in this land. And it is influence which we want.

The remarks that have been made by some few speakers, seem to turn as a matter of interest to only one or two branches of the Presbyterian Churches. There are matters of universal interest, that are to be considered in this Convention, and which touch every heart, and interest every branch of the Presbyterian Church. The practicability of the reunion of these fragments of the Church of Christ, turns upon the question of how desirable it seems to us, to be united. It is entirely practicable, sir, if our desires are strong enough. And it is of course impracticable, if our desires are not strong enough for it.

It seems, sir, that we ought to keep before our minds, the prayer of our blessed Lord, on that last night before He suffered, in which He prayed—repeating the words several times—that His Church might be one, in order that the world might believe that He was the Son of God; and not only that they might believe that, but He put it in stronger words than these—in order that they might *know* that He was the Son of God. This shows, how, on that night preceding the agony, it lay upon His mind that there was a danger to the Church—that it might not be *one*.

And it seems to me that we ought to enter into the spirit of that prayer. That we ought to feel that there is a danger to the Church, and to the salvation of the world, that the Church should not be one! The possibility that it should not be one, in the sense in which He prayed for its union, is evident from the fact that He was afraid. Now, sir, do we pray this prayer in our pulpits—in that connection—with the frequency, and urgency, and importunateness which are suggested by the fact of this being the last prayer before the last scene? And do we consider the connection between the unity of the Church and the salvation of the world, with that tenderness and that pressure upon the heart, with which it was evidently considered by Him?

I am afraid, sir, that we do not. But I believe that there is now a deep sigh for a reunion of the broken fragments of the Church of Christ, filling every heart with deeper and deeper seriousness and tenderness. It is for this that I thank God; it is in this that I take courage. What is it that keeps us apart? Let any man stand up here, and say that there is reason that God justifies the standing apart, in separate organization, of a hundred sects of the Presbyterian Church! I do not know whether there are a hundred or not. [A voice, "Eleven in this country."] Dr. McIlvaine:—That is enough, sir. It seems to me, sir, that we have in detail, an exposition of every creed and faith—not only the Westminster Confession and Catechism—adequate enough to bind the consciences of good men. But rogues can get in anywhere; you never could keep them out by any words or possible forms. With one more remark I will close:

Do we consider that the doctrine of the unity of the Church is one of the fundamental doctrines of the Gospel? "I believe in the Holy Catholic Church!" That was the way it was put to the first Christians.

The "Universal Church"—the Church that could include all of God's people. And this movement looks to that in the end. There is no palpable reason why they should stand apart—these great Presbyterian branches of the Church—the greatest in the country! I believe, sir, with one of the venerable speakers, that we are right; that stronger measures than these which have been recommended in these papers, should be concerted. I hope they will be referred to the Committee to consider, but not as forms of instruction. I think, too, our prayers, Mr. Moderator, should accompany the sending of these papers, for a rich and abundant pouring out of the Holy Ghost upon this Assembly. And pray for that spirit of unity which constitutes the Church of Christ. When inequalities fall, in the united strength of the Church, the people cannot keep apart, but will come together.

President Stuart put the motion on the reference of the two papers without instruction, which was carried.

(At the suggestion of the President, the Convention spent two minutes in silent devotion, after which Rev. Dr. Booth, of New York, led in a fervent and impressive audible prayer).

Rev. W. C. McCune, (Old School), said:—Mr. Chairman, I have a preamble and resolutions which I wish to read! It has been assumed universally in this Convention, that union is a duty, and that division is a sin. I think it would be well if we would be more explicit, and give more formal and explicit expressions to the conviction that union is a duty, and division a sin, and to that end I read the following:

Whereas, Jesus Christ, our Saviour, prayed for such a measure of oneness as would necessarily involve the organic union of all Christians living in the same place:

Whereas, The Church of the inspired Apostles was organically one:

Whereas, Our divisions enable the Apostate Roman Catholic Church, which has not the true spiritual oneness, to say that Protestants admit that the Church should be organically one, and as *she is this one,* she is the *true* Church:

Whereas, These divisions enable every United Evangelical Sect plausibly to say, that it is one of the sects in which the true Protestant Church is divided:

Whereas, The Roman Catholic Church on the one hand, and the United Evangelical sects on the other, are constantly increasing in membership, and seem to be aided in their work by our divisions:

Whereas, Our divisions have caused us to organize two or three congregations in various places in this land, where one would be more efficient in the cause of Christ than two or three, thereby shamefully and recklessly wasting means and labor which, if spent in the destitute places of the earth, might, by the blessing of God, result, from year to year, in the translation of many precious souls: and,

Whereas, The more nearly the branches of the Church approach each other, in faith, order, and worship, the greater is the sin which separates them: therefore,

Resolved, First, that the division of Presbyterians, into various branches, is a great and grievous sin; standing in the way of salvation, murdering souls, and hindering the conversion of the world:

Resolved, Second, that no measure of brotherly love or co-operation in our work, in our divided state, can release us from the obligation to forsake the sin of division:

Resolved, Third, that we have faith in God, that if we go humbly to His Word, and humbly to His throne, He will show us the way out of this sin.

Rev. Dr. Steele, (Old School):—I would suggest that the phrase "shameless and reckless," be stricken out.

This was accepted.

It was moved that this paper be referred to the Committee on the "Basis of Union."

It was also moved that the reference of this paper should be to the Business Committee.

Rev. Mr. McCune:—I had thought that perhaps this preamble and resolutions would express the unanimous conviction of the assembly, and be adopted without reference. Perhaps I am mistaken, but it strikes me as hardly necessary to refer this paper.

A Delegate said:—Instead of that reference alone, I should like to see a committee appointed—or leave it with the Business Committee, as suggested—to report this afternoon an address upon the necessity of union, and of the desirableness of it. We feel that all the churches are one. And there is another point which seems to us a reason why we should come together. Three of us returned Missionaries, from China, went by this Church yesterday afternoon, and we determined to try if we could not roll in our burden upon this Convention of four million human beings. I stand up in the presence of this august meeting to do a duty which I feel, as a returned Missionary from China, and say that there are necessities of a different quality, which demand that we ought to be United; and I hope that the address to be prepared by some committee will set forth the urgent necessity to all the churches for union.

Rev. Wm. Davidson D.D. (United Pres.) said:—Instead of referring this paper to any committee now existing, I rise to make a motion that it be referred to a committee to be appointed one from each of the bodies here represented, whose duty it shall be to prepare an address to the Churches on the subject of union.

This motion was amended to the effect that there should be one elder and one minister from each of the bodies represented, and was adopted.

Rev. Dr. Beatty took the chair while President Stuart made out the Committee.

Rev. A. G. Wallace (U. P.):—I think it would be desirable to make arrangements for holding another Convention next year. There will be need of it. And it is better to have a convention held at the call of this convention than at the call of any one church. If it be in order, I move that the Business Committee be directed to report the time and place for holding a convention similar to this, next year, and also the basis of representation.

THE CHAIRMAN:—The committee will undoubtedly have the whole matter before them.

REV. DR. STEELE, D.D. (O. S.)—Let that committee have the subject in its own hands.

The motion of Mr. Wallace was withdrawn.

PRESIDENT STUART, on again taking the chair, said:—I felt that this committee—to prepare an address—was a very important one, and my first impulse was to consult a higher and greater friend for direction. And if I know my own heart, I have made this appointment under the ye of the great Head of the Church, and by direction of the Spirit of God. I will announce the committee as appointed:—

United Pres.,	Rev. Wm. Davidson, D.D.,
	Elder William Getty.
Old School,	Rev. G. W. Musgrave, D.D.,
	Elder Charles S. Drake.
New School,	Rev. R. R. Booth, D.D.,
	Elder Edward Miller.
Reformed Pres.,	Rev. William S. Bratton,
	Elder Thomas Smith.
Reformed Prot. Dutch,	Rev. J. H. Suydam,
	Elder James Peters.
Cumberland Pres.,	Rev. A. D. Miller, D.D.,
	Elder Robert Carr.

Col. Blake then offered a feeling prayer for God's blessing upon the labors of this important committee.

PRESIDENT STUART:—I hope all the members will be present between 9 and 10 o'clock this evening. I don't say what is to be done, neither do I give notice; I merely suggest it. Something of interest may, or may not transpire.

Rev. Dr. D. V. McLean notified the members to proceed to the front of the church immediately after adjournment to have the photographic picture taken.

The Convention then adjourned until 3 o'clock, P. M., with a prayer by Rev. Dr. S. W. Crawford, (R. P.)

Same place, Nov. 7th, 3 o'clock, P. M.

The Convention met and was opened with prayer by Rev. J. Howard Suydam.

A short season was spent in devotional exercise, under the direction of the President.

The minutes of the Morning session were read and approved.

A communication was read from the Annual Meeting of Clergy and Laity of the Protestant Episcopal Church in session in the city, stating that they would send a delegation to visit the Presbyterian Convention, and desiring to know if the latter would be in session on Friday morning.

THE PRESIDENT:—It more properly belongs to our Committee to make a report of their visit; yet I will state that the Episcopal Convention received our Committee most heartily. I will make no reference to what transpired; though I was told it was one of the most touching and moving scenes ever witnessed. They have appointed Bishop McIlvaine and others as their Committee to appear before us to-morrow morning at 10 o'clock, if the hour is convenient.

A DELEGATE:—Mr. President, we need only say we will not adjourn before to-morrow at 10 o'clock.

The suggestion was unanimously concurred in.

REV. DR. GOODALE (Old School):—I would say a single word. I came from my Presbytery with the earnest prayers, I have no doubt at all, of the ministers, and elders, and brothers, that this Convention may result in greatly advancing the cause of Christian unity. Thirty years ago, I was sent as a delegate by the same Presbytery to the General Convention, in this city, and it was an extraordinary meeting; but I thank God I am spared to be sent here, after these many years, on this mission of Christian union and love! I naturally desire to be spared long enough to see these bodies come together as brethren of a united Church. ["Speak louder."] I will speak louder if I can. I say, I only desire to be spared to represent once more that Presbytery in the united Church. It seems to me, then, I should say, "O, Lord, let now thy servant depart in peace." I expect, if I am spared, to live to see the consummation of this glorious result. I hope I shall be honored with the privilege of sitting down in that united body. That this Convention may hasten that day, it has our earnest prayers. We hardly know, sir, how fervently all the hearts of Christian people beat in harmony with us this day. I am satisfied that we do not come up at all to the cherished desires that exist in our Churches. I have seldom witnessed a more touching scene than I witnessed on the Sunday, when, in compliance with the request of the Committee, I read that notice before my prayer, and asked my people to join with me in lifting up our hearts to God. Every single heart in that assembly was touched, and I saw, even before I commenced leading their devotions, the tears begin to run down their faces. That is the feeling among our people. When you touch this question of union, you touch the deep spring of Christian piety and Christian love. I am thankful that I am permitted to meet and speak to my brethren on this question.

REV. SAMUEL L. SAWYER, (New School):—Mr. President, the Presbyterian churches in East Tennessee would be very much gratified to hear of some action on the part of this Convention that would bring us together in one organic body. They have suffered very much from division. It has been said that such an organic union cannot be accomplished; it has been said that it is not practical. Mr. Chairman, I have been where I have seen the thing done; the thing has been already done. As the colored people have a way of saying in that part of the country, "*It is done done.*" The thing has been accomplished; but not by friends of the loyal Presbyterian Church. The rebel element has already fused into union; there is an organic union already accomplished between the Old School and the New School South. People that have been warring against each other for thirty odd years, under the wonderfully fusing power of treason, have combined, and they are one; and all around them they are doing everything that they can to break down the feeble loyal churches there. We have seen the thing accomplished. There is a movement, also, to unite with the Cumberland Presbyterians; and they will accomplish that union, in all probability, all through that region. I have seen people come from eighteen to twenty miles. People that have been warring upon each other for twenty odd years, will come from twenty miles to attend the preaching of men they have been fighting all that time. Under the sympathy they have for treason, they are all fusing into union.

Now, what are we to do? We are called upon as lovers of Jesus Christ, as lovers of Presbyterianism, to elevate our banners, and, under these circumstances, to unite all those who love Christ, and the Stars and Stripes. How can we breast these combined forces of the enemies of Christ and union, unless united ourselves? There was the Rev. Mr. Vance—one of the noble heroes of that State, belonging to a different denomination than my own, who stood up bravely for years—who has at last preached his farewell sermon, and bade his people good-bye, to make his home in the far West. You must unite the Presbyteries; you must combine. It is the condition of life. We will die out without the union of the denominations. There are great counties in our region, all around us, that have not a single Presbyterian Church within them. One, two, three, four, five, six; I think I can count over eleven counties in my section of the State, that have not a single Presbyterian minister in them. All those counties are calling for ministers; and, in our distracted condition, how can we furnish them? By a little co-operation we can supply them, and build up our Presbyterian College there, and send out our candidates for the ministry. Those Presbyteries that have gone against us in the national struggle, have united, and they are working against us now. Cannot the friends of Jesus Christ co-operate, if the enemies of the country can unite to weaken the Church? It seems as though some answer might be given; that this Convention might encourage us, and that we might have the zealous co-operation of all our brethren extended over those regions, and down throughout the Gulf States. East Tennessee sends cheering words to the friends of union from her Synod. She has given twenty thousand white majority in favor of negro suffrage, and she will, with your help, carry the principles of Presbyterianism and civil liberty clear to the Gulf of Mexico.

Rev. Dr. H. B. Smith, chairman of the committee to wait upon the Episcopal Annual Meeting, said:

Mr. President:—The Committee, according to appointment, waited upon the Assembly of Episcopal clergy and Laymen now in session in this city, and conveyed to them your Christian salutations in the terms contained in the resolution. The business before the meeting was suspended in order that we might be received. We expressed to them, as Christian brethren our cordial felicitations and salutations, in our unity in Christian work. We specially referred to that part of the work in which we have a common interest; namely, so far forth as we are equally assailed by infidelity, superstition and Romanism. (See Appendix II. for full report of Dr. Smith's speech.)

The address was responded to by the call of the Chairman of that meeting, Bishop McIlvaine, in the most cordial and fraternal terms. I only wish that this Presbyterian assembly could have heard the eulogy which that venerable Bishop pronounced upon our Presbyterian standards of doctrine and order, and the cordiality with which he expressed the hope that they were to hear of our speedy approach to reunion. Another member of the Committee, the Hon. Mr. Drake, from Missouri, also addressed them in our behalf, and with an especial appeal to the laity. These statements were responded to from various quarters; and at last a committee of five was appointed, on motion of the Rev. S. H. Tyng, Jr., of New York, to meet us personally. If I understand the resolution, the meeting was proposed to be to-morrow morning at ten o'clock; and among the members of the committee are Bishops McIlvaine and Lee. I have only to add that our reception was most cordial, and that after the addresses had been made, they all crowded around us with the most friendly greetings, and expressed personally their joy in our having made this movement. They only regretted that we had made it first; and that they had not had the privilege of taking the initiative.

On motion, the report of the commitee was unanimously accepted.

Hon. Elder Chas. D. Drake, a member of the committee, on invitation from the Chair, came upon the platform and spoke as follows:

Mr. President, Fathers, and Brethren, I would a great deal rather face another kind of meeting of five thousand men and women than this whole church full. I am not accustomed to the platform; that has become second nature to our worthy President. I felt my insufficiency for such occasions this morning, in the other church, when it devolved upon me to add some words to those that had been previously so well spoken by Rev. Dr. Smith. But the open Bible lay before me there, and I had no difficulty then in finding something with which to address that assembly; nor can I have any difficulty, my friends, with this open Book before me here, to find something upon which to base a few remarks to you this afternoon. I shall be very brief.

There is our foundation; and no matter what may be the divisions of Presbyterians in their order; no matter what may be the space that separates the Presbyterian from the Episcopalian, we all stand and we all must stand on this broad and universal foundation of faith and hope.

There is a wonderful idea in connection with the hope that we all, as Christians have; and that is, that in all our diversities there is essential unity. Nothing under the sky has unity over the whole world but the religion of Jesus Christ—I mean the essential points of that religion.

It matters not, brother, whether you and I sing Rouse's version, or some other version; it matters not whether we have close communion, or open communion. If in fact, we are one in the faith of the Gospel, we may go as we please; we may wander away from each other as we please, and we may differ upon minor questions as we please, in this world; but when it comes to the last, then the great splendid unity will break upon us, and in the unity of the Trinity we shall be no longer Presbyterians or Episcopalians, Dutch Reformed or Associate Reformed. We are all one in the fulness of the Godhead that shall then burst upon us. And Oh, in view of this fact, my brethren, how petty and how poor appear all the divisions that keep Christians in this world apart. One Lord, one faith, one baptism, one God and Father of us all. That is unity; here there is diversity; but there shall be eternal unity hereafter.

My friends, there is something in the principle of union avowed here, which will attract the attention of the Christian world. The attention of the Christians of this nation is now aroused, and the evidence of it is in the fact that you find from so many great bodies the idea of coming back to union into one. It was not so in other days; it was not so in the young days of the oldest men here; it was not so in my young manhood. The important matter is, that it is coming *now*, coming when Romanism and infidelity are marshalling their forces to bear down upon the Church of Christ, and to root out from the hearts of men the faith that rests upon the Word of God alone. While they are thus marshalling, the several members of the great Presbyterian family are rallying together under the banner of our Lord Jesus Christ, to fight anew the great fight of faith, and to carry forward His Gospel to victory here, and to final triumph over the whole earth. Who will stand dismayed when the Christian world is thus clustering around this glorious principle of unity in the faith of Christ? Who shall fear what is to come from infidelity, from superstition, from Romanism, or from any other form of false doctrines? Who shall fear it? Brethren, gather, gather, gather from all the bodies, around the sun of our religious system, the Bible, and the Cross of Christ. Let us banish the differences which belong to different bodies, when the great essential is the same. Let us all do the work which the Lord calls us to do, and hasten the time when His glory shall fill the earth. Brethren, we have met here in the unity of the spirit and in the bonds of peace, and we shall never again meet in this world. Never will all this body be assembled again here; but I hope we shall all be assembled again above. While we are here on earth, let us carry the influence of the deliberations and devotions of this place with us, looking for the day to come, assured that it will come in answer to prayer, when all these bodies of Presbyterians shall be but one body, and when that body shall bear aloft the banner of the Saviour more gloriously than it has ever been before, and when more than ever before, the leaven of unadulterated Presbyterianism shall leaven the whole lump. [Applause.]

Rev. W. E. Schenck, D.D., (Old School) said:—I wish to make a motion at this period. The report of the Committee is one of the most important brought before us. We should have it, I think in writing, and have it incorporated in the minutes of this Convention.

The motion was unanimously adopted.

Elder Robert M. Carter, one of the Committee, also, in response to a call from the President, offered prayer.

The Written Report of the Committee was afterwards presented and is as follows:

We performed the grateful duty assigned us, and received a most cordial and fraternal welcome. We assured them of the gratification with which we heard of their offering supplications in our behalf, and that we hastened to respond to their fraternal sympathy. We also expressed to them the high honor in which we held their Church, and our desire to work with them for all common ends and objects, as well as against our common foes.

Our reception was most gratifying. Bishop McIlvaine responded in a warm and eloquent address; and your Committee only regret that all the Convention did not hear the noble eulogy he pronounced on our Presbyterian faith and order. Senator Drake also addressed the Assembly in fitting and earnest words: various responses were made, and on motion of the Rev. S. H. Tyng, Junior, a large committee, consisting, in part, of Bishops McIlvaine and Lee, was appointed to visit our Convention to-morrow. The only regret expressed by any was, that they had not the honor of taking the initiative in such fraternal greetings and recognitions. After singing and prayer, the members of the body crowded around your Delegation, expressing, personally, their heartfelt thanks and fellowship.

Thus ended this delightful Christian Communion.

Respectfully submitted,

HENRY B. SMITH, *Chairman of Committee.*

REV. J. H. SUYDAM, (Reformed Dutch,) said:—Mr. President, I feel it due to the Convention here assembled, as well as to the body of Christians that I represent upon this floor, that the position of the Reformed Dutch Church at this present time should be properly defined. We feel here as if we stood rather in the outer court of the temple, not being distinctively known as Presbyterians. Yet we believe that we are Presbyterians; and by reason of our system of a rotary eldership a little more Presbyterian than yourselves. The Reformed Presbyterian Church, as to the several other branches here represented, so also extended an invitation to the General Synod of the Reformed Protestant Dutch Church, to meet with the others officially, by representatives in this council. It was deemed expedient at the last session of the Synod, not to accept this invitation. The reason for this action is not generally understood. It is proper that I should explain. For some years past, there has been a movement made in our denomination to expunge the word "Dutch" from its title, as we have believed it to be a hinderance to the growth of our church in this land; and since I have had my residence in Philadelphia, I have become fully convinced that this name is a most serious obstacle.

The people persistently misunderstand the term, and continually confound us, not with the Germans *as such* for we have no hesitation, and no delicacy about being classed with that noble race of people—but with those derisively spoken of as "*Dutch*," some of whom are said to reside in the interior of this State. We protest against this, and we find that this confusion has its evil effects everywhere beyond the States of New York and New Jersey where we are known historically.

We represent here to-day only a small section of the General Synod, viz: The Classis of Philadelphia; and in presenting our credentials, and being received among you, I have no doubt, sir, we shall be deemed as acting in rather a revolutionary manner, in as much as the General Synod has not sent any delegates to this body. The reason why it did not, is simply this: Action was being taken in reference to expelling this term *Dutch* from our Church title, and it was feared by those engaged in advocating that movement, that if we met at this time in this Convention, that act would be considered to be the first step toward organic union. And this might enable the opponents of the measure to rally a stronger force. It was a stroke of expediency. It was a sort of political movement, and which I have reason to believe, many of the members of the Synod have since regretted.

The Reformed Dutch Church has a history—a Continental history—with which this intelligent assembly is no doubt very familiar. You know that the great battle for Protestantism was fought in Holland against the forces of Rome, under the leadership of the Duke of Alva, just as well as you know that your fathers contended in the glens of Scotland for Presbyterianism as against a hierarchy. You vindicated that great principle, and we vindicated it; and although not organically one, we have been in spirit one from that day to this. There are in the Dutch Church at this time, I verily believe, a great number, perhaps a majority, who are desirous to come with the great Presbyterian body on a common platform. (Applause.) I have assurances from many who are leaders in the body I represent, and who make opinion there, that they ardently look for this consummation. I know a great number who like myself, voted for the expulsion of the obnoxious word, "Dutch," from our Church title, with the hope that it might be a means of drawing together these bodies of one common faith and order.

Mr. President, there are difficulties in the way. Many of our brethren suppose that by adopting our old name, "Reformed," distinctively the name belonging to us, and yet comprehensive enough to take in nearly all Protestant Christendom, that they are going to do it by this fact. We have standards which you adopt; and I see no parallel to this Convention better than that assembly of divines which adopted the Westminster Confession; unless I go back to Continental Europe, and instance the Synod of Dort, where our denomination received its standard, which gave it its distinction as *Reformed*. In that Synod were representatives from your own body, from the various Reformed Churches of Europe, and also from the Church of England, to a branch of which you have to-day borne fraternal greetings, and from which to-morrow you expect to receive a return expression of Christian love and courtesy.

O, let us with one heart and one purpose aim to effect, if not immediately, yet at no distant day an *organic union*. And let us now present such a platform upon which all who love the glorious doctrines of grace may stand together; and not merely shake hands at a distance, but with locked shields present an unbroken front to the enemies of the Church, who are rising with all their forces to oppose us. Who can but admire the unity and strength of the Roman Catholic Church? Who can but admire the admirable machinery which is operated by the Methodist Episcopal Church? What strides they are making! And shall not we, who are the disciples of Calvin—and which is only another way of saying it—the disciples, followers, believers in the doctrines embraced in this Blessed Word;—O shall *we* not lay aside all minor differences, such as psalmody, and matters of Church order, and different non-essential interpretations of the same Confession of Faith, and as *one* press forward the cause of our Lord and Saviour Jesus Christ, whom we profess to love and serve! I was reminded yesterday morning, during the hour of devotion, of an apt illustration of that which now prevents us from uniting. Two little urchins came here and took a seat upon the pulpit-stairs waiting to receive copy from these reporters. You know by what name they are called. O be sure, brethren, it is the devil on the pulpit stairs, and *in* the pulpit, who has prevented our union heretofore.

It is not the fault of the *people;* they are ready for it. It is the *ministry* who are quibbling upon these minor matters when the great truth of the Cross should be set forth, and when thousands and millions of souls are demanding from us the bread of life. Shall we not come together? I answer for the great mass of the Church that I represent that they are ready to *go forward.* (Applause.)

Rev. Dr. Eagleson, Chairman of the Committee on the Basis of Union, presented the following report.

The Committee appointed to prepare and report a Basis of Union to be submitted for consideration by the various branches of the Presbyterian Church represented in this Convention, submit the following as such a Basis, viz:

1. An acknowledgment of the Scriptures of the Old and New Testament to be the Word of God.

2. That in the United Church the Westminster Confession of Faith shall be received and adopted, as containing the system of doctrine taught in the holy Scriptures.

While the committee recommend the foregoing basis of doctrine, they do not wish to be understood as impugning the orthodoxy of the Heidelberg Catechism, and the canons of the Synod of Dort.

3. That the United Church shall receive and adopt the Presbyterian form of church government.

4. The Book of Psalms, which is of divine inspiration, is well adapted to the state of the Church in all ages and circumstances, and should be used in social worship; but, as various collections of psalmody are used in the different churches, a change in this respect shall not be required.

5. That the sessions of each Church shall have the right to determine who shall join in communion in the particular church committed to their care.

The committee recommend the adoption of the following resolutions:

1. That we unite in requesting our respective churches in their supreme judicatories, to appoint a committee of five each, which shall constitute a joint committee, whose duty it shall be to meet, at a time and place agreed on, and proceed with all convenient despatch, in an attempt to form a basis of union, according to the principles of this report, which basis they shall submit to the churches for their consideration and adoption; it being understood that this is not designed to interfere with the existing arrangements for reunion between two of the larger bodies represented in this Convention.

2. As there is so much agreement among all the churches here represented, in all essential matters of faith, discipline, and order, it is recommended that friendly and fraternal intercourse be cultivated, by interchange of pulpits, by fellowship with one another in social religious meetings, and by communion with each other at the Lord's Table, subject to the regulations of each particular branch of the Church.

3. In case the above paper should be adopted, that a committee be appointed to lay this action of the Convention before the highest judicatories of the various branches of the Church here represented.

4. That the members of the Convention who may vote for the foregoing basis of union to be laid before the churches, shall not thereby be regarded as being committed to advocate its adoption when laid before the branches of the Church respectively, but shall be free to act, according to the indication of Providence at the time.

By order of the Committee.

JOHN EAGLESON, *Chairman.*

The report was, on motion, unanimously accepted.

THE PRESIDENT:—Before proceeding to the discussion of the report of the Committee on the Basis of Union, the Chair would respectfully suggest that we spend a few moments in prayer to God, who has thus far guided the Convention, and delivered us when we were in perplexity. We will spend two minutes in silent devotion; and when I strike this bell, Rev. Dr. Musgrave will lead the Convention in audible prayer. The vast audience was several moments absorbed in silent prayer, after which Rev. Dr. Musgrave followed in an impressive appeal for Divine guidance and unanimity in the deliberations.

Rev. Dr. Eagleson:—Mr. President, will you permit me to say that this report was drawn up very hastily, and may not be as terse as it would have been if we had had a little more time? Moreover, we had a diversity of views to consult, and had to bring views together that at first seemed heterogeneous.

Rev. Dr. Monfort (Old School):—I would move, sir, to change a single phrase. Instead of "existing arrangements," which is used with reference to the movements for reunion between the Old and New School branches, I would substitute, "pending negotiations."

The Committee accepted the amendment.

Rev. Dr. R. Davidson (Old School):—Mr. President, I wish to offer one or two amendments. I think this is an admirable paper, an excellent one, almost perfect; but like every thing human, it may be a little improved. I would like to see it a little more definite to this effect:

"That letters of admission from one Church to another be considered as valid among all Churches embraced in this union." I do not think that idea is brought out sufficiently. Another thing I would like is, that after "interchange of pulpits" be inserted the words "or occasional intercommunion." I do not think that is sufficiently brought out. There is another amendment I have to offer, because I think there is nothing said about the Westminster Catechism. I should like to see that incorporated. I offer these amendments; if the Committee will accept them, I have nothing more to say.

Rev. A. S. McMaster (Old School) moved the adoption of the Report. At the request of members it was again read, and then on motion of Rev. H. B. Smith, D.D., it was taken up for consideration, article by article.

Rev. Cyrus Dickson, D.D., offered a motion of inquiry as to the meaning of the order already adopted in regard to the manner of voting on any questions connected with the Basis of Union. The President, with the unanimous agreement of the house, decided, that in accordance with the literal sense of the terms of the order, all votes on every such question must be by Churches,—that is, each branch of the Church represented in the Convention shall cast its vote separately, and the majority thereof determine its vote, whether for or against the article voted on; and a majority of the Churches voting shall decide the question.

Rev. Dr. Eagleson, Chairman of the Committee, addressed the Convention, in explanation of the Report, as follows:

Mr. Presidhnt:—The first item in this basis is this: "That in the United Church there would be required 'an acknowledgment of the

Scriptures of the Old and New Testament to be the Word of God.'" It is taught in our Catechism, that the Scriptures are the only rule of practice; and it is included in the Confession of Faith, especially if we add the Catechism. To this the committee have no objection; we did not suppose that the Catechisms would be demanded in addition to the statements of doctrines set forth in the Confession of Faith.

Personally, I would prefer just adhering to the Confession of Faith, which is drawn up in the form of a standard of Faith for every purpose, and which includes all the great fundamental doctrines of the Bible set forth in the Catechism, and in the appropriate form to be adopted by persons who are received into the church, and inducted into the fold of the ministry. I was not present when the amendment was proposed to add the Catechisms of the Church, the Larger and Less. Those would work awkwardly in practice. I would therefore not introduce the Catechisms, Larger and Less as a basis in this platform; because all that is included in the Catechism is included in the Confession of Faith, in the most specific form, and better adapted to practical use. It is more simple than if we add to the Confession of Faith, the Catechism, as that would reduplicate the same thing.

In reference to this statement of things touching the Heidelberg Catechism and the Synod of Dort, it is made with special reference to the Dutch Reformed Church. As they adhere to these standards, it is supposed that this will be the means of conciliating many of the members and ministry of that Church to the scheme proposed for union; and it was put in at the request of the members of that Church who were on the committee. Shall we not concede this much for the sake of having their harmonious co-operation?

The next point is touching the form of government. So much for the doctrines of the Church. Touching the form of government we say it shall be Presbyterian. We presume it is clearly understood by all Presbyterian denominations, what is included in the Presbyterian form of government; and substantially, if not in every item, the Presbyterian form of government to which all these branches of the Church have been accustomed, is precisely the same.

The next item is touching the psalmody of the Church. Now, can we not yield as much as will be required in adopting this; here the Scripture psalms are explicitly stated as suitable to be used in all ages and all lands by the people to the end of time; and to these we have the privilege of adding others, as stated in the latter part of this report? Will those who are in favor of the old psalms as they have been accustomed to them, stand upon giving that liberty to use the other versions? If they stand out upon the ground of absolute exclusiveness, then all union with any other branch of the Church here represented, is out of the question. Will they not give that up? If they will not, on how narrow ground they stand.

The next concerns the subject of inter-communion; and we adopted the basis that we supposed would settle that difficulty though not solve that difficult question. That is, that each Church Session shall be the judge of those who shall communicate in its particular care and communion. This does not make them responsible for those admitted in another church or denomination, and under the practical jurisdiction of another church for which they are not responsible. This was designed to solve the difficulty of open communion.

We have in these five planks, or items, laid on this platform, the broad fundamental principles of Christian truth and Presbyterian government. The Church of God is designed to be the pillar and ground of the truth so represented in the basis of union before us. We can meet upon this platform, and keep safely and perfectly the pillar and ground of truth as we are now. All the great fundamental truths of the Gospel, are to be held through the testimony of this united Church; not a single one should be omitted.

These subsequent resolutions have reference to the method of carrying out this arrangement. If it should be adopted, it will go then to the highest judicatories of our Church, the General Assemblies and higher Synods, for their consideration. The first resolution proposes to raise a committee of five from each of these higher judicatories to confer together, and in pursuance of the principles laid down in this report, adopt a more perfect basis of union, if they can. This report was drawn up very hastily during this forenoon; and the joint committee from the judicatories, perhaps, may make this more perfect, and perhaps add a few additions for harmony.

We recommend also in this Report the appointment of a Committee to go to these highest judicatories and lay this action of the Convention before them. If we just pass this Basis of Union, and have it printed and thrown out to the world, it may die a barren, silent death; though I have no doubt but the people who love unity, even though the ministry should be disposed to neglect it, will not be willing to allow it. I trust the people will press their ministers forward, and make the responsibility of this solemn movement rest upon them. I consider this a momentous and impressively solemn time for the Church. If we are successful in thus uniting, we shall go forward in the strength of God's love, in the unity of belief in God, and a loving, faithful desire to promote His glorious kingdom. The Lord grant that His hosts may go forth in unity and mutual love until the world shall be united in Christ. I have been transacting business in the judicatories of the Church for thirty-four years, during which I have held pastoral offices. I was pained and humbled when the division took place between the Old and New Schools. I am free to acknowledge I took an active part in the Convention, and in all the documents regarding the discussions prior to the separation of the Church; and if I had had the thirty-four or thirty-five years' experience in the ministry which I have had since, I would have been more kind and alive to the interests of the Church, more careful and tender than I was then. The Church God made is an institution which does not bear handling. All these denominations are Presbyterians. Were they one, how soon might we expect the Angel of the Covenant would be seen flying through the heavens, having the Gospel to proclaim through the earth; and soon it would be proclaimed —never before—that the millenium had come, that the kingdoms of the world had become the kingdom of Jesus Christ. [Applause.]

The hour of adjournment having arrived, the President announced that he had been officially notified that to-morrow at 10 o'clock, A. M., the meeting of the Clergy and Laity of the Protestant Episcopal Church, now in session in this city, would, in a body, and by its representatives, Rev. Bishops McIlvaine, Lee, and others, visit this Convention.

The President also announced a cordial invitation from the Committee of Arrangements to members of the Convention, and then ladies, and also to corresponding members, to be preseut in the Sabbath School room of this Church, this evening at 10 o'clock, to join in the social reunion to be then and there provided.

Adjourned until 7½ o'clock.

Closed with prayer by the Rev. J. I. Stearns, D. D.

Same Place, November 7, 7½ *o'clock, P. M.*

The Convention was called to order by the President, and opened with prayer by Rev. Dr. Stevenson.

Minutes of the last session were read and approved.

THE PRESIDENT:—The Convention adjourned pending the discussion on the Basis of Union. It was by common consent understood that the members of that committee should be heard first. Rev. Dr. Eagleson has concluded his remarks and we are now prepared to hear from the other members.

REV. DR. EAGLESON:—I would only make this additional remark. If in the progress of the discussion it should appear we might make important amendments by having the paper back, we would be pleased to have it recommitted to make the amendments. We desire that the paper should be perfected, as it was but hastily drafted.

REV. DR. S. W. FISHER (New School) a member of the Committee, said:—

Mr. Chairman, I would say that the foregoing report was hastily prepared, and in its style, perhaps, is not such a paper as the Convention should send forth. Perhaps, it may be well after we have discussed its principles, to have it re-committed and somewhat recast in reference to style, the same principles being preserved.

I have only heard of two points, or two suggestions amendatory to the Report, which I wish here to mention. To the statement in the first article (that the Scriptures are the word of God,) should be added these words: "the only infallible rule of faith and practice."

The second suggestion has been that in the terms of subscription, the Catechisms of the Church, the Larger and Shorter Catechisms should be added. I would state that the Committee took this ground in reference to the matter: that the ministers and elders of our churches, at least of two of the larger branches of the Church, are required simply to assent to the first article. We have, therefore, inserted subscription to the Confession of Faith, as containing the system of doctrine taught in the Holy Scriptures; and thought that might have been sufficient as a basis of union.

Now, in reference to this whole matter of union, as contained in this report and basis, there are two points especially on which we are all anxious. Presbyterianism rests on two pillars, so far as form is concerned; the first doctrine; the second its order. In the subscription to the Confession of Faith lies the doctrinal basis of the Presbyterian Church; for I may say, the faith of the Presbyterian Church everywhere, with few exceptions, not only in this country, but in Scotland, in Ireland, in Holland, and among the Reformed churches, is preserved and represented in it. I hold that there is a family likeness running all through these Presbyterian Churches; and that likeness is produced by the Spirit of God, in connection with the great doctrines which Calvin enunciated, as did Augustine partially before him, and which we have since thrown into this special form.

I ought, perhaps, to go a little further, and state that any other basis of union will, I think, be rejected very heartily by a large majority of the Presbyterian churches everywhere. I do not believe that, if any set of men attempt to put any of their philosophical definitions and explanations into any confession of faith, the people will assent to it, or the ministry at large. If a man is willing honestly to say that he subscribes to the Confession of Faith, as containing the system of doctrine taught in the Holy Scriptures, according to the plain meaning of those terms, answerable to his God, no man has a right beyond that to question him; except indeed his own Presbytery, to see whether he does believe it. If he holds the Confession as a term of subscription, that is sufficient. Of course we all believe in this body, that each Presbytery, when it licenses or ordains a minister, must examine him personally, in regard to his knowledge of these doctrines.

I have heard it whispered, that it is necessary in order to guard against the influences of the doctrines of Pelagianism and Arminianism, and those of a similar tendency, that you should erect additional barriers, in order to keep out those influences. You may erect the barriers, but you cannot keep them out. If men are insincere and wicked enough to subscribe to that declaration in terms, they will be insincere and wicked enough to subscribe to anything you may put before them.

But as to our basis of union, we are, in this respect, catholic, and mean to be. The Presbyterian Church is a church not of narrowness, but of liberty. We believe in diversity of doctrine; in unity in the great fundamentals. And this diversity of doctrine produces stalwart men, strong men. Who wants to see the professors in Auburn, Newburg, the Union Seminary, and Princeton, all cast exactly in the same mould, like men having every feature of countenance exactly the same? I would rather see one man with a Roman nose, and another a Grecian nose; they are men, and they will be good-looking men, too. I would rather in our Church, the Presbyterian Church, that one man should look at doctrine from one position; he may magnify it in that position; another man takes it from another point of view, and these views combined constitute the grand whole. No man is capable of looking all around these great truths, and of giving every one just their appropriate representation. No man has ever had a mind great enough to do it in this world, uninspired of God himself.

Nor did Christ any where present them thus in their totality. Christ says, in one case, "Ye will not come to me that you may have life." In another, "Ye cannot come except the Father draw you." And thus these terms balance, and all harmonize together. This Westminster Confession of Faith, we suppose, will be acceptable to all the branches of the Presbyterian Church, who are willing to come into the union; and thus we maintain the great doctrinal position of Presbyterianism, the great Calvinistic doctrines as distinct from all others.

Then, as regards the form of union, we accept the form of government in the Presbyterian Church; the government of the Church by Presbyteries, Synods, and General Assembly; the equality of the ministry, etc.

Let me say that this Report is not a finality. We want to get at principles, looking to each other for assistance, and see whether on these general principles, fairly accepted, we cannot agree. There are difficulties in the way. I will tell you the grand difficulty with the two largest churches; it is just this, nothing else, and the assurance that both parties are heartily sincere, and have perfect confidence in each other. That is the grand difficulty, in my view. In accomplishing a union like this, there are sacrifices to be made; and let me tell you they are not all on one side. There are things which we are willing to forget and forgive. They exist in history; and there they are, difficulties in the way.

But when we think of the union of God's people in our country, men of the same faith and order in worship, we feel as if we were willing to sacrifice every thing but the real truth of God to it. I take this ground—I speak for myself in this matter—that where churches conform to each other in doctrine, in discipline, in order, in the main, then to be separated is schism; because there is nothing that keeps them apart but either the want of confidence, or else the ambition of individuals.

I have said there were difficulties, and they are on both sides. Now, I am perfectly willing, for one, and I think my brethren are, to believe that our Old School brethren are pretty nearly orthodox—pretty nearly. (Laughter). If I wanted to insist upon it rigidly, I would want to bring them up to a point they have not reached yet. In regard to certain great moral questions, we would like to know if they are right in these. One of these God has removed out of the way; and we will pass that by. It looks to me, at this final moment, that the providence of God has brought the two larger branches of the Church gradually together. He has eliminated from the branch of the Church with which I am personally connected, certain elements which were discordant elements, which, unquestionably, gave us trouble, and which gave our brethren of the other branch great occasion for censure. I feel that. I know it to be so. In reference to that, God has taken them out of the way. In regard to our mode of conducting our general ecclesiastical matters, God has brought us to a union in that matter.

And now, accepting the same basis of faith, and the same communion, what keeps us separate but a want of confidence, and the old prejudices away back; and those prejudices the grace of God will remove. Why, God's grace can teach a man, and enable him to do almost anything in this world, in the way of the removal of prejudice.

Let me say a word in regard to what it is that has made us come together. I look back to the great revival in 1857, and 1858. That was God's work, beginning first of all in that union meeting in Fulton street, New York; and it went on from town to town, from church to church. We filled our largest churches, not only with men of one, but of all denominations. I sat in the First Church in Cincinnati, when that large church was crowded, and we had gathered together Methodists, Presbyterians of both schools, Episcopalians, and Baptists. I remember when General Mitchell had the chair, and made a noble address to that congregation, and Bishop McIlvaine followed in a noble prayer. And this spirit, morally speaking, has infected us. No; not *infected* us. I will not use such a term. It has been *breathed into* the hearts of Christian men; and thus God, through the men of God, the working material in our churches, has worked. I believe the providence of God, by His Spirit, will carry it on, though all the theologians in the world combine their speculations against it. (Cheers.) Think how the Young Men's Christian Associations in this land further this great object. Think how, in the late war, God brought us together, whether we would or not. Maybe some of our good friends, who only love to sing the old Psalms of David, down on the battle-fields beside a dying soldier, who asked to have sung for him, "Rock of Ages, cleft for me," have learned to sing that sweet hymn, and felt it to be as good as a psalm.

I feel that the cause of Christ is involved here. I believe this work is the cause of Christ; and let me tell you, my friends, if there was ever a time when union was needed, it is now. The theological controversies of this country spread over one hundred years; they culminated when I was a boy. I was the son of a minister, heard these discussions, and probably read more of the controversy in ten years, than men now will read in a thousand, unless times change. Then congregations were assembled to hear men discuss fine points of doctrine, like the point of a needle. Can yon get up such discussions now? No. The men who suppose they can do it are living far back; that time is past. We have stopped considering those points, at least for our generation; and all those discussions, if kept up from this time to the Millenium, I do not think will throw much light on the doctrines, or on the problems of philosophy.

Now, then, God is pressing us up to the work. In the first place, He has made our land the land of liberty, to gather in the millions upon millions of every land. We have got to meet them; and it is the great question which presses upon the minds of every one in God's Church, How they shall be saved. Millions of Romanists; millions of infidel rationalists; four millions of blacks enfranchised; millions in our large cities throng our streets, pressing to destruction; it is to save them that the Church of God must unite and labor. Think, is this the time for the Church to be tithing the little mint, and anise, and cummin; is it now that upon minor points, it should stand aloof and say, I am holier than thou, and know more about the Scriptures than thou? Is this the time for work like this? No. It is time for every Christian man and woman to carry on God's work. It is time for ministers not to harp on minor points of doctrine, but to preach the great doctrine of Christ crucified to the hearts of men, that will issue in their salvation, while philosophy alone would be entirely without good effect.

In this scheme for union, we seek the good of the Presbyterian Church. I speak of us all together, feeling the pulse of Christian unity running through this entire Convention. I have rejoiced to meet with brethren whom some would call narrow-minded, who have hearts as large as ever labored in Christ's cause. The Presbyterian Church in these United States occupies a position for active labor and usefulness, if she will devote her energies to it, superior to that of any other denomination of Christians whatever. She has the best order; she has, we believe, the most perfectly expressed system of doctrine; she has piety; she has freedom; she has the intellect in her ministry, and a cultivated intellect in her laity; and the real power, if she has the mind to put it forth, equal, if not superior, to any other Church in the land. But if we are to stand aloof, and spend half of our energies in planting a Church there, and another, differing a little, near by, and another, and another, making three or four churches, differing on minor points—saying, there is the Old School; there is the New School; there the Reformed; there the United; there the Dutch Reformed; we try to occupy the energies of five men, where one can do the work. I believe we are guilty before God, and He will call us to answer for it.

Union is strength. We need this unity for influence, East and West. I trust God will bring it about in His own good time. I do not feel that man can do it; it will come in time, if not just now. When it does come then we can stand up among our united brethren of the Methodists, the Baptists, the Episcopalians, and say to them, "We are not divided upon these little matters; we are united as you are." We are strong in faith; strong in discipline; strong to work for the Master; and when the hour comes, I trust it will be found that this Church in which I was born and reared, and where I have spent my life, will be filled with the Spirit of God and crowned with glory. We may say of our country, in reference to her future prospects, when this union really takes place and Christ is enthroned here,

"Columbia, Columbia, to glory arise."

We will see our united Presbyterian Church prepared to effect more for the glory of our country than all the statesmen of the earth could do. (Cheers.)

Rev. Dr. T. W. J. Wylie (Reformed Presbyterian), as a member of the Committee, addressed the Convention, as follows:—

Mr. President, it gives me so much more pleasure to listen than to speak, that I would prefer being silent on this occasion, were it not that something might be expected from a member of the Committee, representing one of the different bodies of which this Convention is composed. I desire, however, that it should be understood that I speak not as a representative man; for I am merely expressing my own individual opinions.

Most heartily do I concur in those *noble* utterances which we have just heard from the brother who has been speaking. It appears to me that he has touched the very heart of the subject, and that there was not one person in this assembly who must not have felt that the Spirit of God calls upon us to unite together as one mighty phalanx in the army of the Lord Jesus Christ.

Now, sir, I most heartily desire that all these Churches should be one. I desire it, sir, as a Christian man. I have felt that the Spirit of the Lord Jesus Christ is the spirit of union. As the Divine Saviour prayed, ere He was going to his sufferings on the Cross, that all His people might be one, He still presents that prayer at the throne of His Father. It is inexpressibly dear to all who are His people. But I feel an earnest desire for union as a Reformed Presbyterian, and as a Covenanter. [Applause.] If I understand the spirit of the Church that I venerate and love so much—the Church of my ancestors; the Church of my own birth; the Church of my preference, and my hearty admiration—I do feel that it is the spirit of union. The old Covenanters of Scotland, from whom we delight to derive our origin, united together in solemn covenant, in order that they might accomplish the Union of the Church of the Lord Jesus Christ, more than the union of the Presbyterian Churches, for they adopted a covenant which included Independents and Episcopalians, as well as Presbyterians.

Sir, if we had the spirit of those old Covenanters, our hearts would long for union of this character; we would desire all the Churches of the Lord Jesus Christ to be brought into one body. I feel that I am standing on correct ground as a Covenanter, when I am an advocate for union. At the same time, I would desire no union that would require me to give up any points of belief found in God's most holy Word, or any practice which I consider that Word sanctions; but, when I look at the plan now proposed, I cannot see that there is one principle which I would need to abandon, or one practice I would need to change, if all these denominations in the Convention were united. [Applause.] And, really, members of the Reformed Presbyterian Church, in the United Church, would not know there was any change if they were not told. According to this basis, there is no sacrifice required on our part. We only are to agree that others shall have liberty of conscience and of practice for themselves. [Applause.]

Two points, especially, I may refer to for a moment. In reference to the subject of psalmody, as presented in that report, as I understand it, there is no single principle of the old Covenanters, and of the Reformed Presbyterian Church, as their lineal representative, abandoned. It says that the Book of Psalms—and in love for them I yield to no man—is to be used in the Church throughout all time; yet if there be persons who think that they may conscientiously sing something else, we will not interfere with them. Now, I do not expect as long as I have the honor and happiness of being minister of the congregation meeting in this place, that we will ever sing from this pulpit anything but the one hundred and fifty psalms; but I am willing that persons who go elsewhere may sing what they please. That is the purport of the report: let us not misunderstand it. It does not require us to say that it is right or that it is wrong. It merely gives the liberty to people to do as their consciences dictate. I understand, though I was not present at the time, that a Hymn was sung in this Church this morning. This was entirely unexpected; and yet the building did not fall. I believe no impious Uzzah was struck dead. No, sir, I do not think Christians should be kept apart by psalmody; for the Church has no right to prohibit anything that Christ has not prohibited. If the Church prohibits anything that Christ has not prohibited, I will do what Christ allows me to do, even if the Church says I ought not to do it. In the Reformed Presbyterian Church there is an increase of liberal opinion in regard to this matter. I think nearly one-half of our ministers, and a very large proportion of our members, fully agree with the sentiments I have expressed on this occasion. Sir, you yourself can bear testimony that a man may be presented before the General Synod of the Reformed Presbyterian Church for singing a hymn, and not be subjected to discipline. [Laughter and applause.] We have, sir, a G. H. S., a Great

Hymn Singer, among us. The brother who complained on this subject has not been sustained, and I do not think there is the slightest probability that he will be. The General Synod of the Reformed Presbyterian Church, gave the person who offered that resolution the liberty of withdrawing it. [Applause]

In regard to this matter, in all love and tenderness to the brethren of my own and other churches, who may differ from us, let me say, that nothing that is not to be considered a sin should be considered a barrier to Christian union. Is there a man, woman, or child in this congregation who will stand up here and say, It is a sin against God to sing:

> "All hail the power of Jesus' name;
> Let angels prostrate fall;
> Bring forth the royal diadem,
> And crown him Lord of all?"

We all believe the shorter catechism, and the shorter catechism says, "Every sin deserves God's wrath and curse, both in this life and that which is to come." Well, sir, is there a person prepared to say that if I sing,

> "Just as I am, without one plea;"

or that hymn which my brother so well referred to,

> "Rock of ages, cleft for me,
> Let me hide myself in Thee,"

which so many of the dearest children of God have sung with their dying breath almost, that I am guilty of that which deserves God's wrath and curse both in this life and that which is to come? Is there one, is there one of this assembly who would say so?

I believe I am standing historically, on the true ground of my own Church. I hold in my hand a Psalm Book used by the old Covenanters in Scotland. (A small dingy volume was here shown.) I turn to it, sir, and find, in addition to the Psalmody, quite a number of hymns there. (Laughter.) Quite a number. I see that this Psalm Book has the music along with it, and specific directions, thus; sing this hymn as the Hundredth Psalm, or, "Sing this as the Fiftieth Psalm." There is no doubt then that they used these hymns. And after the version of Psalms which we now use was introduced, they appointed a person to prepare versions of other parts of the Bible; and it is recorded in the "Scots' Worthies," of one of the most eminent of the old Covenanters, that he prepared the hymn,

> "Oh, Mother dear, Jerusalem?"

to be used as an addition to the Plalmody.

I am standing, in regard to this matter, on the ground of the old Covenanters of Scotland.

The other subject which has been referred to is Communion. I do not think that there need be much difficulty in regard to this. If all were one Church, it would be a Communion with their own Church. If there is any Session which would forbid one to obey his Saviour's dying command, "Do this in remembrance of Me," because he sings an Evangelical hymn, I suppose we must leave it to that Session. But the Westminster Assembly declares in the Confession of Faith, that Communion in the Lord's Supper should be extended to all everywhere who call on the Lord Jesus; and they say, "We never did, nor shall deny any members of our congregations to hear or communicate occasionally elsewhere." John Owen says, "Members of Christian Churches shall receive each other to communion, accepting them on the ground of their Christian standing as *pro-tempore* members." Our Sessions could take in *pro-tempore* members. It has been done in many of our churches, and I have never heard of any evils of consequence resulting from it.

In presenting these views, I am in accord with one of the most venerable ministers of the Reformed Presbyterian Church, the late Dr. Gilbert McMasters.

He says: "In the times of the Reformation, rallying around their respective standards, there was no hostility felt or expressed towards each other, by the churches, the best reformed. Why not thus still? Let the children of the Presbyterian Reformation, nearly allied as they are to one another, drink more deeply into the spirit of the fathers of that Reformation, rise to the eminence on which they stood, and act, according to the measure of their ability, as they acted. Knox, and Melville, and Henderson, in their respective days, had no ecclesiastical communion from which they would have excluded Calvin, Beza, or Turretin. Cameron received ordination by the laying on of the hands—the united hands—of the ministry of the Scotch and Holland Churches. Renwick, the youngest and last, but not the least of Presbyterian Martyrs, received ordination from a classis—a presbytery—of the Holland Church, they remaining under the banner of their own Constitution, while they committed the ministry to him upon his own confession of faith. The common ground covered by the two Churches was broad, firm, and consistent enough to sustain the united communion."

Here is something from Renwick, whom Dr. McMasters styles, "the last but not the least of the Martyrs of the Covenant." In a publication containing his letters, we find a memoir by Dr. Huston, well known, among Covenanters as a distinguished minister of the Reformed Presbyterian Church in Ireland. Speaking of the Catholic spirit of Renwick and the Covenanters of those days, he says: "In the spirit of Christian brotherhood they say, 'On the communion of saints let us impose no new restriction. Though others differ from us in the word of their special testimony, let us embrace and love them, and acknowledge fellowship with them as Christian brethren.' In these noble utterances, says Dr. Huston, "we have strikingly exemplified the true spirit of Christian brotherhood and Catholic communion. This is the genuine import of the vow of the Solemn League and Covenant, which binds Covenanters to regard whatever is done to the least of them, as done to all and to every one in particular. While firmly holding fast the Scripture testimonies, and contending earnestly for the faith once delivered to the saints, we should cordially rejoice in the voice of grace in Christ's servants wherever we find them. We should love them, as therein fulfilling the law of Christ by bearing another's burdens; and wish them Christ's spirit in all they do."

I love, dearly love, the Reformed Presbyterian Church. I can well enter into the feelings of those, who, remembering its glorious traditions, its purity of doctrine, and its simplicity of worship, feel regret to find that it is passing away and becoming extinct. But, sir, while this is so, let us recognize the providence of God in regard to this matter. It seems as if a time of disintegration had come. This body and that body is falling into pieces; but there will be a re-crystallization in a better form than any that has existed before. (Applause.) And, sir, if it so be that our own Church is terminating her existence after the struggles through which she has gone for the testimony of the truth as it is in Jesus, what more glorious consummation than to be merged in the Millenial Church which we trust is soon to be organized! (Applause.) The stars—though they shine so brightly, are lost to sight when the sun arises. (Applause.)

"Thus star by star declines,
Till all have passed away;
As morning bright and brighter shines,
From dawn to perfect day."

God has given *you*, my beloved brother, (addressing the President) many honors indeed, not the least of them shall it be found to be for you to have inaugurated a movement which results in the union of all the Presbyterian family. When united, we shall find that there was no real cause of difference; we should wonder why it was we stood apart so long. And when we combine our energies against the common foe—to which such eloquent reference has been made to-night—we go forth as an army of banners to fight the good fight of faith, and to do battle for the Lord Jesus Christ, how strong we shall be.

When another spirit guides us; when, instead of striving to gather members from one another, we go out into the field of *the world*, and endeavor to tell sinners they are lost, and point them to the way of salvation by the Lord Jesus Christ, then our God will bless us! Jesus tells us, that when His people are one, the world will believe that God has sent Him! And if we ask why it is that the world has not believed, the answer is, because His people have not been one! But if we were united we would find that the Lord is in the midst of us, and that by His blessing we would go forth conquering and to conquer; the cause of Christ would be extended throughout every land; we would see the salvation of God, and all the kingdoms of this world, would become the kingdom of our Lord Jesus Christ. (Applause.)

The President.—We will diversify the addresses we have heard from the clergy on the Committee, by one from the laity. Brother Chamberlain, Elder from the Old-School Church, Cincinnati, will now address you.

Elder A. E. Chamberlain, said: I feel, my dear friends, a very great embarrassment in standing before this assemblage to-night, following as I do these brethren who have addressed you, and who have so ably discussed all the principles, as I believe, that are involved in the report of the Committee. Yet I do feel it a very great privilege to stand here in the name of my Master, and thank Him, in the presence of this audience, for what I have witnessed since I came to Philadelphia. It has been the earnest prayer of my life for years, that I might be permitted to live to see the day when all the Presbyterian family should be united in one great Church. And, sir, I have taken very great pleasure in looking through the providence of God for the last ten years, seeing as I have been permitted to do, as I believe, the hand of God moving in this matter from the very beginning. My brother here upon my right, (Dr. Fisher) alluded to that glorious revival that passed all over this land. Before that, you would not see brethren of different denominations coming together, as we have often seen them in Cincinnati; yet all were melted down because the tide had risen so high, by the inflowing of the Spirit of God, that the brethren forgot all their differences when united as one with the Lord of Hosts.

Then, sir, I would come down to this war, as it was my privilege during the war to stand by the side of noble brethren of the United Presbyterian Church, Reformed Presbyterian, Dutch Reformed, and of the Old and New School. In those times, as we stood by the side of the dying soldiers and talked about Christ, then we did not know we were of different churches. I remember one occasion when some brethren who had labored for four weeks, day and night talking about Christ and heaven, were talking of the religious sympathies of our members; and one said he would like to know to what denomination we belonged. One said, I think we are all Old School Presbyterians; and yet when they came to compare notes, he was the only one. And when they compared notes further, it was found they were all of different denominations. Yet they had led many souls to Christ, and I have no doubt some of those who have departed from earth are sitting with Him, singing songs to God and the Lamb.

Oh, when I witness scenes of this kind, it seems that the Master, looking down on this vast assemblage to-night, says, O! shame, brethren, that you have stood apart so long! Is it not time we should be coming together? I want to go back, for one moment, to remark my own experience in this Convention this afternoon. When my name was announced on the committee, I regretted it exceedingly, and went to the chairman to ask to have another brother's name substituted. I feared we would have difficulties in the committee; but we began at the other end of the rope. We began by seeing how we could agree. I thank God, the brethren were praying while we were in the other room, that we might be led to the conclusions that would be to His glory! I believe it was the loving hand of God that brought us to the conclusions that we have presented. It is no merit of the members that they did present them: how could they do otherwise when our brothers here were beseeching God to direct our minds aright! The whole thing as it lies on the table, I know is in answer to your prayers. It was a delightful thought to me, as we discussed these different subjects, that here the brethren's hearts were ascending together, praying we might be guided to wise conclusions, and that all might be to the glory of God, to the honor of Christ, and to the salvation of many souls for ages to come! I believe I would do injustice to my Master, if I should ascribe the conclusions to which we arrived to aught else but the Spirit of the living God.

Now, there were things in that discussion, from time to time, as we passed along, that looked to me like mountains in the distance; but as we approached nearer, we either came up on a higher elevation, or else the mountains became lower; for when we came alongside, we found there were no mountains, but all the way a pleasant plain over which we passed very smoothly. We shook hands at the conclusion; and I believe we can say we were all one. One brother said, We made no sacrifices; another said, We made no sacrifices. And, brethren, no one has made any sacrifices. I do not believe, if that paper is adopted, that any brother in this broad land is called upon to make any such sacrifices as the brethren have imagined.

Now, sir, I am thankful in standing before you here to-night, at the thought that I can go home and say to my brethren there, that the Spirit of God was here, that the Master came with us here to this meeting; that He presided over all our deliberations; that, as in water, face answers to face, so the heart of every Christian to the heart of his brother; that sitting here in amity and love in Christ Jesus, we came to conclusions which will be to the glory of God in the ages to come.

I want to say one word in relation to denominations. I am a Presbyterian. I was born of Presbyterian parents; and yet as my lot has been cast in different sections, in the providence of God, I belonged to the New School Presbyterian Church for a time, and the blessed Spirit of God was poured out there upon souls, and I heartily rejoiced with those brethren. I was a member of the Dutch Reformed Church, of their Consistory, and I saw the same thing there; the same blessed Spirit brought in precious souls full of the love of Christ. We all labored together, and rejoiced to know that God blessed our labors. I am now in the Old School Presbyterian Church, and yet I love all my other brethren with the same tenderness.

I had been greatly troubled before I came to this Cenvention, on one point; which was, that the laity were perhaps too far in advance of the ministry. I believe to-day that if the Presbyterian Church could be canvassed throughout this land—you may think it extravagant, but I believe it to-day—that nine out of ten of all the members, of all the laity of the churches, are ready for Union. (Applause.) Nor is that all; but, brethren, I do not think, with all deference and respect to my brethren, the fathers in the Church, there is in all our section either in the New School or the Old School, or any school of Presbyterians, a single pastor under forty years of age who is not for union.

Mr. President, I know I am taking up the time of this Convention; but I want to say one or two things more. There was an idea that when we came together, we would have to make some sacrifices. No, brethren, there are no sacrifices at all. So far as I feel to-day, I know that if I could sing—which God does not permit me to do in this life; but I hope to do it up yonder—I would just as soon sing the Psalms of David, as anything else. I am pretty much in the fix of a young man who went down to an army hospital; I would not say what denomination he belonged to. He was asked to sing at a prayer-meeting, where thirty of us were singing together; but he could only sing the Psalms, not hymns. Next day, that man went into a hospital, to labor by the side of the sick and the dying. After he had talked and prayed with a dying soldier, the latter said, "There is one thing more I want you to do for me; sing

'Jesus, lover of my soul;'"

and he did sing it for the soldier. A few days after, as I returned from the front, coming back to Nashville, this brother was conducting the exercises. He gave out a hymn, and we all sang it together. I asked him how he came to that conclusion; he said: "When a dying soldier was just about to pass into glory, he asked me to sing a hymn to him. I thought certainly it would not be wrong to sing a hymn anywhere, if

I could sing it as a soul was about to enter those blessed doors, to dwell with God and the Lamb. [Applause.]

Now, brethren, I said before to the brethren of the Committee, I want in this matter, that every brother should have the largest possible liberty. We did not yield, and I would not be willing to yield, a single doctrine or foundation-stone in our glorious Church; but if the question comes upon the union of these communities in one Church, and my brother wants to sing Psalms, I say you can sing those Psalms you love, as I say to those who want to sing hymns—you can do so. I could love to sing with both of them on the common ground of Christian brotherhood. I will go further. If I should go into a Church where communion is being administered, and it would violate the conscience of a brother if I sat with him, I would sit at one side; yet I would not cast a reflection on that brother for what concerns his conscience. But if we were going out together to labor for the salvation of precious souls, there would be no trouble between us on that point; because we believe in that work we shall have God's blessing. He is able to use, to bring people into His fold, all these instruments.

Hence, I am anxious to see this paper, or the substance of it, adopted by this Convention, that when I go home I can say, that some of the fathers in the Church here, some of the venerable and learned men of the Church, who have given tone and character to this Church for years, were melted down by the Spirit of God. We saw there was no real, essential difference between us; and we were willing to unite hand-in-hand, to go forward in the glorious work of bringing souls to Christ.

Brethren, this is the work the Master has given us to do. We have no time to stop to talk about these little differences, when souls all about us are perishing for want of the truth as it is in Jesus. If the Master were here to-night, I believe He would say, Look out on the fields, and see them all white and rich for the harvest! Why are you not thrusting in your sickles, and gathering in the harvest of the Lord?

God grant, brethren, that when we go from this place we may go to pray earnestly that the whole Church may receive the baptism of the Holy Ghost! May we feel and rejoice, as we go out from this meeting, that we go out as loving and united brethren, to preach Christ wherever we go. May the cross of Christ be elevated by all His people, and may precious souls all over the land be brought into His communion.

THE PRESIDENT:—Brethren, let us spend a few moments in silent prayer; and I will ask that, at the signal of the bell, the representative of the oldest Covenanter family I know in this country, Rev. John McMillan, of Allegheny, lead us in audible prayer.

After an impressive pause of several moments for silent devotion, in which the whole congregation participated, Mr. McMillan delivered an earnest prayer. The Convention also joined in singing the 148th Psalm, H. M.

ELDER JAS. C. MCMILLAN, (R. P.), of the Committee, said:—My heart responds to every sentiment that has been uttered here to-night; and if I am right in looking over this audience, I may say the same for them. When I was appointed on that Committee, like Brother Chamberlain, I felt like shrinking back, and saying, would that it were some other person. But when I went to my lodgings last evening, before retiring I lifted my heart in solemn prayer to God, to ask Him that I might be enabled to discharge my duty, with all my energies, in that Committee. As you have been already well told by my colleague here, we all felt it was in answer to the prayers of the Assembly, offered while we were deliberating, that we were brought to such a happy and unanimous conclusion; and let me assure you that it was unanimous. We felt that we were drawn along gradually, smoothly, pleasantly. Those mountains that interfered and presented themselves before us at the outset, vanished out of our sight. This was not our doing. It seemed to me that the Lord Himself was doing the work; and, brethren, while we have thus presented you these points here for your consideration, we desire now that each one for himself shall take them home, meditate upon them, and examine them in the light of God's Word.

The first proposition that is laid down here, is that we recognize the Scriptures to be the Word of God. The suggestion has been made, and I have no doubt it will be readily accepted, that "it is the only infallible rule of faith and practice." Who, in this assembly, is not willing to be governed by that? I think that there is not one who is willing to substitute the regulations of men in our Synods, in the place of the infallible Word of God. Whatever we have else, let it be the first in our affections. Can we not, with that as our corner-stone, may we not look forward in anticipation to the rearing of this noble structure, about which we have heard so much to-night, and during the sittings of this Convention?

Brethren, let us take hold of it: let us stand up to it, and see that the brethren, of our Church, throughout our land, go hand-in-hand in bringing about this desirable object. When we think of the prayer of our Saviour, as He was about finishing His work here, can we sit still in our differences, and not do what we can to accomplish the great desire of His heart? When our Saviour prayed that we might be all one—shall we not do here what we can to have this glorious result brought about? Shall we not do what we can by our lives, and our conversation, that shall be to the glory of the Triune God? I think it is needless, then, for me to waste your time; I think the matter has been presented very forcibly. I do not know but every member of the Committee will say they are ready to thank God that such a happy conclusion, such a unanimous report was brought before you; and that we had not a dissenting voice when the vote came to be taken thereon.

I think nothing more is needed for this assembly to-night than to adopt this basis. I ask the members of this Convention to take this paper with them, and let it be presented to our respective denominations. We all have somewhat regretted our separation. I claim to have regretted it, as well as others; therefore it shall be my aim, as it should be the aim of all of us, to do what can be done to bring about this union, which we all feel and know ought to be accomplished. I trust those who are here to-night—though we may never meet each other again in the flesh—may see it consummated: that ere we leave this world, and are taken to the upper heaven, we may see the work thus inaugurated by our worthy President, result in doing great good, not only in gathering the family of God into one, but in giving strength and force to this

Church, and in carrying the Gospel of our blessed Saviour to the ends of the earth. No doubt you have already heard much on the subject of carrying the Gospel to our Western country. But in union there is strength; and we need union in order to meet the tide of Romanism and Infidelity spreading through this land. Let us, then, close up our ranks, brethren. I say close them up, and let us march on as brethren in one family.

ELDER WILLIAM GETTY (U. P.) also of the committee:—I was afraid, Mr. President, you and the Convention might think the United Presbyterians had disappeared; but we want this whole Convention to be United Presbyterians. This meeting to-night reminds me of a meeting I had the pleasure of attending in May, 1858, in the city of Pittsburgh. There were two churches met there in conference on the subject of union; and the brethren began to talk with each other about their differences. Then, afterwards, they began to talk about their agreements, and one brother after another began to be full of the Spirit of the Master. You could see over the whole of that assembly that a new feeling was filling every man, flowing from heart to heart and making them regard one another as brethren. I remember one beloved brother, who has gone home, got up; and you could see almost inspiration in his features. He was willing there to engage in a covenant with God, and asked them to pledge themselves to be faithful to Jesus and each other.

It seems to me the assembly here to-night has much of the same spirit; and if it were proposed to us now to unite as brethren, we would say, Yes, brothers; we are all willing to unite as one church. I believe that the spirit of the Master pervades every heart here, and that one feeling animates each brother now present. Oh, there is in the Bible enough to encourage us! Our Saviour says, "Whosoever believeth on me, shall be saved." One of the Apostles says, "Whosoever believeth that Jesus is the Christ, is born of God." Dear brethren, do you not all believe that Jesus is the Christ? Are we not all born of God? If we are all born of God, are we not all in the same family? Have we not Jesus as our elder brother? Yet we hold each other aloof, and say, I will have nothing to do with the Old School men, with the New School men, with the United brethren; and yet we are all born of God, and Jesus is our elder brother. Is that right? Do you think Jesus regards us with favor when we separate from each other in that way? Oh, when we go to our glorious common home, will the Saviour ask us of what denomination we are? Oh, no; but he will ask, Did you love and serve me?

Another thing, Mr. Chairman, we have union enough in the Convention to make us one; we have the strongest arguments showing that we are one. I heard venerable fathers in the church praying last night, and they prayed the same language. They spoke to our Father in heaven and to Jesus just alike. If you were to shut your eyes, you could not tell but what they were the same men. If we were to pray to-night, we would all pray alike. Now, why cannot we live alike, and recognize each other as brethren, if we have the likeness of Jesus so stamped upon us that our words come out alike in the language of heaven? Oh, when we begin to pray, then we forget to what we belong! When those brothers were on the battle-field, they forgot all about what church they belonged to. When we come near to the Throne, we only think of Jesus. Oh, that the spirit of the Master may come to-night, and pervade each heart so fully that we may determine here that, from this time forth, we will labor until the union of these churches is effected; and make our prayers effectual so that the time may not be long. I felt sad the other day in thinking that our good President here might never see the union accomplished. I want to see the union. I believe that this Convention can accomplish a mighty work; and I pray God we may all be spared—even the oldest brother in this Convention, I hope God will spare his life—to see the union of all these Churches! (Applause.) I believe that He will. I believe that He will permit you, aged fathers here, to help it on; and that your lives will be gladdened in seeing God hasten the time of Union.

ELDER W. M. FRANCIS (O. S.):—Mr. President, the hour has come and passed at which we were to adjourn. Is it not best, as we have such an abundance of God's influence upon us, to adjourn? My reason for suggesting this is owing to a thought brought to my mind of what occurred a great many years ago. Just about twenty-nine years ago, I was married. (Laughter.) I went on a pleasant trip to the house of a friend, an uncle of my wife, that I thought much of then, but a great deal more of now, because I know him better. One evening we were invited out to a party, and he told me that the rule there was that every one invited must eat something of everything set before him. There was a bountiful table spread, and I went at it. Well, sir, I did not rest well after it. (Laughter.) Now, sir, if there comes much more of this excellent thing that I relish so much, I shall not rest well. There is too much of it; keep some of it for the morning.

REV. DR. GOODALE (O. S.):—I have a motion to make which is this:—

That in the future discussions of this basis the members of this Convention be confined to five minute speeches. We have had a fine specimen of one just now. There are so many here who wish to speak, that I think the motion is necessary.

THE PRESIDENT:—Brother, wait till the members of the Committee are through, they have nearly all spoken.

REV. DR. MILLER of the Cumb. Pres. Church:—Dear brethren, I feel myself unable to speak so as to be heard by this very large audience; in addition, I deem it unadvisable that I should take up much of the time of the Convention. We claim to be Presbyterians, that being our principle of government. We do not, however, like the other branches of the Presbyterian Church here represented, hold the Westminster Confession; that is to say we have modified it. Like you and many who have expressed themselves upon the floor of this house, we feel that God in His providence is saying to the branches of the Church in this country, unite. We have taken steps in this matter; and the question now with us is, Where shall our home be? Some of our judicatories have moved in this matter. We feel that your church—I mean now the Presbyterian Church generally—is dear to us; because as I said we are Presbyterians. But we are not Calvinists to the extent that you are.

I cannot say that the terms proposed to this Convention will be acceptable to my church. Indeed, I am constrained to admit that I believe they will not be acceptable; nor did I think before coming here that any terms could be secured that would embrace the humble denomination with which I am connected.

My dear brethren, permit me, before I take my seat to express to you my heartfelt gratitude for the Christian magnanimity you have manifested towards the few members of my denomination who are present with you on this occasion. When the vote is to be taken—I speak of the few of us who are here present—we will vote in the negative. By that we mean simply, that we believe the terms will not be acceptable to our Church; but we rejoice in this great union movement with you. When you came to act as a Committee, I was surprised myself, I confess, to see how little there was to keep these denominations apart; and if I can feel afterwards that I have contributed in the humblest degree to help you to union, I shall feel that I have been greatly honored of God. For that reason I feel that it would be a pleasure to me to allow my name to appear with the other members of the Committee to that report. Now, with the explanation I have made, I believe that to allow my name to continue to that report will not commit me in such a manner as to place me in a false light, either before my Church or before this Convention.

I heartily approve that report, brethren, as a basis upon which, I think, all the Presbyterian bodies in the United States, receiving the Westminster Catechism, can and ought to unite. I will heartily rejoice with you, if it shall appear that the day is just at hand when, as one brother has said, instead of all these stars which give a great deal of light now, we shall have the great sun in one united Church, that will fill the land with its light and its glory.

Rev. Dr. H. B. Smith (New School):—Mr. President, fathers, and brethren, I think we may mark this day with a white stone. I think the report of this Committee, even as it now stands, has lifted a weight from our hearts, and has made us feel that we are breathing a higher and a rarer air. It seems to me that report shows distinctly that we are advancing directly in a line for forming a basis on which we, as Presbyterians and as Calvinists can stand, and realize the end for which we are here convened. We have all had grave doubts. The obstacles seemed serious, and have really been serious. Now, we are coming to the time when, so far as the influence of this Convention may reach, we are to decide; to decide not only in view of the past, but to decide in view of the present, and in view of the future.

We have all felt the elevating influence of that spirit of re-union which is abroad, and animates all of us, making us in many respects—in most respects; we can almost say in all respects, as far as the objects of the Convention are concerned—of one heart and of one mind.

We ought to be suspicious of mere excitement and feeling generated by a crowded assemblage. We ought to be suspicious of those feelings which come to us through the excitations of the nervous system; but after all it is in the deep feelings of the soul that we have the centre of our moral and our religious life. Even when the deepest feelings are stirred within us, we can distinguish what is permanent and what is merely brief. Do not we know that these common feelings that now animate us, come not from man but from God; that they are the response of Christ's voice to us, exhorting us to come together and do His work here on the earth?

What is the call in the movement that has brought together this assembly, as grave and as influential, I believe, as any that has ever met together for ecclesiastical purposes in these United States? There are four instincts which are contained in it, and which may be said to define it. 1. The instinct of our common Christianity. 2. The instinct of our common Presbyterianism. 3. The instinct arising from our common work, and in view of what we are doing for our common Lord. 4. The instinct which comes from a sense of our common danger, in view of those foes by which we are encompassed, and with which we are contending for the mastery of this land.

And what is the deepest sense of this great movement which is now carrying us onward? I believe, Mr. President, that it is this: That as a nation we have come to a stadium of our national progress and career. We have begun, as a nation, our real history in regenerating this land, and making this continent a Christian republic. This Convention is one of the signs that the churches of this land are preparing themselves to do this great work, in these new circumstances of our beloved country. (Applause.) It is an indication that they believe and know, that this work can only be done, not as they remain apart, but only as they come together in one heart and in one mind, to unite all their forces, all their powers, with a loving faith, in the service of our common Lord and Master. It is a movement to be hailed alike by all Christian hearts. Let us have, and well understand, our doctrinal basis. Let us have it that we may all know just where we stand, in reference to the terms on which those doctrines are accepted. But let us also know that on that basis we may, and as disciples of Christ we are bound to come together. This is to be hailed as a day of joy and gladness, for which we should ever praise God.

THE PRESIDENT:—The question before the house is the adoption of the Report of the Committee on the Basis of Union.

REV. DR. J. F. STEARNS (N. S.):—Mr. President, have we not already agreed to take up the report, article by article?

THE PRESIDENT:—I am much obliged to the member; that is the motion before the house. The first article will be read.

REV. DR. MARSHALL (O. S.):—I am not going to make any remarks on the first article. I think we are ready to adopt that. There is an article here I would like to have modified, not on my own account, however. Perhaps, I may as well say now what I have to say, on that point. In regard to the great body of the report, I approve it entirely; it has my hearty concurrence. I believe that God's Spirit, in answer to prayer, led the Committee; but there are points to which I wish to direct the attention of the house. I would like to see some modification in regard to the fourth part of that report; that is in regard to the matter of the Psalmody. I have a real difficulty, not on my own account, but on account of two branches represented here of the Presbyterian family. I refer to the Reformed Presbyterian, and the United Presbyterian Churches. In regard to the Dutch Reformed, to the Old School and to the New School, there would certainly be no difficulty. The Committee recommend, as I understand, that each party shall have its own Psalmody. That is all very well, at first sight; but they recommend in connection with that, that we exchange pulpits. Well, that is delightful, and what I want to see; but here is where the difficulty comes in. These two branches of the Church prefer the Old Psalms; we use a different version of the Psalms, in connection with, as you know, a large number of hymns. Now, suppose we exchange pulpits, a difficulty arises. If I go into one of the Churches, where the old version of the Psalms is solely used, I can sing them with all my heart, without any difficulty; but when a brother from the United Presbyterian branch, who sings the old Psalmody, comes into my pulpit, he cannot use the Psalmody in use by us. If the Committee had recommended the best possible version of the one hundred and fifty Psalms to be prepared, that it might be used in all our pulpits, to be incorporated in the Psalmody —that we could all sing, we could then have our meetings in common with each other.

Rev. Dr. Beatty (O. S.):—Mr. President, I desire, beforc we proceed to the final adoption of this report, that it be recommitted to the Committee, to be in some respects recast. There has been some objection to some of the phraseology, and the brother himself who brought it in, says it was a hasty production, and not in the form in which he would desire to have it. Sir, that is to be a most important document. It is to go before our Churches; it is to go before the world. It will go down in history; and, therefore, we should endeavor to obtain a document, not in the fewest words, it is true, but as brief as possible. It should express, in the clearest and best language, what we really mean. I do not mean that there should be any change in the great sentiments there uttered; but that we should have them clothed in the most happy language. Therefore, I move, as we will not probably come to a vote to-night, that before we adjourn, this paper, with the suggestion about the first article, which has been accepted, with all the other suggestions made, be recommitted to a Committee from the several denominations, that they may bring in a report to-morrow morning, in the best possible form.

Rev. Dr. Stearns (N. S.):—Mr. President, it seems to me, we would save time if we would pursue the course we have already resolved upon. It is very likely there may be some suggestions in the way of amendments to different articles; therefore, the best way to get at the wishes of the house in regard to that matter is to pass upon these articles in general. We may then refer it to the Committee, in order that they may make a new draft, and adjust the matter in the best phraseology possible. It appears to me that the Committee will stand in the same position when they receive these articles, in which they were when the Committee formed it. There have been almost no suggestions made by the house, and there are no indications of the pleasure of the house in regard to the alterations to be made. Therefore it seems to me superfluous at this stage of the business, to recommit it. The better way, as it seems to me, would be to follow the course we have already resolved upon, so as to get the mind of the house in regard to the substance of the articles; then we can have it recast afterwards.

Rev. Dr. Musgrave, (O. S.):—Sir, I am opposed to this motion, and I hope the mover will withdraw it. How do we know, at this stage, that we shall want the committee to do this? Certain individuals here seem to express the belief that the basis is the right one; but the house has expressed no opinion. Let us wait until we find the document is what we want, before we re-commit it.

Brethren, we have reached practically a glorious result; that report has seemed to me to have received the approbation of the house generally. How do you know, how can any man foretell, how another report differently expressed will meet the views of this house? Why, sir, it seems to me that we are flying into the very difficulties that we wish to obviate. We are now about to spend our time on style and rhetoric, and get into difficulties about different phraseologies. Sir, we have got above that now. (Applause.) I beg the brethren not to risk it.

Besides it seems to me to be rather discourteous, though I know my venerable brother never intends to be discourteous to anybody, for, he is too kind, and good, and polite. Yet it does seem to me to be rather discourteous to the former committee, to take it out of their hands and place it in the hands of others. I am so much in earnest in this thing, that I want to go for the practical rather than the theoretical. Sir, let us go on as we have begun. We are in the right line now; let us take it up, and if anybody wants to alter the language of a phrase, let him come forward, state his objection, and make his motion. Then, after we have got through, perhaps it will be just finished and we will all say it is exactly right.

I do not like this motion: it looks like a damper. We have all been thinking that report was almost inspired; that it was in answer to prayer; that the Spirit of God indited it; and behold somebody gets up, and declares it is a very faulty thing. If the Spirit of God has led us to that report with such unanimity, let us be very cautious how we undertake to mend it. Let us be cautious. I beg my brethren now to be cautious; because I am satisfied that when that report was read, it met a hearty response from all this convention. I believe it meets the aprobation of a large majority just as it is. There may be some little minutiæ, that will not affect it materially; and that can be suggested. Do not risk that report of the committee by placing it in other hands; they may bring it back in a shape that will not at all suit us.

Rev. Dr. Beatty:—Mr. President, I always listen to that brother with a great deal of interest, and I ask leave of this house to withdraw my motion. (Loud applause.)

The President:—There is no feeling but one here, and that is the feeling of love to each other in that we are led by the Spirit of God, step by step. Now and then we may get out of the right path, but God will bring us back. We got out yesterday afternoon, but how we came back at night. If we had not had that incident, we would have forgotten we were of different denominations. The question is on the First Article.

Rev. Cyrus Dickson, D.D., (O. S.,) moved to amend by inserting the word *inspired* before the phrase "Word of God," and adding to it the words, *the only infallible rule of faith and practice*, which amendment, by unanimous consent of the House, the Committee adopted.

Rev. Dr. Musgrave, (O. S.):—Mr. President, I rise to a point of order. Is it necessary for us to vote, at this stage of the business, by churches? It strikes me it is not necessary at present, and that we may thus save time.

THE PRESIDENT:—The question is upon the adoption of the article. I hope that you will vote without losing time.

The question was put to vote *viva voce*, and unanimously adopted.

REV. A. ERDMAN, (N. S.):—I would like to suggest that you take this vote standing.

THE PRESIDENT:—Oh no. It is very distinct. We have taken the vote, and that is all over.

REV. J. W. EDMISTON, (C. P.):—It is not my understanding that we are to take the votes in any other way than by denominations.

THE PRESIDENT:—When we come to adopt it as a whole, then the question will be, How do the separate churches vote? We are merely paving the way.

REV. DR. CANDEE, (O. S.):—I cannot but think that, with reference to voting by denominations, it is better to hear the expressed opinions of the denominations as such on the individual clauses. When we come to vote on the whole paper, there will probably be hardly a dissenting voice; but there may be, at first, in regard to particular clauses. But it appears to me that now is the time to put into practice the principle of voting by the churches separately.

THE PRESIDENT:—The Moderator has decided the question.

REV. S. W. CRITTENDEN, (N. S.):—I appeal from the decision of the Chair, for this reason. I can vote heartily to accept all, and hope to do so; yet I want the privilege of rising to vote on every distinct proposition, with an Aye and an Amen! I wish, then, to have the privilege of voting on the whole, Aye; but I wish to grant every brother the same privilege I ask for myself. If any brother in this assembly, of any denomination, wishes to vote aye to one proposition, and no to another, I wish to allow him that privilege; and I wish to allow him the privilege of rising and showing his vote, and not be held to do it at the last. Now, sir, I appeal from the decision of the Chair, because I have not occupied the time of this assembly before.

THE PRESIDENT:—Allow me to speak. I have said I would govern this body by common sense. If it is the wish of the house to vote now by denominations, I will withdraw my decision, as I want merely to save time. The brethren will vote, then, upon these questions by denominations. The Chair is trying to guide you along, and when he makes a wrong decision he is willing to substitute a right one.

REV. DR. T. W. J. WYLIE, (R. P.):—I am heartily prepared to vote on this matter myself; but I think we should be very cautious not to take any step that would seem to do the slightest injustice to the wishes or feelings of any brother. I know there are brothers here who wish to vote directly on certain propositions; and instead of compelling them to call for those special clauses, let us go over the report by denominations.

REV. MR. CRITTENDEN:—That is just what I was about to say when interrupted by the Moderator. We agreed to vote on every important question by churches.

THE PRESIDENT:—The decision of the Chair is this: The question before the house is upon the adoption of the article read; and according to the ruling and decision of the Chair, it shall be taken by denominations.

The Convention then proceeded to vote by Churches, and Article First was adopted unanimously, as follows:

I. An acknowledgment of the Old and New Testament to be the inspired Word of God, and the only infallible rule of faith and practice.

The Second Article was then read.

Rev. H. B. Smith, D.D., (New School):—Mr. Moderator, it seems to me that in this article we have reached the central point, and that here we need to be careful and circumspect; because we have come to the article where there has been the most controversy. There will be the most difficulty, in respect to the terms of subscription to the sense in which we assent to the doctrines presented, and receive the Confession of Faith as containing the doctrines taught in the Holy Scriptures. I move that the following words be added to that article; namely:

"It being understood, that this Confession is received in its proper historical—that is, the Calvinistic or Reformed sense."

The Article as amended, was read.

Rev. Dr. McIlvaine, (O. S.):—Mr. President, whilst I hold to the Confession of Faith, in the proper historical—the Calvinistic, or Reformed sense, as strongly as any one, I would very much prefer the resolution as it stood at first. There are strong reasons why we should not set up any interpretations of the Confession of Faith, as if that detailed statement of doctrine was a feather which could be blown about one way or the other. The words of that Confession of Faith must forever bind the consciences of honest men who receive it, in the sense which has been called the historical sense. You cannot get any interpretations of the Confession of Faith which will bind the consciences of good men any more than the Confession of Faith itself will do. Therefore, I feel we shall be stronger every way to say that Confession of Faith shall be the one basis of union. I am satisfied with the Confession of Faith as the basis of our union. I do not want to argue one statement of facts upon it, and make that the basis of union. If the others are satisfied with the Confession of Faith as the basis of union, I am satisfied with the Confession of Faith as the basis of union. With these few remarks I will sit down.

The Convention was adjourned with prayer by Rev. Dr. J. Few Smith, (N. S.)

FIRST REFORMED PRESBYTERIAN CHURCH, PHILADELPHIA.
Friday, November 8th, 1867, 9 *A. M.*

The Convention met, as per adjournment, and spent a season in devotional exercises, being led therein by Rev. Cyrus Dickson, D.D.

The services were opened by singing the 68th Psalm. The Chairman then read the 12th chapter of Isaiah, and the 5th of Matthew. Let us sing, said he, with full hearts, to God, the 36th Psalm. It will probably be the last time that we will have such an opportunity for exhortation and praise. This Convention will, in all probability, adjourn before another morning. The Psalm was sung.

A DELEGATE said:—Mr. President, it has done my heart good, and I have felt it leap within me with joy, at the manifestation of God's Spirit here. I have always put God first, everywhere and every time. I love the Presbyterian name. I love the Calvinistic order, and I love the communion of saints. I thank God, that we are becoming harmonious, feeling the same great need of the unity of the Church. I believe in that great sentiment that was enunciated from the pulpit by Dr. Duff; that this great assembly is like the ancient tribes coming up to Jerusalem; and the nearer they get to Jerusalem, the nearer they get to one another; and when they get on the Mount of Zion, then they are on the same platform.

REV. DR. MONFORT (Old School):—I believe this, sir, that we should act as did the disciples of old, when their Saviour, asking them to follow Him, said: "Let the dead bury their dead." And so I feel, that we are in a great work; a work inspired of God; a work in which we should press forward; and I feel like saying to those who will not come with us, Let the dead bury their dead; as for us we will accomplish the great unity of the Church. We have been speaking all along with reference to our disagreements; let us now, for a time, consider those things wherein we are one, and on which we all agree! It is not for us to know what God's purposes are, but we are now about knowing that Christian unity is being perfected. This is the most solemn day in my life, as a minister of the Gospel. And I pray God, that harmony may prevail, and that a unity of spirit may prevail, and that the good work may be consummated.

REV. DR. STEVENSON (O. S.):—Perhaps it may be well to turn our thoughts for a moment—as our brethren of the Episcopal Convention are to be here in ten minutes—to the subject of even a wider union. I confess, I am amazed at the evidence of God's Spirit here; amazed to see five or six denominations together as we are. But let us remember that there is another great body—a Protestant body—a Calvinistic body—a noble church of Jesus Christ, whose delegates are to be present with us here in a few moments; a body that has the love of the blessed Jesus in all their hearts. May we not hope that eventually the border of this organic union may extend beyond these five or six denominations? We are all one body! All one body in Christ Jesus! Then brothers as we are one body—let our minds and hearts go out to our Christian brethren of the same body. Not only that—we are of the same Spirit: in-dwelt by the same Holy Ghost; and many of us have precisely the same characteristics.

During these exercises the Clergy and Laity of the Annual Meeting of the Evangelical Anniversaries of the Protestant Episcopal Church in session in this city, consisting of Rev. Drs. Newton and Butler, and Rev. Phillips Brooks and others, entered the house.

President Stuart took the chair and said:—We are to have one grand union of the Millennial Church one of these days!

The 133d Psalm was sung,

"Behold how good a thing it is,
And how becoming well;
Together such as brethren are,
In unity to dwell."

The President:—Paul in his Epistle to the Ephesians, thus writes: —"I therefore the prisoner of the Lord, beseech you that ye walk worthy of the vocation wherewith ye are called. * * * * * * * * *

"Till we come in the unity of the faith, and of the knowledge of the Son of God, unto a perfect man, unto the measure of the stature of the fullness of Christ."

Brethren, we were in the midst of devotional services, when the beloved brothers of the Episcopal Convention entered the church. We shall continue the services for a few moments longer. Will the Rev. Dr. Newton, of the Protestant Episcopal Church, lead the Convention in prayer?

Rev. Dr. Newton:—Let us pray.

Lord Jesus Christ, Thou great Head of Thy church we thank Thee for this Thy church on earth. We thank Thee that Thou hast revealed Thyself as the foundation of hope and trust. We thank Thee that Thou hast revealed Thyself as the only common Saviour to ruined sinners everywhere. And we thank Thee for the grand, precious truth on which Thy people can stand. Truth centering in Thee! Truth in Thee! And we thank Thee that Thou art the life and embodiment of the truth in which our souls can live.

We thank Thee that there is so much in Thy Blessed Book, which any man can receive of the truth that will save. We thank Thee that we are getting to see more and more of the things which we hold in God, and that we are coming to yield more in obedience to them.

Blessed Saviour, may the time come when not only the watchmen on the walls of Zion, but all who dwell within those walls shall see, eye to eye, the glorious light of their Redeemer. We thank Thee for the privilege of mingling together, and engaging thus in views and sentiments worthy of the great interests that are mutual to us.

We pray Thee, blessed Saviour, that Thou wilt shed down more and more of the spirit of love and unity into the hearts of Thy people everywhere. We pray that Thou wilt bless Thy servants who assemble here, consulting together for the mutual interests of that portion of Thy Church committed to their care. We thank Thee that we are permitted in the goodness of Thy providence, to come in the midst of them. Guide their assemblies! control their councils! and lead them to such results as shall glorify Thy name!

We thank Thee that Thou hast brought this meeting together. We pray that Thou wilt bless all; and may we feel that we are brethren; that we are poor ruined sinners, who are saved but by our common, glorious Saviour; who have no foundation or hope but Thee. Thou wast sacrificed that we might live. May we feel that we are complete in Jesus, and incomplete in our outward organization. Incomplete in those things by which we differ from one another, but complete when we can arise to those things which are of Thy divine nature. May we feel that we are all one in Christ Jesus, our precious, precious, precious Saviour!

Be with us now! Direct this hour! Direct what may be said and done. May we all feel that we are in Thy presence, and that Thou art looking down with favor and approbation upon us. Shed down Thy blessing upon every waiting soul here. May we be brought more and more to love Thee and Thy precious truth. May we be brought nearer and nearer to one another. May these, Thy brethren, be united as a band, and further Thy kingdom and Thy cause. Hear us, and then give us Thy blessing, and Thy presence. Guide us, and may we at last be united as a body of the Church in Christ, and finally be received into Thy glorious kingdom, to sing the triumphs of the Redeemer's life. *Amen.*

The Committee appointed by the annual meeting, consisting of

The Rt. Rev. Charles P. McIlvaine, D.D.,
" " Alfred Lee, D.D.,
The Rev. Stephen H. Tyng, Jun.,
" Hon. Judge Conyngham,
" " Felix R. Brunot,

then appeared, and were received upon the platform—the Convention standing.

The following action of the body represented by the Committee was received and recorded.

CHURCH OF THE EPIPHANY, *Phila., November 7th.*

Annual Meeting of the clergymen and laymen in attendance at our Evangelical Anniversaries.

WHEREAS, This Convention has welcomed with unfeigned pleasure, a delegation coming to visit us, with the cordial greetings of the Presbyterian Convention now assembled in this city,

Resolved, That a committee of five, consisting of the Rt. Rev. Chas. P. McIlvaine, D.D., Rt. Rev. Alfred Lee, D.D., Rev. S. H. Tyng, Jr., and Lay Members, Hon. Judge Conyngham and Hon. Felix R. Brunot, are hereby appointed to return the hearty Christian greetings of this body, and our cordial congratulations at the prospect of the speedy reunion of the various Churches into which the Presbyterian Denomination is divided.

Attest, ROBERT J. PARVIN, *Secretary*.

PRESIDENT STUART said:—The Deputation from the Convention of the Protestant Episcopal Church will be introduced by the Chairman of our Committee, that was sent to present our saluation of brotherly love to that body—the Rev. H. B. Smith, D.D., of New York.

REV. DR. SMITH:—Mr. President, I have already spoken to you and this Convention, of the mode in which we were received by the Episcopal brethren; of the hearty and grateful reception we had from them. In response I now have the pleasure of introducing them to you. They will address you upon the subjects that come before us in connection with this auspicious occasion.

PRESIDENT STUART, advancing to Bishop McIlvaine, said:—I am most happy, Brother McIlvaine—I shall not call you Bishop, now, for we are all brothers in Christ Jesus—in welcoming you and your colleagues to this platform, which I hope may be found strong enough to hold the whole Church of Christ!

BISHOP MCILVAINE came forward amid great applause, and said:—I am glad to find presiding over this august body my old friend, Mr. Stuart:—Christian Brethren, of the various bodies comprising the great Christian interests of the whole Presbyterian Church in the United States of America. The several bodies that have been assembled, representing in a certain sense, the religious interests of the Protestant Episcopal Church in the United States, assembled together in this city during the present week. At their morning meeting for prayer, they had their hearts drawn out in supplication and fraternal love toward you, brethren, assembled here, in consideration of the exceedingly important business by which you are gathered together, in which business and for the furtherance of the same, our hearts were deeply interested with yours. We were rejoiced to hear that you have heard of our prayers in your behalf, and reciprocated the interest; and amongst yourselves, did engage before the Throne of Grace, for us. Those prayers are answered. Not directly, but perhaps more auspiciously than any of us could have anticipated.

The prayer of the Christian heart is all concentrated and comprehended in the gift of the Holy Ghost. And we believe that God has answered those prayers in giving to us all a spirit of love and fraternal sympathy in the common cause of our Lord Jesus Christ! You have reciprocated them. You were so kind and so good as to send to us the deputation of brethren who appeared before us yesterday morning. It was a surprise; but indeed, it was a most grateful surprise; and every heart was opened at once to meet and welcome them. And I trust, as I have heard from the brother who introduced us this morning—I trust that the report was such as to indicate that there could not possibly be a mistake, in regard to the unanimity and perfect openness of heart, and warm Christian sympathy and regard, with which we greeted your representatives. (Applause).

We are here to-day as a committee, appointed by that particular body which was in session yesterday, for the purpose of expressing, in return, our feelings, our regards and love, and desire; in response to those to which you called us to listen!

It may seem to you, as it does to me, a very remarkable indication of Providence, in this connection, when I tell you that when the General Convention of the Episcopal Church was in session in this very City almost ten years ago—in the year 1856—the matter of promoting any measures for bringing about a better understanding and nearer communion among the Protestant Churches, was very pointedly and directly brought before the House of Bishops, and earnestly agitated. A Committee of five bishops was appointed at that time, which Committee should be a standing one, to take advantage of any opportunity that might arise, or that God in His providence might appoint, for the purpose of promoting a nearer communion, and better co-operation among all the Protestant orders.

It is remarkable, that I am the only surviving member of that committee. The rest have gone to the blessed communion above. And I rejoice to think that as the end of life approaches,—and I am very near that end,—it is reserved for me to stand in this place and discharge that duty in reference to the opening, which I believe to be precisely of that style that was then contemplated. Just such an opportunity we were waiting for when the right hand of fellowship should be extended from one to the other,—first in prayer, and then afterwards in the manner in which we are now met together. Just the opportunity we anticipated, and precisely the sentiments and expressions that were then intended! I stand here now to do the work of that committee, in the name of the House of Bishops, that appointed it, and greet you, dear brethren, in the name of the Lord Jesus Christ. (Prolonged applause.)

The committee who appeared before us, yesterday, in the happy addresses to which we listened—more especially that of the reverend brother who led,—were wise in saying that while they came to us in the spirit of brotherly love, for the promotion of a better union and concord, —yet it did not seem to them that the time had come, when any opportunity was open in which we could see that the Lord had cast down and taken out of the way, all such barriers to the entire union as still existed.

I am happy, exceedingly happy, to express my own personal opinion—as I know it is thought by those from whom I come, that these barriers, whatever there may be on their side, are purely of an external and visible character, and have no entrance within the sacred precincts of the matters of Faith, and salvation in Jesus Christ. (Applause.)

These are times, dear brethren, when instead of there being any principal desire in any Christian heart to magnify differences of that sort, the great tendency and inquiry on all sides should be how we may see them conscientiously and truthfully, in their least important and difficult aspect, and how, in spite of them, upon any great common ground of Christian truth and Christian love, we may come together and tramp them down, remembering that whilst they divide us denominationally, they do not divide us as Christians, and whilst they have a position separate in certain respects, they have no position at all, whereby to separate us in regard to the great matter of love to God, and faith in Jesus Christ, and more especially with regard to each arena of Christian labor, and ministerial effort common to the whole Christian Church. And with regard to which there comes a voice so loud, at the present time, that all Christian people should enter and work together for the glory of God and salvation of man! The foundation of God standeth sure! "and other foundation can no man lay than that is laid, which is Jesus Christ." The foundation is not in this or that external order! The foundation is in the personality of Christ! The foundation is the personality of Christ, crucified: who was once dead, and now liveth at the right hand of God to make intercession for all them that come unto God Almighty. The foundation of the Church of God, is in the personality, and work of Jesus Christ. And the foundation of Christian faith and hope in Jesus Christ has not only come to us all—you here, and we, and whom we represent—but we stand here to acknowledge our unity; not merely as individual volunteers, but as churches, Presbyterian and Episcopal; erect, standing upon this single foundation. (Applause.) Then we are not to look to external things, but to those internal things, which should ever be true—built upon the solid foundation of Christ Jesus.

Now then, brethren beloved, we live together in the most—not merely remarkable—but most solemn age. You, and we, and all that love our Lord Jesus Christ, in sincerity, and desire to work for Him in this world —not only for the great work of to-day, but whatever offers in the future— must meet the dangers successfully. And the dangers are alike common to us all. They assail the very foundation of Gospel truth. They assail the very foundation of spiritual life. We have to war against Infidelity under the name of Rationalism. We have to war against the power of Lust, which ever since the beginning of the Gospel of Christ, has developed itself from time to time, and at last it has come out in the monster—POPERY! And now in its new life, and in its new vigor, standing in its panoply—and a wonderful panoply it is!—it has almost everywhere more especially, fixed its eye upon the great Protestant light and faith:—in England, and in this land; and it will almost surrender everything else to make its footing certain here.

I say, at this time we have got a great work to do. And we must go at the work, heart to heart, and shoulder to shoulder, to fight against this enemy of our Lord. I tell you, dear brethren, there is no possible rivalry in the right judgment of any mind—between us, in this matter, except the rivalry of endeavoring, each to do the most possible in this work, for his Master. And just in proportion as God by His Spirit shall come forward, and by your instrumentality, increase the simple teaching and preaching of Jesus Christ and Him crucified, and the simple reception of Christ into the sinner's heart, so that men shall live by faith in Jesus Christ,— just so far will the only work of true religion be spread amongst you; and just in that proportion may we rejoice, because it has interested, not merely the Presbyterian Church, but because the whole Christian Church has been interested and strengthened! We therefore do earnestly desire God's blessing amongst you. We desire to see brought to a successful conclusion, the object for which you have gathered. May God prompt you to finish it aright!

We pray that the great Head of the Church—the great Head and Master of us all—in whom is our only life—Jesus at the right hand of God, whither He ascended to make intercession for us—will bless all our hearts, and give us new strength to go on in the good and great work! We pray that we may be blessed with this new life, and be workers together for Him! There is no glory or honor like that of being a worker with Him. I have only to say: "Let brotherly love continue." God's grace be with all them that love our Lord Jesus Christ in sincerity. (Applause.)

PRESIDENT STUART:—May we have many successions of such Bishops to the Protestant Episcopal Church!

BISHOP McILVAINE:—I have now, Mr. President—knowing that two voices are better than one—to ask that you will listen to my Brother, Bishop Lee, of Delaware, who will address you.

PRESIDENT STUART: (welcoming Bishop Lee,) said:—

I can remember well the last time we met. It was when you, Sir, and Bishop McIlvaine, and myself, were knocking at the gates of Richmond, asking Jefferson Davis to allow us to go in and minister to the spiritual and temporal wants of our starving Union prisoners, who had been battling for their country. (Applause.) We are here to-day with a country restored. We have one country—may we soon have one church! (Applause.)

BISHOP LEE:—Gentlemen, it is an additional gratification to be welcomed at this time by one whom I have so long known, and highly esteemed and loved for his work's sake. You, Sir, and the brethren will pardon emotion, which, however it fills the heart, does not always find its way so readily to the lips! I have felt that it was a privilege to be associated in that committee which brings you—as I say the word—our grateful reciprocation of those sympathies of Christian concord extended to us yesterday. I feel, in common with my blessed brother and father who has addressed you, that an interchange of fellowship and Christian love—so unpremeditated and so unexpected, can be attributed only to the wisdom and goodness of the Almighty! I cannot but recognize in it the providence of Almighty God and the work of that Holy Spirit—whose fruit is love!

As we entered your doors this morning, I heard in the voice of prayer ascending to the Throne of Grace, the words: "Unto Him who loved us, and washed us from our sins in His blood, and hath made us kings and priests, unto God and the Father be glory and dominion forever!" In these words, Mr. President and brethren beloved, we have the key-note of Christian sympathy. These are words which we learn to repeat and sing, when as penitent sinners we lay down our burden at the foot of the Mercy Seat, and the Cross! These are the words which we hope to sing when we stand before the throne of a revealed Emanuel, coming down in His power to reign where once He suffered! And in these words shall it not be our privilege and our happiness to unite our hearts and voices? "Unto Him who loved us!" Did He not love us all? "Who loved us and washed us from our sins in his own blood." And is not that blood as precious and efficacious to save one as another? And have we not all a share in that royal priesthood which He hath instituted—those who are to reign with Him hereafter in his kingdom of glory?

One of your delegates, (Senator Drake) in his remarks yesterday, laid his hands upon the Book that was spread open there as it is spread open here, and spoke of it as the centre of our union and our hope! That word is our common heritage—every syllable and letter. For we have not only the same original Scriptures, and the same time-honored version, but we read the same blessed and saving truths together, in words that we drink in, and which comfort and console us to our latest hour. And we remember too, that those who bear your name, and those who bear our name, contended for the liberty to read that Book, and to preach from it; to sow broad-cast that precious seed which was brought through the fiery trial, and was baptized in the blood of the glorious Reformation. We glory, brethren, that the truths which were then vindicated at such great price, and with the precious blood of those who laid down their lives for Jesus, have been maintained with unshrinking fidelity and faithfulness by your communion. We rejoice in the thought that our Lord Jesus Christ has servants and fathers so true and faithful in this sin-burdened and sin-stricken world! And that in the battle that is waged between the God of heaven and the god of this world, between Christ and Belial, the great Captain of our salvation marshalls you and us in His common host! (Applause.) We feel, Mr. Chairman, how deeply we are interested—as American citizens, in your prosperity and in your advance. We cannot be blind! We desire gratefully to acknowledge the debt which we owe as citizens of the great Republic, to the manner in which the ministers and the laity of the Presbyterian Church, have maintained the great principles of morality—publicly and privately, the sanctity of the Lord's day, and the great principles of Christian truth, as well as of social duty and order; and how much they have done to repress the torrent of licentiousness, worldliness, and vice, that has threatened to sweep over and engulf the land. We honor them for all they have done for the kingdom of our Lord and Saviour, and we trust that they will be prospered and strengthened to accomplish more and greater things for the honor of His name.

Mr. President, on that day when the Lord shall be revealed in the brightness of His glory and when the joy of His salvation in those who shall be blessed shall be seen; when all shall stand at the right-hand of the Throne, how insignificant will be those things which divided and obstructed the heirs to the kingdom, during their passage through this wilderness world! All hearts will overflow with increased love and fellowship towards the Redeemer, and unite in a lofty tone, in that hymn of praise to which I have already alluded; they will magnify that Christ which hath brought them out of the horrible pit, and miry clay, and out of corruption and sin, to sit in heavenly places, in the courts of angels; and will love to remember any occasion in which they were enabled to give each other a fraternal grasp, and acknowledge each other as brothers in Christ Jesus, their Lord and Saviour.

With these expressions, then, Mr. President, I thank you and all this assembly for the fraternal and courteous greeting you have given us, and say, in the words of my brother, "Grace, mercy, and peace to all them that call upon the name of the Lord Jesus Christ"—their Lord and ours. (Applause.)

The President:—Delaware is one of the smallest bishoprics, but she has one of the largest Bishops!

At the suggestion of the Rev. Alfred Nevin, D.D., (Old School), a corresponding member, the Convention was, at this point, led in the recitation of the Apostles' Creed, by Rev. H. B. Smith, D.D. The Hymn,

"Blest be the tie that binds, etc.,"

was then sung.

President Stuart:—One of the sweetest of spirits that it was ever my privilege to be associated with in America, is now in glory! clothed in white robes; but he is to-day rejoicing in spirit over this scene of communion on earth. His name was Dudley A. Tyng. His dying words—the watchwords for the young men of Christ throughout the world—were: "Stand up for Jesus." It is not in the programme of our brethren that his beloved brother should speak to-day, but as I am the Bishop of this Diocese (Laughter) I call upon my young brother, whom I love from the bottom of my heart, Rev. Stephen H. Tyng, Jr., to say a few words to the Convention.

Rev. Mr. Tyng:—I shall only say one word, and that will be from my heart; for we have distinguished representatives of the laity, who are expected, on the part of the laity of our Church, to reciprocate the greeting of the honorable gentlemen whom you sent to our body. Let me say, that when we entered these doors, there was one in the deputation who knew, by the very atmosphere, and by the very spirit manifested here, that he was in his Father's house; when the word was spoken in love from this place, the truth as it is in Jesus, he knew that he was in his Father's house; when the thrill of Christian love ran through this vast assemblage, he knew that he was in his Father's house, and that all here were brethren, bound to each other by the magnetic name of Jesus, living and loving under the common constraint of grateful affection to Christ. It seems to me, as we came here, from different fields of work, and different methods of work, that this was but the repetition of that scene when the disciples were gathered from their wanderings and many missions, about Jesus' feet, to give a report to Him of their work, and to tell Him that, "Even spirits were subject unto them."

Dear brethren, though our work has been weak, and in a wandering way, though we are conscious of our infirmities and failures, God alone knows it, and the heart, in its relation to God, only realizes it in part; yet may we not say that, in this great work for Christ, "Spirits have, through Jesus' power, been made subject unto us?" And yet, in the language of such rejoicing, we may hear the Saviour's voice speak: "Rather rejoice that your names are written in heaven!" (Applause.)

The President:—Judge Conyngham, of the Laity of the Episcopal Church, will address you. If we had such judges every where, we would not now be mourning over the prospect of a desecrated Sabbath.

Judge Conyngham:—My dear brethren! Layman as I am, with one common hope with all the rest of you that are here, I am permitted to call you "brethren." I come before you simply to assent to the remarks that have been made by the Rt. Rev. Fathers who have addressed you, as one of the delegation, from the body to which I have the honor to belong, and which received the kind, the Christian, and the loving greeting which was yesterday sent to us. We received it in the same manner and spirit in which it was sent. It must have been in the same spirit, for I believe the whole was the result of prayer, moving, with the Spirit of God, the hearts of men to seek to do honor to God. (Applause). I feel, in such an assemblage as this, that I know not what to say, but cry: "Thanks be to God that brethren can meet together in unity and in love."

Yes! it is well known to all here we had prayed constantly that all Christians should come together in the unity of the Spirit, and in the bonds of peace, holding the same blessed truths. And now, when we all here look to the same Triune God—the Father, the Son, and the Blessed Spirit—where are the differences that existed among us? Oh! they are nothing now. But the time will come—no, sir, the time will never come for it will be when time shall be no more—when all the petty differences of this earth are to be done away, and the distinctions prevailing now shall be lost. Then will it be that all, clothed in that white raiment, washed in the blood of the Lamb, shall be singing praises to the Redeemer forever. Oh, let us then, when we think of these differences, look forward, look beyond these sublunary scenes, and look aloft! Then will this rule of faith,—the rule of faith in your church and mine,—be the rule of faith there, where faith shall be made perfect, where all shall be found alike.

But, my brethren, I rejoice to see this day—and feel that this is a day—when we can all come together. It is not a new thing to me to work with my Presbyterian brethren, shoulder to shoulder, in those societies in which we can unite—even with all our differences. We do work together in the place in which I live, shoulder to shoulder, against the great enemy, and to spread abroad a knowledge of the truth. And sir, let us pray in our ignorance—knowing that though ignorant here, hereafter we shall know even as we are known—let us pray that Almighty God will hasten the time when all shall call upon the name of Jesus, and when all as beloved Christian brothers shall bless that name!

The President:—There is one other name not unknown to the country; and surely in the last great day, I doubt not, many a poor soldier may rejoice to meet Felix R. Brunot, Esq., who labored from the commencement of the war to its close, to minister to the men who were fighting our battles. (Applause.)

Felix R. Brunot, Esq., of Pittsburg:—I may say, sir, that I am surprised and embarrassed by your unexpected presentment of my name to this assembly; for I did not expect—nor was it a part of our programme—that I should have anything to say. I will not trespass upon the attention of the brethren, but simply make a single remark which may be thought not quite in the province of a layman.

I noticed, sir, when we all joined in that noble creed in which the belief of every heart was so solemnly expressed—that our leader, at one place interpolated that which I hardly thought belonged there, "I believe in the Holy Catholic Church, the Communion of Saints"—there is a comma there which should not be there. It should read: "I believe in the Holy Catholic Church—the Communion of Saints."

President Stuart:—Right Rev. fathers, and brethren, dearly beloved for Christ's sake, we thank you in the name of this National Presbyterian Convention, for the words of cordial greeting and Christian sympathy, which you have been permitted to bear to us this morning, as the representatives of one of the great Protestant churches of our country. We heartily reciprocate all that you have said, in the name of this Convention. We say to you, moreover, that all your trials are our trials. That when you are assailed, we feel that we are assailed. That you and we are fighting the same battle of secular and religious liberty. That we have the same great doctrines of Jesus Christ to proclaim to a dying world. That we have the same blessed hopes of immortality. We rejoice to know that there are fields in which we can labor together. And I hope this Convention will pardon me for intruding upon its time, if for a single moment I refer to one single incident, in connection with the chairman of this Deputation. You,—Bishop McIlvaine—my beloved father in Christ, have often been highly honored by your church; honored in representing her not only in courts abroad but in all her own religious councils. But I question if ever you walked more gloriously in your Master's steps, than when on the banks of the Potomac, when the rain was falling from heaven on that uncovered head, you preached from the saddle, the blessed Gospel of Jesus Christ to those thirteen hundred prisoners captured by our army, who were on their way to prison. (Applause.) Or, sir, when at the hour of midnight, in the garret of the Planters' Hotel, in Fredericksburg, you knelt down over that gallant young captain of Harrisburg, who had sent for some one to speak words of comfort; you came to him, sir, with the same message that we preach—the message of salvation—the only message that can be preached to a dying sinner.

And, sir, on the next morning, when we went to take final leave of the young captain, and found that he had passed into glory some hours before, we stood opposite the coffin, in the entry of the Planters' Hotel, and looking into the bar-room—the place where they had been accustomed to sell that which sends men's souls to hell!—through the door which stood ajar, we saw a dying "son of the forest,"—a Michigan sharp-shooter—unable to talk much to us in our language. And there, again, we saw you, Bishop McIlvaine, kneeling down upon the tavern floor, and bending over the dying Indian, who had been fighting the battles of his country. You were then occupying a position higher than any which ever your Church, or our Government called you to occupy! [Applause.] But, I cannot trespass further upon the attention of the audience. There are brethren here whom I desire to ask to speak. We have no special bishops in our Presbyterian body, because all our ministers are bishops. But, sir, we have some who are commanders-in-chief, and rather than trespass upon the time of the audience, I will call upon one or two of those generals, who will present to you, in fitting words, the salutations and greetings of these six Presbyterian bodies, who have been upon the mount of communion for the last two days. I want to tell you, before the speakers are announced, that we have had such a meeting as I never could have anticipated on earth. All our differences seem to have almost vanished, and we are nearly ready now to unite in one great Presbyterian family. [Applause.]

The Rev. Charles Hodge, D.D., of Princeton, was brought forward by the President, and greeted with great applause. He said:—

Gentlemen and brothers: honored and beloved; I am called upon, as you hear, to present to you, in the name of this Convention, their hearty greeting and salutation. You here see around you, sirs, the representatives of six Presbyterian organizations of this country, comprising in the aggregate, at least five thousand ministers of Jesus, an equal number of Christian Churches, and at least one million of Christians, who have been baptized in the name of Jesus Christ. It is not only, therefore, as the organ of this Convention, but for the moment, the mouth-piece of this vast body of ministers and public Christian men—that we, sirs, were commissioned to present to you our cordial and affectionate Christian salutations.

We wish to assure you, sirs, that your names are just as familiar to our people, as to your own! That we appreciate as highly your services in the cause of our common Master, as the people of your own honored Church. And, sirs, we rejoice with them, in all that God has accomplished through your instrumentality.

I hope this audience will pardon a reference that might seem too personal under any other circumstances than the present. The honored President of this Convention might easily have selected some more suitable person to be the mouth-piece of this body, but on the ground of one consideration, perhaps, the choice of myself to be that organ, is not altogether inappropriate.

You, Bishop McIlvaine, and Bishop Johns, whom I had hoped to see with you here to-day—you and I, sir, were boys together, in Princeton College, fifty odd years ago. Often, at evening, have we knelt together in prayer. We passed through, sir, the baptism of that wonderful revival in the Institution, of 1815. We sat together, year after year, side by side, in the same class-room. We were instructed through our theological course, by the same venerable teachers. You, sir, have gone your way, and I have gone mine; and I will venture to say in the presence of this audience, that I do not believe you have preached one sermon on any point of doctrine, or Christian experience, which I would not have rejoiced to have uttered. [Applause.] And I feel fully confident that I never preached a sermon, the sentiments of which, you would not have publicly and cordially endorsed. [Applause.]

And now, sir, after these fifty odd years, here we stand, gray-headed, side by side, for the moment, representatives of these two great bodies of organized Christians. Feeling for each other the same intimate, cordial love, and mutual confidence; looking not backward,—not downward to the grave at our very feet,—but onward, to the coming glory. Brethren, pardon this personal allusion; but is there not something that may be regarded as symbolical in this? Has not your Church, and our Church been rocked in the same cradle? [Applause.] Did they not pass through the same Red Sea, receiving the same baptism of Spirit, and of fire? Have they not uttered, from those days of the Reformation to the present time, the same great testimony for Christ and His Gospel? What difference, sir, is there between your thirty-nine articles and our Confession of Faith, other than the difference between one part and another of the same great Cathedral anthem that arises from earth to heaven? [Applause.] Does not this seem to indicate, sir, that these Churches are coming together? We stand here, sir, to say to the whole world that we are one in faith, one in baptism, one in life, and one in our allegiance to your Lord and to our Lord. [Applause.]

Rev. J. F. Stearns, D.D., (New School), of Newark, N. J., was also introduced, and said:—

My Brethren, Bishop McIlvaine, Bishop Lee—and brethren and fathers in the Lord, in rising to add my testimony to the words of the Reverend Dr. Hodge, in regard to the cordiality with which we welcome you on this occasion, I am conscious of emotions and impressions as strange as they are sweet. I seem to catch a glimpse of that far-off glorious unity of the Church, whose beauty, the King Himself, greatly desired.

As you have said, sir, there is something peculiarly impressive in the circumstances under which we are brought together, at present. It was not from us that the impulse came which produced this deputation from our brethren of the Episcopal Church! No! it was from you; not directly, but through that Trinity of God, the Son, and the Holy Spirit, who heard the supplications ascending to the throne.

It went up in prayer; it came down in the blessings of the Holy Spirit, which we all felt, and which humbled all our hearts. That was the initiative of these experiences of fraternal salutations and congratulations. And we have reason to thank our Heavenly Father, that He put it into your hearts to pray for us, and answered those prayers, as we believe, with blessings on our souls.

A few months ago, I had the honor and pleasure to be engaged with a large joint committee of the two principal branches of the Presbyterian Church, which parted almost in anger, thirty years ago,—in trying to devise a platform on which they might come together, and harmonize all their difficulties. For ten days we were hard at work, from morning until late at night consulting and praying; and scarcely had we reached the first stage in our progress, and were prepared to report to our brethren what we regarded as a fair indication of grounds on which we might come to an understanding as a united Church, when voices rose up all around us, from smaller bodies saying that they had no intercourse, or very little, at least, since they came to this, our common land,—saying that we all were Presbyterians, and exclaiming: "Is there to be a union? Come then and we will unite too." And we gathered together, here, sir, six denominations of Presbyterians, consulting as to the particular platform on which we all could stand together as a united Presbyterian Church! We had not dreamed of the sympathy that was felt outside of our own denomination; and it came upon us like the dew from heaven when we were informed that the Episcopal convention had had it in their heart to turn aside from their special business and unite in fervent prayer to Almighty God, for the success of our endeavor. We could not choose but to stop and pray too. (Applause.) Sir, it has pleased God, in His mysterious wisdom, unexplainable to us, to send our Protestant churches, or permit them to go apart, now for these many centuries, in their efforts to promote the interest of the Redeemer's kingdom. He has suffered us, for some wise reason, to be divided into denominations, and known by distinctive names. He saw that we were not prepared yet to form one grand organic Church of the Lord Jesus Christ: that there was a preliminary work to be accomplished. And so He gave us each our task, and sent us into the mountain to hew timber, to hew stone, to prepare posts for the great edifice, against the day when He would come and cause it to be carried to its completion. We do not know the plan which the great Head of the Church has in view in the building of His universal Church. Perhaps He will use less of our work! Then He may assign it a less conspicuous and honored place, and we know not how much He will take from you, or how much from us. But we should labor on at the task, the great Task Master has set us, assured that if we labor faithfully, we shall not have labored in vain. And the day is coming, I said "not far off," and the indications here seem to me to almost compel the belief that it is not far, but near, when we shall see a Church arise here, such as the world has never seen before: beautiful as Tirza, comely as Jerusalem, and terrible to the foes of Christ as an army with banners.

We love and honor the Episcopal Church, both in Europe and America! We love her for the noble stand which she has taken in the advance of our common Protestantism! We love her for her rich and varied instruction, and religious literature, from the fountain of which we have all drunk and been refreshed! We love her especially, for her martyr history; wherein she stood, side by side, with the ancestral worthies of our Church *while* they stood side by side, with *hers*. But, sir, we have our affections strengthened, and our respect greatly heightened, as we have looked on in these days of degeneracy, and seen a noble band among them, standing up with firm resolve to resist the tide of Ritualism! (Applause), and excessive ecclesiasticism, which so threatened to sweep the Protestant foundations, and carry the young men who are coming up, far off to Rome!

Our sympathies are with you, brethren! They are with you in this noble endeavor. And I can reciprocate what has already been said, that not only your prosperity is our prosperity, and your joy is our joy, but that the time is not far distant, when if we are not one organic church, we shall be standing side by side with each other, battling for the same cause! And we shall need all each other's strength as well as, all each other's prayers.

But this hour is one that we shall remember as long as we live! We shall remember it when we go to stand in the General Assembly of the church of the First Born! It will be one of the spots to which we look back—this church—where now we are gathered! It will be one of the spots to which we shall look back when we bow around the throne of our Master above! When we all come in the unity of the faith and knowledge of the Son of God, unto a perfect man, and unto the measure of the stature of the fullness of Christ!

And Sir, and brethren, assembled here as a deputation representing the Episcopal Church, let me assure you, that we feel now that there is a bond of union stronger than ever we have felt before! You and we are no more strangers, and foreigners as regards each other,—but fellow-citizens, with the saints and of the Household of God! (Applause.) And we know that you are building, and we, on the same foundation of the apostles and prophets, Jesus Christ himself being the chief cornerstone. "In whom all the building fitly framed groweth unto an holy temple in the Lord." (Applause.)

President Stuart:—Let us all bow, for two or three minutes, in silent prayer together. After which the Rt. Rev. Bishop McIlvaine of Ohio, will kindly lead us audibly in prayer to the Throne of Grace, asking God's blessing on this Convention, to grant us a happy deliverance from all difficulties, that we may make a right Basis of Union. And immediately following him, without any interruption, the Rev. Dr. John Hall, late of Dublin, Ireland, but now of New York, will invoke the blessing of God upon the Episcopal Church of America, and their brethren of the Church of Great Britain and Ireland.

The Convention then bowed in silent prayer after which:

Bishop McIlvaine:—We desire to bring Thee, our offerings of praise and glory! Thou didst promise, and Thou dost fulfil Thy promise, that wherever two or three are gathered together in Thy name, there wilt Thou be in the midst of them! We desire unitedly to recognize and bless Thee for Thy presence here with us now! For causing us thus to meet together, and so uniting our hearts together, and blessing us with the experience of Thy love in our souls,—we thank Thee: we bless Thee: we glorify Thee, O, Lord Jesus, now the high-priest forever to make intercession for us! And we thank Thee, gracious Lord for what Thou didst accomplish in Thy gracious providence, in regard to us, in having given us the opportunity and the enjoyment of our present meeting together. We pray Thee so to bless out of the unsearchable riches of Thy grace —so to continue—so to enlarge—so to prosper—so to guide and so in all things, according to Thy wisdom, to control us as that the glory of Thy name may prompt to the gathering together of all hearts in Thy glorious work,—and that Thy name may be magnified, and a larger conversion of souls to Thee, and a wider spread of Thy righteousness, and goodness, and love, and the light of Thy Gospel may in Thy good time take place.

And we beseech Thee, blessed Master, that Thou wouldest look down upon these brethren assembled together, in this place, for the purpose of concerting together in Thy name, and for Thy glory, a nearer communion and fellowship among themselves, as members assigned to the same great body and Church. We thank Thee, O Lord, for what Thou hast done in enabling them to see more eye to eye, and to feel heart to heart; and we pray that they may yet see more plainly, and feel yet so much the more heart to heart, as that unnecessary barriers may be cast down, and entire union be effected; and that they may stand forth together, undivided in the great work and the common salvation!

Hear us, O Lord, in this our supplication and prayer! and grant that when the shadows of this present life are passed away, and the valley of the Shadow of Death shall have been passed, and the great banquet shall be prepared in Thy kingdom, and Thy blessed ones shall be gathered around it, and all here have laid aside the flesh, and the entanglements of the flesh, and infirmities, and wants of the present life, and see no more through a glass darkly, but face to face, that beholding the emancipated Saviour in all the fullness of Thy glory—every one here may have a place at that glorious table of redeemed love, and that we may rejoice forever together in Thy blessed presence. All of which we humbly beg, Heavenly Father, in the name and mediation of Jesus Christ, our most blessed Lord and Saviour.—*Amen!!*

Rev. Dr. John Hall:—O God, our Heavenly Father, Thou hast been our dwelling-place through all generations. Thou art the God and Father of our Lord Jesus Christ. For our being, and our continuance in being, for all mercies vouchsafed, for the light, help, and deliverance Thou hast given us, we unite in praising Thee. We thank Thee for the Christian fellowship of this happy hour, for the happiness of having revealed to us the depth and fervor of brotherly love in the hearts of Thy people. We here, in Thy holy presence, confess all our sins against such fellowship. If we have ever felt any joy at the embarrassments of our brethren, if we have ever put any thing in the way of their work for Thee, Father forgive us, "for we knew not what we were doing." Bless with Thy special favor and love the church, and the various societies of the same who have here visited us in Thy name. Bless them in their prayers, in their preaching, in all their efforts to spread the knowledge of our Lord Jesus Christ, and that multitudes may be turned from darkness to light and from the kingdom of Satan unto God.

We pray for these our brethren in England and in Europe; and now, especially, when new controversies are springing up, and they must enter into them to maintain Thy truth, O give them wisdom and firmness, and direct them how and what to do.

We come as the priesthood of God's house to call upon Thee. O, Holy Ghost, too often grieved and forgotten, come Thou unto us, and rule us and dwell in our souls. Be Thou a spirit of love in heart and lip, in power and life. We wait on Thee: we have been wayward and rebellious, but Thou hast ever been kind and indulgent toward us, and wilt keep us unto the end. And O may that happy end be the gathering of all our souls into the fold of their great and gracious Shepherd and Bishop, our Lord Jesus Christ; and unto Him who is able to keep us from falling, and to present us before the throne of His glory with exceeding joy, to the only wise God our Saviour, be all glory and dominion, world without end. AMEN.

Bishop Lee then recited the Lord's Prayer, the whole assembly rising and joining in it!

President Stuart, now grasped Bishop McIlvaine by the hand, and addressing the committee through him, uttered farewell words and recited the beautiful benediction of the Old Testament Church, from Numbers: 6, 24, etc.

The Lord bless thee and keep thee.

The Lord make his face to shine upon thee, and be gracious to thee.

The Lord lift up the light of His countenance upon thee and give thee peace.

During the reading of these words, a solemn stillness fell over the Convention, and continued when they were finished. A member broke the silence by raising the well known Doxology,

"Praise God, from whom all blessings flow,"

which was sung with thrilling emphasis and earnestness.

The solemn and memorable services were brought to a conclusion by Bishop McIlvaine, who pronounced the benediction of the New Testament Church; and the Convention, by common consent, amid prayers, thanksgivings, and tears of rejoicing, participated in by a vast congregation which crowded every part of the church edifice, adjourned to 3 o'clock, P. M.

Same Place, November 8th, 3 o'clock, P. M.

The Convention assembled, President Stuart in the chair.

Prayer was offered, as follows, by the Rev. Mr. Edmiston, of the Cumberland Presbyterian Church:

O Thou Eternal, Invisible, and All-wise God, our Father! What shall we render unto Thee for what our eyes have seen, and our hearts felt since we have been together as a Convention! We praise God that when we were without strength, Christ died for the ungodly, and has brought about an everlasting righteousness for us. And being made children of God, in that common Redeemer, it is our privilege to daily come and unite, and to love one another! And as our Saviour prayed that we might be one, may it be the hearty response of the heart of every elder, and minister, and spectator present this afternoon, that Thy Church may ultimately be one in her organic form.

But O God, we are now divided; we lament the evils of our position. We supplicate pardon, and humbly ask now in behalf of the Presbyterian family represented here, that though an organic union may not be speedily consummated, we may nevertheless exercise great forbearance, one towards another, keeping united in the Spirit and in the bonds of peace; and we pray that Thy Church may become more and more powerful in her influence against the powers of darkness, and may the world in time be compelled to exclaim: "Behold how these brethren love one another."

Bless us, and accept us in the Redeemer. Amen!

The President:—The members of the Convention will come to order. The Secretary will read the Minutes of last evening's and this morning's sessions.

The Minutes were read, and after corrections, alterations, etc., were approved.

The President:—This Convention adjourned last evening, pend ing the discussion of the amendment of one of the articles proposed by Rev. Dr. Smith, of New York.

Rev. W. P. Breed, D.D., (O. S.), a corresponding member, said:—I rise to make a request which I hope some member of the body will put in the form of a motion, and that the motion will be passed. It is greatly desired by a great many Christians of Philadelphia, that a large portion of this Body will remain over the Lord's Day. I heard a lady remark, as I went out this morning: "I hope they will remain over the Sabbath; for we have delightful guests at our house,"—and that is the general expression. And, therefore, I request that when this Body adjourns its business sessions, it adjourn to Sabbath afternoon, at the West Spruce Street Presbyterian Church, for closing exercises.

It is usual, after an ordinary dinner, to serve up a delicate dessert. May we not expect that the Lord may visit us, and we shall have a fitting close to these delightful services. We have here had the solid meat of discussion, and we have here had the grand old Psalms sung! May we not meet, then, after this Convention, and have a delightful season of religious exercises there, where each one may sing Psalms and tunes of exaltation, and forget all else but that we are all Christian brethren together. And if you will only grant this request, and if these brethren will remain, I have no doubt it will be said not as it was 1800 years ago, that every man setteth forth his good wine first, and when men have well drunk, then setteth after that which is worse, but that unto this time the best wine is kept.

You may tell me that you have reached the top of the mountain of Zion, during the morning service, but let me tell you, that the mountain is a great deal higher than you think it is. When the disciples on Mount Tabor had seen their Lord, they came down and said, "Well this is the very climax. We shall never see Him as we have seen Him." But, beloved, when they came to that upper chamber, and the sound of a rushing mighty wind fell about the place, and fiery tongues came down upon them, and three thousand souls were converted, they believed that "Tabor" was only the first step toward the top of the mountain.

I do trust that God will send down his Holy Spirit and most Holy benediction upon this marvelous Convention. There are inducements why the brethren should remain. The Rev. Newman Hall, of London, will preach three or four times, next Sabbath, and our brothers have not seen half of Philadelphia yet, and have not got into the depths of brotherly love with its citizens yet. I hope the motion will be made.

REV. DR. KEMPSHALL (O. S.):—I am delighted to hear these words from my good brother: but most of us have got to go to our homes by 5 o'clock—and will have to leave this house at that time.

On motion of the Rev. M. C. Sutphen, O. S., it was,

Resolved, That in case the Convention adjourn its business sessions, the members remaining in the city, meet in the West Spruce St. Church, (Rev. Dr. Breed's,) on Sabbath afternoon, at 3½ o'clock, for a farewell meeting of Conference and Prayer. (See Appendix III.)

DR. KEMPSHALL:—I would make a motion that the speeches to be made upon the pending business, be limited to five minutes, each; and that if the fathers shall occupy the floor for a longer time, that we shall suspend the rule. I make the motion as one of urgent necessity.

The motion was carried.

The members were here informed that an Autograph book, to be preserved as an historical relic, was in the ante-room, and that it was earnestly desired to have in it, the signature of every member of the Convention.

PRESIDENT STUART:—The question before the house is upon the amendment to the second article.

THE SECRETARY read the second article as follows:

"That in the United Church, the Westminster Confession of Faith shall be received and adopted as containing the system of doctrines taught in the Holy Scriptures."

The Secretary also read the following amendment made by Rev. H. B. Smith, D.D.

"It being understood that this Confession is received in its proper historical—that is, in the Calvinistic or Reformed sense."

The Rev. D. V. McLean, D.D., (O. S.) moved to lay the amendment on the table, as being wholly unnecessary; which motion was lost.

Rev. Dr. Musgrave (O. S.) said:—

I weuld never have offered such an addition to the report of our committee. I would have been perfectly satisfied to have it as it originally stood. But now that it has been introduced, and that by a respected brother of the New School, I find sir, it would be impolitic to withdraw or vote it down, because, sir, it expresses precisely what the Old School would regard as entirely satisfactory. Now, I am a practical man, and I wish this union consummated. If you vote this down you will excite suspicion, and it will be said, when the test is made, the Convention will not allow it to be put. Suspicion, if it extends widely, will certainly frustrate all attempts to carry a union, and for that reason I would not have introduced it here. I would have been fearful that I might give offence to my New School brethren, by such a proposition as they might have supposed it implied a want of confidence in them. In the next place, I do not regard our action here as a finality. There is nothing binding on the churches, and we could settle all these things when we come to agree upon the terms of re-union.

But, sir, you need not doubt that when the time comes for the settlement, actually, of all these questions, there will be a large body of men in the Old School Church that will insist upon some such explanatory note or term. Now, sir, if we were to propose it, it might be regarded as offensive to our New School brethren, and they could not receive it on such terms. But, if the representatives of the Calvinistic world in this country—if that is not a Hibernicism—if the representatives of all the Calvinistic Presbyterian Churches in this land declare that they accept a paper on a satisfactory basis; then both of these great branches of the Presbyterian Church can honorably propose and accept that basis. Because, then, it will not imply any suspicion or want of confidence; but it will be just acting upon the suggestion of the whole body of Calvinists in this country, as here represented.

Now, sir, I would not throw a straw in the way of the actual and speedy settlement and consummation of this matter. Some of my brethren have wondered at my zeal. It is my nature. I cannot be driven an inch, nor made to wink, unless my judgment and conscience approve of the thing. But when I do approve of it, I am no half-way man. I go for it with my whole soul. I am satisfied, now, that the time is come when this thing should be done upon a proper basis, and, therefore, I give it my whole heart and might. (Applause.) I don't wish to switch off and stop the train, to burnish the locomotive. [Applause.] I don't care for the criticism as to the rudeness of the cars that brought us, only so we get into the grand Temple, and feel that after all, under God, we are one. It is because my whole heart is in the views of the Old School. This is not the first Convention I have béen in. I was in the Convention of '37; I know the history of this thing; and I was heart and soul with my son, Robert J. Breckinridge. [Laughter.] I say my son, in the

Apostolic sense. That hand (stretching out his right hand) was laid upon his head at his ordination, and I gave him the charge, and was then called a mild man. I saw something belligerent in the spirit of the young man. [Laughter.] I recollect that I emphatically charged him as his duty to seek "the peace and union of the Presbyterian Church."

Now, brethren, I know the spirit of my clan. I know it thoroughly, and if you are sincere—I will take that little word "if" away; it might give offence, and say, *as* you are sincere in this basis, then we are satisfied. Why, sir, my brother Hodge privately whispered to me, that he would approve of it. [Applause and laughter.] It is exactly what he aims at; and I have asked him as an old friend, to say a few words of that kind, in order that you may all see that we are acting upon a hearty ground. Sir, if we become one, I want to have a name above all suspicion and jealousy. I want it to be a union—a real union—steady and permanent. Let us then retain this amendment; and mark the prediction, that if you do, this union will be consummated.

Rev. Dr. Hodge of Princeton, was welcomed upon the platform with hearty applause, and spoke as follows:—

Mr. President, I came to this Convention under an entire misapprehension, and I presume that this same is true of the majority of my Old School brethren. We inferred from the wording of the call that the object of this meeting was prayer and conference, with the view of promoting Christian fellowship and harmonious action between the several bodies here represented. We thought it probable that some plan of federal union, which would allow each member of the confederation to retain its own peculiarities, and to revolve in its own sphere, might be proposed and recommended. But we did not expect that any plan of organic union, embracing all the Presbyterian Churches in our land, would be for a moment thought of. We were confirmed in this impression as to the design of the Convention by the fact that the call came from the Synod of the Reformed Presbyterian Church. We supposed that the peculiar views of that body as to Psalmody and communion, put any organic union with Churches which did not adopt those views out of the question.

But, sir, from the first hour of our coming together, with the solitary exception of the remarks of Dr. R. J. Breckinridge, on the first day of the Convention, I have not heard a word uttered, nor a prayer offered from the members of any of the bodies here represented, which did assume that the organic union of all the Presbyterian Churches of our land was the object contemplated and desired.

Such being the case, I have taken no part in your deliberations, but have sat in silence, waiting to see what God, by His providence and Spirit, would bring to pass. When the committee appointed to bring in a Basis for the organic union of all these Churches, reported a unanimous agreement, (except, of course, on the part of the delegate of the Cumberland Presbyterians,) I was greatly surprised. There was nothing in the report, as it seemed to me, to which any Old School man could object. The ground of union proposed was that on which we, as a Church, had always stood. The great majority of Old School men, as appears from the almost unanimous declarations of our Presbyteries, are in favor of organic union upon terms which would satisfy their conscience. They are unanimous also in declaring those terms to be the sincere adoption of our standards of doctrine and order.

The great question, however, is, What is meant by "the system of doctrine" taught in the Westminster Confession which we all profess to adopt? On this point not only difference of opinion, but no little misapprehension appears to prevail. I understood Dr. Fisher the other evening to allude to his Old School brethren, when he spoke of philosophical theories and theological speculations to which assent was demanded as a condition of union. And we have heard it said on this floor, as well as elsewhere, that commentaries were written on the Confession of Faith, and the adoption of these explanatory comments was insisted upon. This, Mr. President, is an entire mistake. Old School men are satisfied with our standards. They are willing they should be adopted without note or comment. If a man comes to us, and he adopts "the system of doctrine" taught in our Confession, we have a right to ask him, Do you believe there "are three persons in the Godhead, the Father, the Son, and the Holy Ghost, and these three are one God, the same in substance, equal in power and glory?" If he says Yes, we are satisfied. We do not call upon him to explain *how* three persons are one God; or to determine what relations in the awful mysteries of the Godhead, are indicated by the terms Father, Son, and Holy Ghost.

If we ask, do you believe that "God created man, male and female, after his own image, in knowledge, righteousness, and holiness, with dominion over the creatures?" and he answers Yes, we are satisfied. If he says he believes that "the covenant being made with Adam, not only for himself, but for all his posterity, all mankind descending from him by ordinary generation, sinned in him, and fell with him in his first transgression," we are satisfied. If he says that he believes that "the sinfulness of that estate whereinto man fell, consists in the guilt of Adam's first sin, the want of original righteousness, and the corruption of his whole nature, which is commonly called original sin, together with all actual transgressions which proceed from it," we are satisfied. If he says, "Christ executes the office of a priest, in His once offering Himself a sacrifice to satisfy divine justice, and reconcile us to God, and in making continual intercession for us," we are satisfied. If he says he believes justification to be "an act of God's free grace, wherein He pardoneth all our sins, and accepteth us as righteous in His sight, only for the righteousness of Christ imputed to us, and received by faith alone," we are satisfied. Mr. President, will you allow me to ask my brother, Fisher, whether there is any metaphysics in this?

Dr. Fisher:—"No, I agree to all of that."

Dr. Hodge:—I give you my hand. [Here Dr. Hodge and Dr. Fisher grasped each other's hands, amid great applause.] Mr. President, I now appeal to every man in this house, is not this simple, reasonable, and right? Is not this what is meant when a man says he adopts our "system of doctrine?" Is not this—nothing more and nothing less—that which we are authorized and bound to require? God grant that we may unite on terms so simple, so reasonable, and I must hope so satisfactory to every sincere, humble Christian brother. (Applause.)

President Stuart:—The President has the floor. I believe he has always a perfect right to speak. One reference of Dr. Hodge touched my heart. From the opening of this Convention down to its closing speech, there has not been a single jarring note but one, and that is a personal matter with myself. And if there is a man in America that I have respected and honored for the great services he has done to the Church and to our country, it is Dr. Robert J. Breckinridge. I wish here at this point to ask the meeting to go with one heart to the Throne of Grace, not only to give thanks for God's blessing vouchsafed to us, but also to implore especially His goodness and mercy to our brother Breckinridge, who has been prevented from attending our meetings since the first day by reason of sickness. I will ask the Rev. Dr. Smith of New York to lead in prayer.

Dr. Smith responded in a fervent prayer.

Rev. Dr. S. W. Fisher (N. S.) said:—Mr. President, I desire to make a word of explanation. I wish to say, in taking Dr. Hodge's hand on that basis, I stand just as I have stood all through life, as my father took that Confession of Faith, and as I took it when I was ordained. I wish further to say, that as I have assisted in the licensing and ordination of many young men, I have never yet given a vote, —wherever I have been a member of a Presbytery that has given a vote,—to any one who has not subscribed to the Confession of Faith in that way. And while I am not authorized to speak for my brethren here connected with our branch of the Church, I think it will be generally admitted by them that the same is true with all our Presbyteries. I ought also to say this: Dr. Hodge was my instructor in the knowledge of the Word of God; and if there is any man on earth I am bound to respect and love, next perhaps, to old Dr. Alexander, it is Dr. Hodge. (Applause).

Rev. Dr. T. W. J. Wylie (R. P.):—I would make a suggestion to Dr. Smith, that he should withdraw the proposition he has offered.

Rev. George Junkin, D.D. (O. S.) corresponding member:—Mr. Moderator, I desire to say a word as a corresponding member. Before I eat my breakfast this morning, I noted down several little items which I wish to use in making my remarks. I cannot follow them out, but shall briefly refer to them.

On the question of Church union, I have heard a passage of the fourth chapter of Ephesians quoted in remarks here, entirely aside from its meaning. Any man who looks at that chapter, will say that it is the unity of faith that is discoursed of there. "Endeavoring to keep the unity of the Spirit in the bond of peace." Spiritual unity. He exhorts spiritual unity to be brought about here by that ministry the Saviour has sent down to the Church. They are to receive the gift of the same gospel, the same precious message of Jesus, until all are come into the unity of faith. Now, I say there is no unity of the Spirit to be preceded by the unity of the faith. The whole chapter is the discussion of the indispensable necessity of unity in the doctrine of salvation. That is the subject discussed there; and it has only a remote and secondary bearing on the question of organic unity. Organic unity—unity of faith—how is that to be brought about? I have already said until we come into the unity of faith and of the articles, we will be drifting about by the very want of doctrine. Stability is the characteristic of Presbyterianism; stability, firmness, and fixedness in the doctrine of salvation.

Now, my friends, I deny also, the appropriate exercise of that part of our Lord's Prayer, properly so called, "That they all may be one; as Thou, Father, art in me, and I in Thee." What! Do you call that organic unity? Surely not; it is a spiritual unity, simply a spiritual unity, and not an organic union thus mentioned. These passages of Scripture have been quoted, I don't know how many times, in support of the constituent ideas of organic union, by which is meant the association of persons in Presbyterian assemblies; but that organization, I say, is an organic unity. Constitutional law is organic law; our Confession of Faith is our organic law; and the unity of belief in that, secures unity and co-operation in the Church. Now, that is an entirely different thing from the spiritual unity mentioned in the three verses of that chapter. We have had illustrated throughout the meeting, but especially this morning, the important unity. "Endeavoring to keep the unity of the Spirit in the bond of peace." No better demonstration can be shown than by that of the position I occupy, that organic union is not at all the union for us, "keeping the unity of the Spirit in the bond of peace." Here, gentlemen were persons from another denomination, entirely differing in the order of Church government; and yet we felt ourselves all one. What! organically? No! no! no organic union about it; but "the unity of the Spirit in the bond of peace." We felt it; we rejoiced in it. I have never been in a situation in which I felt that unity more powerfully exhibited. Now, sir, this is what I felt; "the unity of the Spirit in the bond of peace." But you can have that without unity of doctrine. I want to say why I am opposed to organic unity. Organic—

THE PRESIDENT:—Dr. Junkin, the Chair has no discretion. There is no man in the whole church he has more respect for, but it is the opinion of the Chair now that you have exceeded the rule. Our time has become valuable and the members should observe the limit.

REV. DR. D. X. JUNKIN (O. S.) said:—I represent a Presbytery in Western Pennsylvania, and came four hundred miles to attend your meeting. I was prevented from getting here earlier; but I have been deeply delighted and profoundly moved by the meeting. I have met my brothers, whom I highly esteem and love, with the gag law that restricts me in the utterance of my sentiments. I only remark here that I think it a little unfair that after a five-minutes talk, brethren who only come sixty miles should prevent those from being heard who have come four hundred; that is all. I am opposed to the passage of the amendment before you. I differ "*toto cœlo*" with my brother George, and my brother Musgrave; I differ totally with them. Pass that resolution, pass that amendment, and you kill what I understand to be, the object of this meeting—the organic union which is to result therefrom. It is possible, sir, to reach an organic union, in "the unity of the Spirit and the bond of peace," manifesting itself in outward forms; but if we are to have the bed of Procrustes, if we are thus to have the Westminster Confession, then we should fairly accept the fact that we cannot have an organic union. But if you will agree in those numerous points, in which you do agree, and agree to differ in those in which you do differ; if you will not attempt otherwise by the force of public sentiment to be raised here and elsewhere, then you can reach an organic union. I think it to be a sin for the great Presbyterian family to overcome the great principle which God has embodied in the very bosom of our faith, and which points us along the path of practical organic unity. The principle that is embodied in the doctrine of federative government;

the principle of representation; the principle which I have seen practically illustrated in 1856, so as to bring the representative world on the floor of one general assembly. Africa was there; Asia was there; America was there; England was there; and the continent of Europe was there; all were represented. We did not all perfectly agree in all our conclusions; but we agreed in so many things that all else was forgotten.

Now, sir, you can reach an organic union that will place you as one in the house of God's elect; one in opposition to Rome, one grand protesting, Protestant Presbyterianism, if you will not attempt too much. I think you are attempting too much in asking us to adopt fully the narrowed Westminster Confession. If you will adopt a plan by which each denomination will be suffered to run its own machinery—to use a departed President's phraseology—and have a National Council or General Assembly, in which all these bodies can be united, and in which they will agree to unite on the great principles in which they do agree, and agree to differ on those they cannot agree upon; then, sir, you can have an organic union. We have the great principle which is proclaimed on our national banner, "*E Pluribus Unum;*" and it is the only practicable unity. It is the only practical system of government on the earth, "one out of many!" And we have no organization that has an absolute union.

In reference to the text to which the distinguished brother refers, I will make a single remark. If you give the interpretation to it I have heard upon this floor, you are Unitarians without knowing it. If the Church is to be one as the Father and the Son are one—an absolute unity—an organic unity—why every mind that comprehends our doctrine of the Trinity starts back at the idea. That is a unity of substance; and we are to become one, as the Father and the Son are one, by the Spirit, and by overcoming our divisions. Sir I love union; I came four hundred miles to plan and think of union; I am ready for it. I think that an organic union is practicable—I differ with my venerable brother. I think it is practicable, and I want to reach it; but I do not want to rely upon any perversions of some most precious texts of Scripture in order to secure it. I want that Bible before you to be rightly interpreted; and the difficulties under which we are striving, need to be reached by using the means which are not interpretations *ad captandum.*

Rev. Mr. Morton (R. P.):—I do not wish to make a speech, but offer a paper as a substitute for the second article. It is evident we are not agreed as to what the Confession of Faith is; some of us suppose it to be one thing, and some another. I offer this paper as a substitute, so that we may have some understanding as to what our views are on that article. I move that in explanation of the Westminster Confession of Faith, "the Catechisms, Larger and Shorter," be added; as these were admitted, by the Westminster Confession, to be agreeable to, and founded on the Word of God.

On the question whether the house would entertain the substitute, it was rejected.

The amendment to the Second Article, proposed by Rev. Dr. Smith, was again read.

On the question of the adoption of the amendment, the Old School

Presbyterian Church voted sixty-eight ayes to twenty-seven nays.

On a reconsideration to make the vote unanimous, there were three nays.

The New School Presbyterian Church voted forty-six ayes to two nays. On re-consideration the vote stood the same.

The United Presbyterian Church voted ten ayes to one nay.

The Reformed Presbyterian Church voted three nays.

The Reformed Dutch Church voted one aye.

The Cumberland Presbyterian Church declined to vote.

The Secretary announced the vote to be, one hundred and twenty-five for the amendment, to thirty-three against. On re-consideration the vote was one hundred and forty-nine ayes, and nine nays. For the Amendment, Old School, New School, United Presbyterian, and Reformed Dutch. Against it, Reformed Presbyterian. Declined to vote, Cumberland Presbyterian.

REV. DR. WYLIE (R. P.):—I did not vote, Mr. President, because I thought it was entirely superfluous. If, however, the brethren, both of the Old and New School, think it is desirable, I have no objection to vote. I think it is probable that the other brethren of our own Church might be willing to do the same. I would say that I think, in regard to voting by churches on this or any other question that comes up, that the Chairman would be entitled to give his vote. He loses none of his rights by occupying this position. I hope that in this case, he will do so.

The Reformed Presbyterian Church, on a re-consideration of their vote, stood three ayes to four nays.

REV. W. W. BARR (United Presbyterian):—Mr. President, I rise to make an amendment by adding the words, " with the Larger and Shorter Catechism."

On the question of the adoption of the Amendment, the vote was as follows: In favor, New School and Reformed Dutch. Against, Old School, United Presbyterian, and Reformed Presbyterian.

A DELEGATE (U. P.):—I spoke against the adoption of this, and yet voted for the Amendment. That might seem to be inconsistent; but if you adopt the Westminster Confession of Faith, I want you to go the whole figure. I wish you to adopt it in its historical sense; but I do not wish to have it adopted at all until you come together upon some basis of organic union that will take the Reformed Presbyterian and Cumberland Presbyterian with the rest.

REV. DR. MARSHALL (O. S.):—I want to say from the result of this vote, that certainly the New School brethren are ahead of us of the Old School in orthodoxy.

On a reconsideration of the question of the adoption of the amendment, the vote was as follows:

Old School, ninety-four ayes to one nay (Dr. Junkin); New School, unanimous; United Presbyterian, nine ayes to one nay; Reformed Presbyterian, two ayes to six nays; Reformed Dutch, one aye; Cumberland Presbyterian Church, a negative vote.

The following personal explanations were made during the vote:

A Delegate (U. P.):—I vote against this, simply because I know this is dear to the heart of the United Presbyterian Church, and I fear it will hinder the union.

Rev. Dr. Crawford (R. P.):—Is the Westminster Confession of Faith, as here referred to, that as amended by the Old School; or is it the Westminster Confession of Faith?

The President:—Doctor, you are getting too deep in theological questions for me.

Dr. Crawford:—I wish to vote intelligently, and wish to know if I am to vote for the Westminster Confession of Faith, as I understand it, or for the Westminster Confession of Faith, as the Old School understands it?

A Delegate:—For the latter.

Dr. Wylie:—Every one takes it as he understands it.

Dr. Marshall:—I vote against it as interpreted.

The President:—I gave no interpretation; I said I could not define it.

Dr. Wylie:—The Chairman does not decide upon that question; it is left to each individual, as I understand it. That question came up in the Committee, Mr. Moderator, and we agreed to leave it to be understood as the Church understands it.

Rev. J. Morton (R. P.) said:—I vote against the adoption of that amendment; because I do not know what was understood to be the "Confession of Faith," by the Bodies represented here. I offered a substitute to test matters. The Convention has not entertained it, and I do not know what you are voting for.

Rev. Mr. Suydam, (R. D.):—I noticed there was a passing compliment to the Heidelberg Catechism and the Canons of the Synod of Dort. I do not know what action my body will take upon it; but in view of the fact that I can endorse the Confession of Faith fully—while I am not prepared to commit myself as finally for it—in regard to the Heidelberg Catechism, I vote aye.

Rev. Mr. Edmiston (Cumb. P.):—It is not in my heart to make remarks to you. We all meet as members of the Presbyterian family. We wish you God speed in your work to consummate the organic union of your bodies. In explanation of the reasons which at present lead the members of the Cumberland Presbyterian Church I represent in this body, to vote in the negative, we have simply this statement to make: that of the one hundred and twenty thousand communicants of the Cumberland Presbyterian Church, of more than one thousand ministers, and with eighty Presbyteries, I know of none who are dissatisfied with their theological status. Still, however, we bid you God speed! and rejoice in what we have seen and heard.

Rev. Dr. Musgrave:—I rise to a point of order. I do it with great reluctance, and with conscientious convictions that it is my duty. I would like to do it in the most respectful and delicate manner. But it does strike me that when the representatives of one body publicly declare that they have no wish, as well as no expectation of uniting with the other Presbyterian Churches in forming one body, it is not proper that such a body should be permitted to vote in settling the basis of union of these churches. Why, sir, it may so happen that that body would turn the scale, and thus defeat the majority that would otherwise exist on the very terms that would secure an organic union. Sir, I submit respectfully to the Chair whether it would be proper under the circumstances—for I will not assume the responsibility of declaring that they ought not to be allowed to vote—and whether he will entertain, or the Convention will allow, a motion to be made, that under these circumstances that body should not be permitted to cast a vote as a denomination.

THE PRESIDENT:—The Chair understood the gentlemen representing that body to say as much, when they commenced this matter, as that they were about to decline to vote.

DR. MUSGRAVE:—I think, Mr. President, those brethren will arrive at that conclusion. I do not wish by any vote to exclude them. They have certainly acted very kindly, and we are glad to see they enjoy their communion, and wish us God speed! Now let them consult together, and decide in this matter. It is probable they will request to be excused from voting.

REV. MR. EDMISTON (C. P.):—Our voice has not been heard very often in this assembly. As stated by my worthy brother on the floor, we came to this Convention pursuant to a call. We have been agreeably disappointed. We have seen and heard more of interest than we expected. I said in behalf of my brethren, having had a conference on another point, that we declined voting on the amendment to this main question; but we only declined voting on the amendment. Surely, Mr. President, there is nothing wrong when our denomination declines to accept that as a basis, in our voting. When we arrive at the point for voting upon the proposal as a whole, we have agreed to decline voting; but we want our people throughout the whole western churches, and wherever our churches exist, to know how we vote on the question of adopting the Westminster Confession of Faith, as a basis of union.

REV. A. B. MILLER, D.D. (C. P.):—Mr. Chairman, and dear brethren, as I remarked last evening, we did not expect to take up much of the time of this Convention. I think that the call made embraces us upon the same ground with all the other branches of the Presbyterian Church; and if one branch may vote on any question, upon any point, why may not we, if we choose to exercise the privilege? While we did not expect much from this Convention, we cannot say that we did not desire that something should be done that would embrace us in the organic union.

One brother this afternoon has indicated a course which would have embraced us, as well as the other branches in an organic union. There are some of our people who hope the day is not far distant when some such basis will be adopted, as will admit us into the great family of Presbyterians, and they base their hopes on what they think to be the fact, that many brethren, in the Old and New-School branches especially, in their public ministrations, preach what we believe to be their, and what are our views of theology. Now I should much prefer, at this stage of the Convention, to consult my own feelings; although the propriety of our declining to vote has been suggested to me. I prefer now that we be allowed to vote, unless there can be something shown in the call of the Convention, which excludes us. I expect to vote in the negative upon the question to adopt the report as a whole. I wish to stand before my own Church, and all the branches represented here, as having voted in the negative; because, as some one has alluded to the illustration, you can construct an iron bedstead entirely too narrow and short for us to stretch ourselves upon.

A DELEGATE:—Mr. Moderator, will a vote in the negative of that body peril the report? If it does not, I see no impropriety in taking it; if it does, then it is improper that it should be admitted. They have declared publicly that they do not know any part of their Church that desires a change. They have declared that they are not Calvinists; that they do not accept the Westminster Confession, and that they do not desire a change. Is it possible we will peril this great enterprise by the vote of that body, who come in and declare they do not intend to unite? If their vote does imperil the passage, I think it is improper.

THE PRESIDENT:—I will say, that while I was glad to see my brethren, I had no idea, when I offered the resolution in the Reformed Presbyterian Synod, of inviting,—and it was not intended to include,—any who did not believe in the Westminster Confession of Faith.

REV. DR. D. X. JUNKIN:—I do hope that after the Christian scene in this assembly this morning, we are not to be discourteous to any Christian Assembly. I was sorry the point of order was raised. Their vote cannot imperil anything morally right; and it has been properly said, if one can vote in the affirmative he can certainly in the negative. I hope you will allow the brethren to vote. I will say, I saw and read the call, and I supposed they would come. I am glad to see them, and I am glad to have them here. I represent a Presbytery, and not the Chairman of this Assembly; the Chairman has no right—

The President decided the speaker to be out of order, not having been recognized and announced by the chair.

Dr. Musgrave withdrew his point of order.

The Cumberland Presbyterian Church voted against the second article as amended, which was declared adopted by the vote of four churches in favor, to two against.

Rev. Dr. H. B. Smith, asked the unanimous consent of the house to offer a verbal amendment. Instead of saying, "they do not wish to be understood as impugning the orthodoxy of the Heidelberg Catechism, and of the canons of the Synod of Dort," it would be better to say, *we recognize the orthodoxy*, etc.

Consent of the house was given, and the amendment unanimously adopted.

Rev. Dr. T. W. J. Wylie, asked unanimous consent also, to offer again the amendment rejected a few moments ago, viz: to add after the word orthodoxy, the words *of the Larger and Shorter Catechisms*, which was granted, and the amendment unanimously adopted.

REV. DR. MCMILLAN (Reformed Presbyterian):—Mr. President, if we were allowed to vote again on the article as now amended, I believe our vote would be unanimous on the whole article.

By consent, the vote of the Reformed Presbyterian Church was reconsidered, and the second article as amended was unanimously adopted by the delegates of that Church.

On motion of Rev. Mr. Barr, U. P., the vote of the United Presbyterian Church was also reconsidered, and the article was by them unanimously adopted.

The article was then declared adopted, the Cumberland Presbyterians alone voting in the negative. It is as follows:

ARTICLE II. That in the United Church the Westminster Confession of Faith shall be received and adopted, as containing the system of doctrine taught in the Holy Scriptures; it being understood that this Confession is received in its proper historical, that is, the Calvinistic or Reformed sense.

Whilst the Committee recommend the foregoing basis of doctrine, they wish to be understood as recognizing the orthodoxy of the Larger and Shorter Catechisms; of the Heidelberg Catechism; and of the Canons of the Synod of Dort.

The *third* Article was taken up by the Convention, and by a vote of the Churches, in the same way, unanimously adopted, as follows:

ARTICLE III. That the United Church shall receive and adopt the Presbyterian form of Church government.

THE PRESIDENT:—The question is now upon the fourth Article:

"The Book of Psalms which is of divine inspiration is well adapted to the state of the Church in all ages and circumstances, and should be used in social worship; but as various collections of Psalmody are used in the different Churches, a change in this respect shall not be required."

REV. DR. EAGLESON (O. S.):—Before the question is taken on the adoption of this paper, I wish to make a statement, and read another. During this Convention, a number of the friends of exclusive Psalmody came to me, and intimated that they could not vote for this article in its original form. I conferred with them, and they and I together drew up another form, which pleases the speaker better than the original, and for which these brethren can vote cordially. I therefore ask the liberty to offer this paper as a substitute for the article reported by the Committee.

The Book of Psalms, which is of Divine inspiration, is well adapted to the state of the Church in all ages and circumstances, and should be used in the worship of God. Therefore, we recommend that a new and faithful version of the Book of Psalms be provided as soon as practicable. But inasmuch as various collections of Psalmody are used in the different churches, a change in this respect shall not be required.

The paper was unanimously accepted as a substitute for the original article.

THE PRESIDENT:—I was waited upon by some person who stated that His Excellency, John W. Geary, Governor of Pennsylvania, was anxious to visit the house this evening. He desires to use his influence for God, and to be among Christ's people.

A DELEGATE:—I move that Governor Geary be put upon our roll as an honorary member.

REV. DR. EDWARDS (O. S.):—Mr. President, I wish to amend that motion in this way: that when the Governor enters the house, he be invited by our President to be a corresponding member, and to take his seat upon the platform.

REV. DR. WING (N. S.):—It strikes me it would be much more appropriate when Governor Geary is presented in this house, that we should invite him to speak to us; but to make him a corresponding member of this Convention, is inconsistent with every rule of Presbyterian order we have adopted. He is not an elder or corresponding member in any sense, having united with the Presbyterian Church only three or four weeks ago.

DR. EDWARDS:—Governor Geary is not an elder in any branch of the Presbyterian Church. He is an active, and a worthy Christian; but he is not an elder. I withdraw the first part, and move that when Governor Geary enters the house, the President be requested to ask him to take a seat upon the platform.

The resolution was unanimously adopted.

Resuming the consideration of the fourth article, the Rev. Mr. Blair, (U. P.,) addressed the Convention, but as he could not be distinctly heard, he was requested by the President to write out his remarks to be inserted in the proceedings of the Convention.

REV. DR. STEELE, of Philadelphia, (R. P.) corresponding member:—It is not necessary, Mr. President, at this stage of the proceedings, to make any extended remarks on the subject of Psalmody. It is very evident from the tone of this Convention, as well as from the general harmony that prevails in reference to it, that our views accord on that point; but as a member of the Reformed Presbyterian Church, before this respected and glorious Convention assembled here, I desire to lift up my testimony in favor of what has been the position of the Reformed Presbyterian Church in reference to the subject of Psalmody. I have listened with a great deal of interest to the proceedings of this Convention. I have sometimes thought that there were members of this Convention who did not thoroughly understand the position of the Reformed Presbyterian Church in reference to this subject; otherwise it seems to me that there would have been some concessions made to that Church which has had the honor of calling together this Convention. I have listened with surprise at that basis, as I heard it read here from time to time, and looked in vain for one concession made to that Church which has been honored, under God, for bearing aloft the banner of our Lord, that I trust will be still lifted up faithfully and honorably, until the millenial day shall be gloriously introduced.

Mr. President, we wish it distinctly understood here that it is not the position of the Reformed Presbyterian Church that uninspired compositions should be used in forming the devotional services of our Church. The position of that Church, as I have been taught to understand it, is that the Book of Psalms is of Divine inspiration, and that that is to be used in offering the sacrifice of our praise to God. The Reformed Presbyterian Church necessarily feels the difficulty of putting to one side that faithful translation of that Book of Psalms for any composition of uninspired men, no matter how beautiful that poetical composition may be. I have not a single word to say against those beautiful hymns that have been poured forth, and that have stirred the souls of many, as they have recognized the Scriptures, and they have been highly acceptable to the members of the Church every where. But it should be well understood that the position of the Reformed Presbyterian Church has been that these songs of inspiration shall be exclusively used in offering the sacrifice of praise to God.

Now, sir, there has been some diversity of opinion as to the sources of inspiration. Some say the one hundred and fifty Psalms, exclusively, ought to be used; and some say parts of the New Testament Scriptures ought to be added. Sir, it has not been the position of the Reformed Presbyterian Church—and she would be setting aside her inspired Psalmody if she did—to accept the most beautiful poetical compositions, no matter how much Scriptural truth appeared in them. But the Reformed Presbyterian Church has thought that there might possibly be some such basis of union secured as this: by taking the one hundred and fifty Psalms, and some translations from the New Testament, literally translated, and versified either in prose or metre.

We have thought that the Presbyterian Church could unite upon this basis; but I have looked in vain for such concessions, or anything even tending to it. How could the Reformed Presbyterian Church, as I understand her position here, adopt that basis of union, and send it down to her Synod; for it would justly be regarded before the world, as letting down her testimony in favor of uninspired psalmody? As long as I am to live in this world, whether that be longer or shorter—unless God sends more light from on high on my soul—in view of my connection with that Church, I cannot concur in the proposition that has been here submitted as a basis of union in reference to psalmody? There are many things I would like to say in this connection; especially as some eloquent speeches have been made here in reference to the position of the Reformed Presbyterian Church. Sir, she has not been represented on this floor.

THE PRESIDENT:—The brother must make no reflections, and I feel assured Dr. Steele did not intend to do so. One man must be considered as representing a Church as well as another; their differences must be judged in another court, not here.

REV. DR. WYLIE (R. P.):—I wish to make a remark that will satisfy my respected brother. It is that the very language of the first part of this proposition is taken from the testimony of the Reformed Presbyterian Church. (Applause.) Sir, the proposition was made in the Committee by one of the representatives of the Reformed Presbyterian Church in that Committee, that this should be incorporated. And the remark was made to the Committee, in my hearing, by a member now absent, that he considered it a remarkable concession indeed; and it is so regarded by many, as virtually adopting our ground in reference to psalmody, by declaring that it was fit for use in all time. That, sir, is the position in which that resolution places the subject.

REV. MR. McMILLAN (R. P.):—Mr. President, it occurred to my mind after you called the member to order, that inasmuch as he was not elected by his own presbytery, he could not question the right of those who were elected, and say they had not represented that church on this floor. We have been elected as the delegation here; the brother has not been, and he is not authorized to speak for the delegation, or to speak for himself.

DR. STEELE:—I meant no personal insult, or anything disrespectful to any person connected with the Reformed Presbyterian Church. I made the remark in general, and meant nothing disrespectful.

DR. WYLIE:—We are all satisfied.

REV. W. W. BARR (U. P.):—I would simply ask this Convention not to come to a vote just now; because you are coming to a point at which you must carefully consider your action. Now, my dear brethren, on last evening here we listened to speeches made *ad libitum* in favor of this report of the Committee. It was a thing unprecedented in parliamentary bodies; after a paper has been accepted by a Convention, to allow all the members of the Committee presenting it to make their speeches without limitation, and then when we come to the discussion, to limit us to five minutes, when we have just as much right.

THE PRESIDENT:—The member must not reflect on the house.

MR. BARR:—I want to say that my difficulty in regard to this paper is simply this: As I understand it, it places the Psalms on a level with the compositions of uninspired men. I am correct in this, because in the Psalmody used in general in the Old and New Schools they have got that Psalmody in connection with Hymns. It is authorized in the Church; that being authorized, we simply declare the Psalms of Scripture are proper to be used, and should be used. They come in then on precisely the same level. We cannot, I suppose, occupy this ground, that we recognize the Word of God, as being on the level with compositions of uninspired men. In other words, we recognize the compositions of such persons as Martin as equal to the compositions of God. There is a platform on which we might have stood—the poetical parts of the Bible. Dr. Bonar of Scotland has now published fifty of those psalms; and they are glorious translations. I believe, in the providence of God, they have come to this country to be published by the Carters just at this time, that we may look into this matter. Now, if we would get Dr. Bonar, who is a skilled scholar, to take up and versify these and other portions of the Scriptures, could we not unite on this platform? I am sure it will be a great platform, to stand on the Word of God in our praise, as we stand on it in our faith and our prayers. If we do that, we shall have union without a dissenting voice. There is not one distinctive principle of my Church that can be given up. We are willing to concede something for the sake of union; we are willing to make this concession in regard to psalmody. I believe we could come upon a common platform, if we only be careful on that point; but if you send that paper down to our United Presbyterian Assemblies, you will put this question back ten years. You simply say to our brethren, give up every principle you hold; declare you are wrong. Will they do that? Can you ask your brethren to give up every distinctive principle they have? I do not think that is necessary, nor that they will do it.

REV. DR. DAVIDSON (U. P.):—I was the means of introducing this substitute for conciliation. I thought it would meet the views of the United Presbyterian Church which I honor; for I had a strong desire in my soul to carry them with me. Therefore, I suggested that the committee should recommend a better version than we have of the one hundred and fifty psalms; then those of us who believe in the use of other hymns, or portions of the New Testament, could put them all together. Then, when united with our brethren in worship, when they come to our churches, they can sing the one hundred and fifty psalms, and if they get a little more light, they can go further; so when we go to them we can sing the one hundred and fifty psalms. I want brother Barr to look and see if there is not a great deal of concession. I am willing to make it, and our convention desires to do all it can; because here is a great body of Presbyterians whom we honor and love, and whose influence is weighty. These bodies are all dear to my heart; therefore I suggested this paper offered by Dr. Eagleson, as a substitute for the article which the committee brought in, and Dr. Wylie accepted it. I think there is concession, a great deal of concession, and I hope the brother will not hold to his views.

The Convention was adjourned until 7½, P. M., with prayer by Rev. Dr. Landis, (O. S.), of Danville, Kentucky.

Same place, Nov. 8th, 7½ P. M.

LAST SESSION.

The President took the Chair, and called the Convention to order.

REV. A. G. WALLACE offered the following prayer:—O Lord, our Covenant God! in whom our fathers trusted and were not put to shame; in whom we have trusted, and whom we have found ever the same, faithful, covenant-keeping God; Who hast fulfilled Thy promises to us in the past; Who hast comforted us in the time of trial; Who hast cheered us in our despondency; Who hast sustained us in all the burdens of life, and hast guided us when we have humbly prostrated ourselves before Thee, do Thou, this evening, hear us as we come again before Thee and ask Thy blessing upon us as we engage in deliberations concerning those things that pertain to the glory of Thy Great Name, to the best prosperity and efficiency of Thy Church, and our own personal, spiritual welfare! We thank Thee for all that Thou hast done for us; we thank Thee for all the evidences of Thy favor resting upon us; especially for that spirit of concession, and kind, fraternal love and flowing together of hearts that we have seen on this occasion. And now, as we meet this evening, grant us still more of the spirit of the Lord Jesus Christ! Bind us still more closely. Remove from us everything that would hinder the closest intimacy, the closest union, the utmost confidence, the warmest love. Do Thou, we beseech Thee, guide us into all truth! Guide us, and all Thy people, evermore; and Thy Name, in Christ Jesus, shall have all the praise. Amen!

The minutes of the previous session were read, amended and approved.

Rev. Dr. D. V. McLean remarked, that the wording of the minutes, in one place, seemed to imply that the Convention, as such, would meet on Sunday afternoon for farewell exercises; and wished to know if that was the sense of the Convention.

The Chair explained that it was not; that, however, since many of the delegates proposed staying over the Sabbath, such as desired it should have an opportunity of joining in a farewell meeting.

The question before the House was, the substitute accepted for the fourth article submitted by the Committee on the basis of union.

Rev. Dr. R. Davidson (O. S.,) said:—I only wish to make a brief statement, to pour oil on the troubled waters, not to protract debate. And what I am about to say in two sentences, perhaps, I think will be gratifying to this Convention, and I think it ought to be gratifying to those of our friends who are the advocates of the use of the Psalms. It has been stated on the floor to-day, by some of the brethren, that no concessions have been made from the other side. What I wish to state for the information of the Convention is this: that in The Hymnal just authorized by the Old School General Assembly, the Committee have fifty selections from Rouse's version of the Psalms and the Scottish paraphrases, with the express view of accommodating those of our brethren who have their own peculiar notions on that subject; and this was done in conformity to a letter from a distinguished divine of the United Presbyterian Church. I think it will be gratifying to the Convention to knew that fact.

Rev. Alex. Scott (O. S.):—In passing through Allegheny, the other day, on my way to this Convention, in a conversation with Dr. Elliott, of the Western Theological Seminary,—whose name is a household word among Presbyterians—he made this remark to me: "You may say to the Convention, upon my authority, that old Dr. McMaster" (Gilbert McMaster I believe his name is, whose history you know better than I) "said to me, in a conversation had years ago, that he would be satisfied with a Psalmody containing a metrical version of the Psalms, selections from the Psalms for chanting, and hymns, and that the Churches might have liberty in the use of them."

REV. DR. WILLIAM DAVIDSON (U. P.):—Mr. Chairman, and brethren: It has been with pleasure I have observed that the delegation from our Church has occupied but little time in this Convention. I desire that it may be so in the future. I desire that this matter now before you may be disposed of speedily. I do not look upon our action as final; therefore I am desirous of a speedy disposition of the subject. I wish here to thank this Convention for their kind sentiments expressed toward us, in private and in public, and for the sincere disposition manifested by Christian men from the other bodies represented here, to yield to our wishes so far as might be. I understand, Mr. Chairman, that the delegation from the United Presbyterian Church are ready to vote upon the proposition which is before this Convention. [Applause.] If the Convention itself is willing to vote for this proposition, I am sure that for myself I shall be gratified, and I believe it will be so with very many—with a large proportion of the delegates from that Church. I think, that in all probability, the Convention is ready to vote. [Applause, and cries of "Question! Question!"]

REV. DR. MCMASTER (O. S.) said:—Mr. President, I have occupied less than one minute of the time of this Convention, and I do not expect or wish to occupy much of your time now, or hereafter. And I should not say a word now, merely to express my own opinion, or to define my position; but what I wish to offer may have some influence, perhaps, upon the minds of some of the members of the Convention, or those whom they represent.

I was present at the conversation referred to by the brother who spoke last but one. It occurred twenty-seven years ago last summer, in my own house. I remember the conversation very well.

I will make my speech very short. A brother, the other day, read his speech, that he had written to make more clear, concise, and intelligible; our worthy President advanced upon that, and read his speech in the written words of another; I shall improve, perhaps, a little, even upon that, and read, with your leave, from the printed page.

They are the words of a man who spent his whole long ministry in the respected branch of the Church at whose instance this Convention has been called—the Reformed Presbyterian Church. The first edition of the work was published in 1818; that I now read from is the fourth edition, published less than two years before the death of the author, when in his seventy-fifth year, and in the full exercise of his mental powers. He says:*

"How shall the evil complained of be remedied? The inquiry is reasonable; and to it our response is:

1. "In a faithful version, and with as much elegance as is possible, consistent with fidelity, in *prose* to be chanted; or in *metrical language*—tasteful poetry—to be otherwise sung, restore in its entireness, to the Psalmody of the Church, the Book of Psalms.

2. "If the Church authorize it, collect from the books of inspiration, at large, a volume or volumes" (mark the word; it does not say how many volumes it may be—two, or six, or twelve—the whole Bible, or

---

* On pp. 203 of "An Apology for the Book of Psalms, in Five Letters addressed to the friends of union in the Church of God. By Rev. Gilbert McMaster, D.D. Fourth Edition. Philadelphia: Daniels & Smith, 1852."

any part of it), a volume or volumes of inspired poetic matter, in prose or verse, leaving her ministers and people to use, at pleasure, such collection, or collections.

3. "When the sources of inspired poetry are exhausted," "if any enlightened and sanctified minds wish for more, which is not probable,"—(this was the writer's opinion; you and I may think differently,)—"let the Church, duly impressed with the solemnity of this inquiry, and with the hazard of undertaking to meet that wish, in council endeavor to ascertain what it may, in the case, be *necessary*, *safe*, or *advisable* to do; and thus, by a common consent, settle the *what* and the *how* of the subject of inquiry.

"The version of the Scripture Psalmody, like that of the entire Bible at large, ought not to be a party or a mere sectional affair. It is a matter of general interest, and as such should be viewed and treated." These were the well considered and mature views of the author.

Permit me, in connection with this subject, to refer to the judgment of one whose name is justly of great weight, not only in the whole Presbyterian family, but in many churches and in many lands. May I be permitted with profound reverence and affection to pronounce the illustrious name of DOCTOR JOSEPH ADDISON ALEXANDER, lately of Princeton, New Jersey. In the Introduction to his valuable Translation of, and Commentary on the Psalms, (I have not the book here; if I had my time would not allow me to read: I am confident I can state the substance of what I refer to,) he lays down these four positions, namely:—

1. All the Psalms are poetical: that is, Hebrew poetry, not mere prose.

2. They are all lyrical: that is, designed to be sung with an accompaniment.

3. They are all religious: not merely secular or national. Even those that appear, at first view, to be the most local or national, upon a profounder and fuller examination are found to be religious. And,

4. They are designed to be of permanent use in the church. I do not wish to play upon a word: I understand the term permanent to mean that they are to be used not only through the whole of the Old Testament economy, but through the whole of the New Testament economy as well. All the Psalms are poetical; they are lyrical, that is, designed to be sung; they are religious; they are designed to be permanent, to be used under the Old Testament and under the New. He of course does not say exclusively.

Is there not here a basis upon which all may unite? We have the whole Book of Psalms. We may have a volume, or *volumes*, collected from the Scriptures at large. If enlightened and sanctified minds desire other gospel hymns, the church may do what may be fitting and edifying to be done, all and each being left at liberty to use the whole or any part of the psalmody.

REV. MR. WALLACE of the U. P. Church:—

I wish simply to thank those brethren who not only publicly but privately have spoken to me on the subject under consideration; and I wish them to be assured that even though the basis submitted by the committee should not be adopted by this assembly, that we will always bear in grateful remembrance their kindness and courtesy to us on this occasion. We do most earnestly desire the union of all Presbyterian Churches, and I think that the time of that union is rapidly approaching: though we may differ for a little while, about the basis, it will ultimately be accomplished happily. (Applause.)

Rev. Dr. Harper (U. P.):—I am not authorized, Mr. Chairman, to speak for my Church, the United Presbyterian; I can only speak for myself; but I am free to say that I am pleased with the article under consideration. No union can be formed without some concessions. We might sit here until the millenium before we could form a union, unless we should make up our minds to concede as far as we can on all sides. I believe that that is the spirit that pervades this entire Convention, which on its part has made a concession, I think, in reinstating the Book of Psalms, and giving it a prominence in this article of the basis which it has not had heretofore in the churches—certainly not in the practice of many of these churches. I think that that is a concession, and that it is right. Now, what is asked of the U. P. Church is that we shall bear with our Christian brethren and allow them to sing their hymns if they wish to, if they will allow us to sing our Psalms if we wish to. (Applause.) I will say further that for many years past the U. P. Church has been earnestly seeking a new version of the Psalms. I have myself been on a Committee appointed by the General Assembly of our Church, which has had this matter before them for years, and I will say merely as a matter of information that on last Monday, we ascertained that the U. P. Church had adopted a new version for *eighty-one* of the Psalms, and so I think we are that far on the road toward union. (Applause.) I do not wish to take up any further time, Mr. Chairman; I think that we are prepared to vote.

[Cries of "Question, Question, Question!"]

Rev. Mr. Bratton, (R. P.):—I have been exceedingly sick all day, and not able to be here, and am too sick now to attempt to make any remarks, but I feel, Mr. Chairman, a great deal in regard to this question. I have been one of those who have been called strict, I suppose, in the department of the Church with which I stand connected, and as yet I do not feel like giving up the position occupied by the Reformed Presbyterian Church. I am, as you know, Mr. Chairman, a union man. I have been in favor of union; I am in favor of union; I am in favor of it for many reasons I might state here to-night, that have been stated time and again since this Convention met. I am in favor of it, especially because I feel that there is a necessity that the Church in this country should be united, and united against a common foe. I know that the idea has been rather scouted since we have been here, and yet after all, there is force, in my mind, in an argument like this that scarcely comes from any other. Infidelity in all its shapes and aspects is raising its head in every direction. Not only so, but it is uniting its forces—and I include in infidelity all false religions in the country and world—to do battle against the cause of Christianity; and we need to be united on this account. I need not go on to enumerate many other reasons why the Church ought to be united in this country. And I know too that there can be no union of the Church of God in this country without concession. I am willing to admit that. Not of doctrine, not of truth, however, for there is not one of us ready to give up a single particle of truth; but there must be some concession in the manner of stating and expressing the truth by the various denominations here represented, if we would have union.

It seems that the great difficulty is going to be upon the very matters now under discussion—the psalmody question—and I think, after all, that we have not quite fully understood the position which we occupy toward each other in regard to this matter. We have been disposed I suppose, too much, to think that those who refuse to use the Psalms consider them as unfit for the worship of God; and, on the other hand, they have looked upon us as not really singing the Psalms, but a version of one Rouse. But we do not use Rouse's Psalms; we use a version which, in the first place, was made by one Francis Rouse, to be sure, but which was afterwards revised by the Church of Scotland, and adopted by that Church. We are not sticklers for that version. We know that it is rough and uncouth in language in many places, but, after all, there is a beauty about it which I have not been able to see in any other version of the Psalms. But whenever we shall be able to get a version more smooth, and more agreeable to the times in which we live, and still faithful to the original, we are ready to adopt that. We are ready to unite with the United Presbyterian Church in this, and we appointed a committee two years ago to correspond with the United Presbyterian Committee in regard to that very matter. I believe that we have been scarcely recognized by the committee of that Church, and we have not, as yet, co-operated together, but stand willing to adopt such version. We do not fight for Rouse. We maintain that the Psalms of inspiration should be used in the very best version that can be made, and we are willing to lay down Rouse, or the Scottish version of the Psalms, at any time, and take another.

Now, I would say that I think this matter may be made better, at least; and I would not promise to vote for the proposition, even if the amendment that I am about to offer should be adopted. I have not heard the article, since I have not been able to be here to-day, as I have said. I should like to hear it read.

The Secretary read:—"The Book of Psalms, which is of Divine inspiration, is well adapted to the state of the Church in all ages and circumstances, and should be used in the worship of God; therefore we recommend that a new and faithful version of the Book of Psalms be provided, as soon as practicable. But inasmuch as various collections of Psalmody are used in the different churches, a change in this respect shall not be required."

Mr. Bratton, resuming:—And I would add, "Until the United Church shall prepare a Psalter from the Bible, which shall then be used as the Psalmody of the United Church." I think there can be no danger in adopting an amendment like this. Our action here is not ultimate, and if the United Church does not afterwards please to make such arrangement, why the hymns can be continued. If the Church succeeds in making an arrangement, which can be adapted to the Church, and acceptable to all the branches that may be going into theUnited Church, it does not cut off any liberty. It says "until" the Church shall prepare a Psalter—until the Church, led on by the Spirit of God—led on, as I firmly believe, by the Spirit of God, she will be, at some future day, willing to take the Psalms from the Bible; and if it is not the will of God, or if the Spirit of God does not lead the Church forward; this will never occur. There can be no danger, then, in adopting an amendment like this; and it would go far to unite the minds of members of my Church, and the United Presbyterian Church; and I do think it would be a step in the right direction.

REV. DR. WYLIE (R. P.):—Called for the reading of the Article and Amendment together, and then asked: Do we understand the respected brother, whom we would all exceedingly like to gratify, to be willing to concede the liberty of using hymns until this shall be done?

MR. BRATTON:—I think no other construction could be put upon it.

DR. WYLIE:—Well, that is right. I wanted to ask the brother whether, if this Amendment is adopted, he is willing to vote for the proposition as amended?

MR. BRATTON:—I said at the outset that I was not sure that I would be prepared to vote for it.

REV. G. W. MUSGRAVE, D.D.:—I think it exceedingly unreasonable for the gentleman to want us to make such a concession as that, and yet, at the same time, inform us that he will not vote for it himself. Now, sir, I wish to be perfectly honest and frank in this whole matter. I will neither be entrapped, if I can help it, nor would I entrap anybody else. I will never consent to commit myself to such a principle as that—that the United Church, thus formed, may, by preparing a version of the Psalms that will be agreeable to that gentleman and others who think like him, require its exclusive use. I will never consent to that. I am willing to allow these brethren the fullest liberty to enjoy the privilege of singing their present version, or any other they may prefer; but, surely, it is unreasonable—on some other occasion, and in a different presence, I might even be tempted to say tyrannical—to want to hinder others from the exercise of their liberty. Now, sir, I venerate that version of the Psalms for its antiquity—I speak of the version—I of course profoundly reverence the Book of Psalms indited by the Spirit of God; and I have always been in the habit of using these Psalms, to a very considerable extent, in my public ministry. But, sir, I will never consent to the exclusive use of that Book of Praise. I am no Jew: I am a Christian, I hope. I am not only a Presbyterian, but a Protestant, and I maintain that such a principle is contrary to our published standards, contrary to one of the fundamental principles of our Confession of Faith, which that brother adopts sincerely, I have no doubt, as I do.

Now, sir, when we protest against the authority of popes, and Æcumenical councils, the authority of any human body to legislate on the subject of Christ's laws, what principle do we lay down? On what ground do we raise our protest? Why, upon this: that God alone is Lord of the conscience, and no man, or set of men, has a right to bind my conscience unless they can give me a "thus saith the Lord," for it. Now, sir, if a man says to me, "Thou shalt not sing anything but the Psalms of David," I say to him, "Sir, where is the chapter and verse?" and if he cannot give me Divine authority for such a command, or such a prohibition, as the case may be, I tell him, "Sir, I am a Protestant, and maintain my Christian liberty."

Now, sir, I feel that after all the concession we can make, it will amount to nothing with some people. I do not like either of these articles myself. They are not exactly in accordance with my views and sympathies and feelings. I think that we say very much about the lawfulness not only, but the adaptedness of the Book of Psalms to the public worship of God, as if we would impliedly intimate that our hymnology is not lawful or so well adapted to praise. I love many of the hymns just as I love the Psalms, and if I were to consult my own private views and feelings, whileI would exalt the Book of Psalms, I would speak of the undoubted lawfulness and adaptedness of many of these poetical effusions, these scriptural songs of Zion, to the public worship of God. But, sir, so ardent a lover am I of union, and so desirous am I to accomplish it, that I am willing, perfectly willing, to vote for either of these articles *if*, IF by doing so we can gain these brethren, if they will then, with these articles, consent to unite with us in one Church. If they will not, to what profit will it be to them? saving to laud their own particular psalmody, and throw in the shade our hymnology? I hope now we shall be frank with one another. I am perfectly willing to say what you have said there. But certainly no man has a right to ask us to go further. We cannot do it. That is about as far as a man with my views and feelings and habits can go. *I cannot go any further.* No! Another man says *he* cannot, and there are thousands of men in our churches that cannot.

Now, can we not agree upon that? I am willing to say that, if that will satisfy them. I am willing to say almost anything, except this, that Christians shall not have the privilege of praising God in anything else than Rouse's version of Psalms, or some other version to be approved of by A, B or C. [Cries of "Question! Question!"]

MR. BRATTON rose to explain:—I think that the aged father misapprehends my position and my view altogether. I have listened to a great many addresses made by the father, and am highly pleased, exceedingly pleased with the spirit he has manifested towards all; but I do think that he has misapprehended my intention in making that motion. Now he says that he cannot go any further; he cannot admit this amendment because we intend by it to confine them to the Book of Psalms. Now there is no such intention. It is not a Psalter drawn from the Psalms of the Bible alone, but from the volume of inspiration, that we mean. He says that he loves the hymn. I want to know why? Because it contains Evangelical Scriptural truth. And if you can draw hymns from the Bible; if you can get such translations and such versions from many parts of the Bible, as contain these sentiments, expressed at least as well as in the hymn, as in the Evangelical hymn, I am sure that the father will be ready to adopt it.

As to the vote, I am ready to vote for this proposition, as it is not ultimate, is not a finality, to send it down to the churches. [Continued cries of "Question! Question!"]

ELDER WILLIAM GETTY (U. P.) said:—This afternoon, on this platform, we witnessed what seemed to me the uniting of the two branches of the Presbyterian Church. Now I should like to see something take place in the Convention, to-night, that will get over this difficulty, and this is the great difficulty between the other branches of the Church and the United Presbyterian Church to which I belong. I feel in my heart that the brethren here have conceded far more than I ever expected they would concede. [Applause.] I just want to ask my brethren in the United Presbyterian Church if they are willing to concede *anything?*

Are we to stand on our own platform, and have all the brethren who have been for years, and as long as we have, practising in a different way come over to *our* platform? Do we expect *that* brethren? If they will permit us to sing the old Psalms until we die, is not that enough? [Applause.] And Mr. Chairman, there is no doubt at all, but in the masses of our congregations we will sing the old Psalms as long as we live. ["Good!" and laughter.] And then, what harm can it do our brethren if in the other Churches they sing,

"Rock of ages, cleft for me?"

What harm can it do? Must we have the union on a basis so strong that we would stretch out our hands, and draw them in, and chastise them a little, for singing "Rock of ages?" O, I do earnestly hope and pray that the whole United Presbyterian delegation here this evening will vote unanimously for the article as it stands—as it stands—we do not want any amendment. Let us show that *we* have the spirit that has been in this Convention from the beginning. Let us shake hands with these venerable fathers and brethren here, and consummate the union.

R. C. STEWART, Elder in the U. P. Church:—I am not willing that my brother should express the only sentiments coming from the Eldership of the United Presbyterian Church. I came here, sir, because it has been the ardent wish of my heart for fifteen or twenty years that I might live to see just such a proposition before such a body as this. [Applause.] And I have frankly and candidly expressed my opinion for some years past. For it is fifteen or twenty years since I have been investigating this subject for myself, and for several years my pastor who sits on your right hand will admit and acknowledge that I have frankly stated to him for years past, that just such a proposition as that would satisfy me. [Applause.] I should not have left my family and my business, and travelled well on to six hundred miles, if it had not been for the solitary question before you this moment; and the venerable father on our left (Musgrave) has touched the key-note of the whole subject. [Applause.] I shall never require my brother, in the least degree, to forego his liberty of singing Gospel Evangelical hymns. I would not yield it myself. I sing them now, and I expect to sing them when I go down to my grave! [Continued applause and clapping of hands. Loud cries for "Question!"]

Mr. Bratton was requested to withdraw the amendment, but he declined; the vote was, therefore, taken on it with the following result:

OLD SCHOOL—Unanimous in the negative.

NEW SCHOOL—One in the affirmative.

UNITED PRESBYTERIAN—Unanimous in the negative. (Greeted with applause.)

REFORMED PRESBYTERIAN—Four ayes, six nays.

REFORMED DUTCH—Negative.

CUMBERLAND PRESBYTERIAN—One aye, three nays.

The amendment was declared lost. The main question recurring, the article was read, and the vote taken, as follows:

Old School—Unanimous in favor of it.
New School— " " "
United Presbyterian—Ten ayes, one nay.
Reformed Presbyterian—Six ayes, five nays.
Reformed Dutch—Unanimous in favor of it.
Cumberland Presbyterian— " "

The President declared the article adopted, as follows:

Art. IV. The Book of Psalms, which is of divine inspiration, is well adapted to the state of the Church in all ages and circumstances, and should be used in the worship of God. Therefore, we recommend that a new and faithful version of the Psalms be provided as soon as practicable. But, inasmuch as various collections of Psalmody are used in the different Churches, a change in that respect shall not be required.

The reading of the next article having been called for, the secretary read:

"Art. V.—That the session of each church shall have the right to determine who shall join in communion in the particular Church Committed to their care." [Cries of "Question!"]

Rev. Jonathan Edwards, D.D. (Old School):—I rise, sir, not to discuss that article, but to inquire what it means. I have some difficulty in apprehending the precise object of introducing it. The power of the Session seems to me to be perfectly understood among Presbyterians, and now to introduce a specification of these powers would seem to imply either the introduction of a new element, or some mistake in regard to the history of the Convention. I wish to know what responsibility and risk I am to run by voting that. I am looking back over one article we have adopted, and forward to others, and I can conceive of a case like this, and I wish to know whether the resolution in hand would cover it: If the Session have power over the Communion, is the effect going to be to make the Communion congregational instead of Christian—the table of a particular church rather than the Lord's table in that church? Could a case arise in the United Church where a man of unquestioned standing in his own church, visiting a sister church, could be rejected by that session from sharing in the privileges of the Communion? Could a case arise like this, that a minister assisting the pastor of that church should be left in the pulpit by order of the session, and not permitted to take part in the Sacramental service and Communion? I do not know that anything like this is contemplated, but the introduction of the matter seems to be connected with some point of history not familiar to me.

Elder A. E. Chamberlain (Old School):—I would state that we found in the consultation of the Committee that there were churches, and fathers in the churches, who felt that they ought not to commune with persons who are in the habit of singing hymns. Well brethren, as we went into Convention for the purpose of arranging a basis of union upon which all could stand, we agreed to let these churches determine who should sit at their communion table. It was a compromise, brethren; and yet, for one, I feel in my own heart that it was no compromise at all. I "would not," as Paul said, "eat meat to the end of the world," if it "caused a brother to offend." There are many brethren in these Churches for whom I have a most profound respect, fathers for whom I have the greatest reverence; and, sir, they are conscientious in this matter, and I am willing that thy should enjoy these privileges while they remain upon earth: for I believe that in that glorions Communion of saints above we shall all sit together at one common table, and drink of the fruit of the vine in the Master's Kingdom, without any questions being asked.

It was in order to satisfy the feelings of these brethren that this clause was inserted in the paper.

Rev. Dr. T. W. J. Wylie (Member of the Committee): It was considered that as this paper contemplated a united church, the case which Dr. Edwards supposes was not likely to occur, inasmuch as when all these different denominations should be united in one, then no session would think of making any objection such as he has presented before us; and therefore I think there is no practical difficulty in the matter. There are many in these churches who have been in the habit of practicing close communion, who have adopted the principle that the Communion of the Church should be no more extensive than her discipline; and it is recognizing to a considerable extent that principle and giving to sessions the power which they now claim. Every session at the present time in all these churches, has the authority to admit or to exclude members from the communion; and it is only saying that when we are united, the same authority shall be exercised by the sessions of the United Church. I think, therefore, that there can be no practical difficulty in the matter whatever.

Rev. Dr. Booth (New School):—I rise to state simply, in my own behalf and in behalf, no doubt, of many brethren, that we are touching a principle here, for which, under no circumstances, can we consent to vote. My whole nature—every fibre of my being is opposed to the dogma of close communion in any form. I believe in the Catholic Communion of the Church of Christ; and I am unwilling to be allied, as a New School man, with any such principle as this, or have it introduced into the bond of union, or receive the sanction of this august body, and shall be compelled to vote against it.

Rev. Dr. D. X. Junkin (O. S.):—I thank the brother for his remarks and brother Edwards for his. There is an important principle involved here; and I would be very loath, sir, to have this assembly stultify itself, as it certainly would, by first proposing to form a united church on a broad Catholic basis, and then in the very terms of union making a provision for each session, the least court known to our system, to cut up that church if they see proper, into as many divisions as there are congregations. It is constituting a session of the church with power to make terms of communion and to exclude brethren recognized in other parts of the church as in good standing, from the communion of saints. Whilst with one hand we rear the banner inscribed with that part of the Apostles' Creed, "I believe in the holy Catholic Church, in the communion of saints,"—with the other hand we hold up a motto that some of the saints may be excluded for cause by the lowest court of the Church. Let us not stultify ourselves, sir. No explanation that the committee can give can reconcile me to this position, and it runs far deeper than the Convention has yet perceived, and far deeper than any man of common sense can make plain to those that have not studied the subject, in five minutes. (Applause.)

Rev. George Hill (O. S.):—I have not spoken during the meeting of this Convention, and would not now if it did not seem to me that just as we are coming to that point when we are about to harmonize on a basis, objection is made to a point which I think is of very small importance in comparison with those that we have already passed upon. I wish simply to say that I am an Old School Presbyterian, and that I do hope that the brethren of our denomination at least will not set themselves in opposition to this article of the basis. Our brethren of the Reformed Presbyterian and U. P. Churches have astonished and delighted me, sir, with the spirit of concession, which they have manifested on the subject of Psalmody. When I came here, Mr. Chairman, I had no more thought that we should adopt such a basis on the subject of Psalmody, than I had, scarcely, of flying to my home on wings invented here. And, now, sir, shall we on this subject of communion interpose an obstacle to the harmonizing and uniting of our vote in reference to the basis of union which we are to send down to the churches? I do hope not, Mr. Chairman. It binds no man's conscience. It simply allows a liberty which is now exercised universally in these churches, a liberty which binds none of us that go into it; and as they have allowed us the liberty of singing hymns, contrary to what they themselves practice, shall we not allow them the liberty for the time being (I hope as their minds are enlightened and their hearts expand, the difficulty will melt away) of holding to their communion, as they have allowed us liberty in the singing of hymns?

Rev. Dr. Steele (O. S.):—I have a word to say that may serve to harmonize the brethren. It is, sir, a short amendment. After the words stating that the session shall have the right to determine, etc., add "subject to the review and control of the superior judicatories." According to Presbyterian order these have control of the lower courts. That will make the matter plain and guard against any misapprehension of it.

Rev. W. T. Wylie (N. S.):—I have been placed for a number of years in a position that enables me to understand the full force of that resolution, as I am sure many of the fathers and brethren here cannot understand it; and I think, that a few words of explanation will show all that are concerned in this and have any difficulty in regard to it, that instead of putting chains upon any session, or upon any brethren, this will emancipate and free some who are already held in this difficulty. (Applause.) I have been for ten or twelve years of my ministerial life in connection with the R. P. Church, and during my ministry I have had the privilege of welcoming to the communion table members of other churches, Old School, New School, United Presbyterian, and Methodist brethren, under this view of our standards, that the person who may be admitted to constant fellowship may be admitted to occasional communion; and our session claimed the right to decide whom we would admit to constant fellowship, and whom we would admit to occasional communion; and this gives the session the right. There are many sessions who feel that they would be glad to have this liberty recognized. Instead of restricting we would thus be giving liberty to those who have been deprived of it.

Rev. John Ward (N. S.):—I do not wish to stultify myself, nor do I want any brother to do so. We say the sessions shall have the right—I do not quote the precise words perhaps—to say who shall constitute their communion, and immediately take the right away by the amendment now up. I go against the whole thing. We have lately fought for the Union. We have given hundreds of thousands of our sons and fathers and brothers, who have bathed themselves in blood and death because some States said that they would have rights that the United States did not grant them; and we are saying here to-night that we will grant to sessions a right which this Union Church never can grant to a church within its bounds. I hope this body has too much intelligence to pass a resolution, especially with this amendment, which shall stultify ourselves, and send down the whole matter to the church with a difficulty that we as a New School body, I am sure can never, never adopt.

Rev. Dr. Shedden (O. S.):—I would inquire if in the nature of the case it can be more than temporary if we pass it? I understand by church there not a denomination, but an individual church. If we become a National Church, and are all one as much as an individual church, then shall not the right to say whether a man in good standing in the membership of the National Church shall commune with us be accorded in the regular courts of judicature? Thus, as soon as we become a National Church, sir, the whole thing is settled.

Dr. Wylie:—That is the idea of the Committee.

Rev. Dr. Wm. Davidson (U. P.):—If I knew how to bring this discussion to an end I would speak. I would be pleased, if the Convention were disposed to adopt an amendment of this kind, namely, "that sessions should extend occasional communion to all those whom they would admit to constant fellowship," and just drop it there.

Dr. Wylie:—I would most cordially accept it; it is almost verbatim the language of the testimony of the Reformed Presbyterian Church.

Dr. Davidson:—I would then rather pass that question over. In my Church we get along about as well without that question as with it.

Rev. Dr. Musgrave:—I was going to ask if the Committee would agree to withdraw that article. It is really superfluous.

Rev. J. H. Suydam, (Reformed Dutch Church):—I would move a substitute that the members of each church in the united body shall be considered entitled to commune in any other Church in the united body; and that in respect to other denominations each church session shall be the judge of the qualifications of those whom it shall admit into communion.

The Chair:—The question is upon the amendment of Dr. Steele.

Rev. Dr. Steele:—I would say, in explanation, that every Church session has the power now, to say who may communicate with it; but if this power is abused to do injury to the Church of Christ, the Presbytery has a right to review and control.

Rev. Dr. Henry B. Smith:—I wish to second the suggestion of Dr. Musgrave, that if the session have the power, why need we say a word about it?

Rev. Dr. Davidson:—I move that the whole article be laid upon the table; which was adopted.

The Convention then proceeded to the consideration of the *recommendations* of the Committee, as follows:

1. That we unite in requesting our respective churches in their supreme judicatories, to appoint a committee of five each, which shall constitute a joint committee, whose duty it shall be to meet at a time and place to be agreed upon, and proceed with all convenient dispatch in an attempt to form a basis of union according to the principles of this report, which basis they shall submit to the churches for their consideration and adoption; it being understood that this is not designed to interfere with the pending negotiations for re-union between two of the largest bodies represented in this Convention.

[Unanimously adopted.]

2. As there is so much agreement among all the churches here represented in all essential matters of faith, discipline and order, it is recommended that friendly and fraternal intercourse be cultivated, by interchange of pulpits, by fellowship with one another, in social religious meetings, and by communion with each other at the Lord's table, subject to the regulations of each particular branch of the Church.

THE REV. DR. ALEX. DONALDSON (O. S.):—I am opposed decidedly to this recommendation. We are not now a united body. We propose constraining this body in advance of union to take a position antagonistic to their own views. I would be ashamed of my church if it voted in advance of union to constrain them to depart from their ground. I would be ashamed of myself if I did not solemnly testify against any such thing. My heart is in the matter of union. Our brethren on the other side have conceded nobly. They will have to contend at home with difficulties that some of our brethren know nothing about. They have acted a very noble part; and we would now wish to put upon them the tightest kind of screws that we can apply. My heart would bleed if this house should agree to that, and recommend in the face of their church regulations, and in defiance of their form, that we violate all their rules.

REV. DR. D. X. JUNKIN (O. S.):—That is a good speech, brother. We are only recommending, however, and this resolution only comes from this Convention with the force of a recommendation. And after all, this process herein recommended, is the process by which if we shall ever come to a visible unity, it is to be effected. It is by cultivating the *spirit* of unity. For I tell you, sir, that your body, strong as it is, and much fatigue as it has endured the past few years, would fall apart into many pieces if it was not held together by the Spirit. And our churches would fall to pieces, and ought to fall to pieces, if they are not held together by the Spirit of God. The body of Christ is one by virtue of the indwelling of the Holy Ghost; and I embrace this opportunity in the two or three minutes I have to spare to throw out this idea as a very important one, that we must cultivate "the unity of the Spirit in the bond of peace," if we would ever arrive at visible unity. The Church of God held together by visible unity has been sometimes in her history, that is the nominal church, a curse to the world. When she has had the most perfect visible unity without the spirit of purity and peace, she has been a moral putrefaction, having a Dead Sea beneath her whole surface. The ages that were characterized by the most perfect visible unity were the dark ages. That is history, and we cannot undo it. This recommendation then I look upon as most valuable for the cultivation of peace. You cannot force men to walk together, unless they be agreed. And if agreed—and they will be agreed just in proportion as the Holy Ghost comes down upon them in answer to their earnest prayer, and the people of God speak often one with another in the spirit of this resolution—the Spirit of God will come down and produce heart unity, soul unity, unity in the faith. Then, when brethren are agreed you cannot keep them apart. And we have had demonstration after demonstration here of the danger of attempting too much at once. *Festina lente* ought to be our motto, make haste gently and slowly and with forbearance. I do trust that the remarks of my brother Donaldson will be heeded.

Rev. Dr. W. Davidson (U. P.):—I rise to make a request of the Convention: it is that they strike out the clause "and by communion with each other at the Lord's table," so that it shall read "by interchange of pulpits, and by fellowship with one another in social religious meetings, subject to the regulations of each particular branch of the Church;" and your "regulations," brethren, are to inter-commune with one another when you please; strike that out and you still have your regulations for inter-communion; and it will greatly relieve some of us.

Rev. Dr. T. W. J. Wylie (R. P.):—I feel a great interest in this particular part of the Report, and I think that it is very desirable that we should keep it in the form in which it has been presented. Least of all would I be willing that that portion to which my respected brother, Dr. Davidson, has made objection be omitted.

Dr. Davidson:—I did not make objections, but simply asked for the striking out of the clause for the relief of us at home.

Dr. Wylie:—"For the relief of us at home," I would put it in. Now, I think that we have been brought on by the Spirit of God to feel that we are so much one that we might almost have, if we were here on next Sabbath day, a communion in this Church together. [Applause.] I am fully prepared for that, and would rejoice to see something of that spirit. And I feel that many other brethren of my own church are prepared for it; and I think that the brother who wishes this clause about Communion to be omitted, would not himself have any objection to it! Now, sir, this meets a condition of things, especially in the Reformed Presbyterian Church, which it is very necessary to meet. It is stated in our Testimony that no person should be admitted to occasional communion, who would not be admitted to constant fellowship. This seems to recognize the existence, in our churches, of such a thing as occasional Communion; and I have considered that if there are persons whom we would admit to constant fellowship, those persons we may admit at any time to occasional communion. But, in order to promote our fellowship with one another, in order that we may mingle our Christian sympathies and feelings, in order that we may blend together and be fused into one common mass, it is most desirable to bring us thus together in the Sanctuary, in the ordinary service of the Sabbath, in the social meeting, and, most of all, on the summit of the mount of God, at the Communion table. I feel that this would do very much, indeed, to promote the cause of union, and I have been perfectly astonished that opposition to this has come from the brethren of the Old and New School Presbyterian Churches, who, I had supposed, would at once agree to it, because it is, as I consider it, the principle on which they themselves are acting. They have this interchange of pulpits. They have this mingling together in fellowship meetings. They gather together around the Lord's table. Now, what is this asking from them but what they are already doing, and still intend to do? It appears to me that it recognizes, completely, their position, and is only giving the sanction of this influential Convention to other churches who may not yet be educated up to that, to take the same position.

Let me, now, just read this once more: "As there is so much agreement among all the churches here represented in all essential matters of faith, discipline, and order, it is recommended that friendly and fraternal intercourse be cultivated"—we are all agreed to that, so far. How? There must be some way of doing it. "By interchange of pulpits"—that is done now, I think, in all our churches—"by fellowship with one another in social religious meetings." We do that, "and by communion with each other at the Lord's table"—some of us do that, and some of us do not do that. Now, I would desire very much to have us all brought to do that. That is my heart's wish. Therefore that has been put in this resolution. And in order that none would feel aggrieved, or smaller bodies be compelled to violate their order, it is added: "Subject to the regulations of each particular branch of the Church."

Now in this congregation, when we have communion we have three tables set, one down the middle aisle, and one on each side of the pulpit here. We have tokens given out, cards on which each individual is requested to write his or her name and residence; and when a person wishes to commune with us, that person must apply to the ministers or elders, and get one of these tokens. That gives the liberty to those who are the proper judges, to admit such persons to the Lord's table, and we would still continue to do that according to our own regulations. Now, sir, I think there is no reason why the brethren of these larger churches who themselves practically do all this, should not encourage us also who have not been educated up to the point in this matter. [Applause.]

Rev. Dr. Donaldson (O. S.):—It is very evident that Dr. Wylie has entirely misunderstood, and has lost sight of the proposition to strike off, "subject to the regulation," etc. If that was stricken off, we would recommend the brethren to have intercommunion at the Lord's table. Those brethren who feel tenderly disposed would perhaps come and wish to commune with us under the strength of this direction. If they do so, most assuredly their Presbyteries would take them up and subject them to discipline. There was a proposition that the last clause be stricken out. That would be a recommendation to them to violate the established rules of their Church. That is why we do not wish it. When the way is clear for an intercommunion I shall rejoice, but I do not wish to say to my United Presbyterian brother, "Come and commune with my Body, and risk a trial before your Presbytery to-morrow."

Rev. Dr. George Junkin (O.S.) corresponding member:—My whole fifty-one years of ministerial life have been practiced on that principle. You, sir, with a multitude of the citizens of this city, know what the feeling was here, in the winter before last, when we had a prayer-meeting every afternoon at four o'clock. There never was, within my knowledge of Philadelphia, a state of religious feeling equal to that. At least since I have been acquainted with this city, after fleeing from Virginia, in 1861, there has not been a period in which there has been so much of right Christian feeling, and so large approaches have been made toward a perfect union. This is nature's plan; it is God's plan. There is no other way to unite Christian Churches together, but by having a union *de facto* before you can have a union *pro forma*. Before you have a fact union, you must have union of affection and sentiment. I never missed those meetings, when it was possible for me to attend.

THE CHAIR:—We will have them renewed.

Well: I always attended them, and I became acquainted with a large number of Methodist brethren and Baptist brethren, and I cannot now dwell upon the thought of one dear Baptist brother (Rev. Dr. J. H. Kennard) who is up yonder (in heaven), without the tears starting to my eyes—I saw so much zeal, love and simplicity of holiness in that sainted brother—Kennard—that I cannot think of him without tears. And then I saw many good Methodist brethren in those meetings, Brother Cookman among them, and I have never refused since when called upon to preach for these brethren, whether Methodist, Presbyterian, United Presbyterian, or all,—I have not refused to do so, and by the grace of God I never will. [Applause.] I have preached ten times since the short meeting of our Synod, and am ready to do it again, although I am a little below the mark. I think that this is the way to get together,—to mix in the prayer-meeting, to mix in the pulpit,—by interchanging, and I have been amazed at the few interchanges I hear of in the city of Philadelphia. I hope it will not only receive the approbation, but the warm approbation of this body, and be made the practice of all the brethren who have control of pulpits.

REV. DR. W. E. SCHENCK (O. S.):—I wish to make a suggestion by way of relieving the embarrassment. I think there is danger of consuming a good deal of time needlessly, and of embarrassing some of our brethren by going into particulars without the necessity of doing so. I move, sir, an amendment, that after the words "recommended that friendly and fraternal intercourse be cultivated,"—the words be inserted —"in every practicable way."

REV. DR. M. S. GOODALE (O. S.):—I am, in the providence of God, surrounded by U. P. brethren. They are my nearest neighbors and my best brethren. We act on that principle, and have thus acted for the last few years. We are accustomed to carry out those principles to the full length, and when we came together in our Convention, for there our union began, and along with it the revival of God's work in these churches; and when these brethren appointed seasons of protracted effort, and we went in, and preached and labored with them, and then sat down at the communion table and admitted the converts, it was a union *de facto*, in spirit and in truth. We found no difficulty in acting upon that principle; and it will be like a message from heaven if you can just adopt that resolution, I have no question at all in that region. They are among our very best brethren, and I feel exceedingly anxious that we here assembled shall recommend the whole article, without at all abridging it. I believe it is just what we need.

REV. DR. D. V. MC LEAN (O. S.):—I would like to make an inquiry here, Mr. President. Is this resolution to be recommended to the several supreme judicatories as a part of the Basis of Union in accordance with the resolution we passed before? Or is it a temporary expedient to be adopted in the meantime, until something is done to cultivate this friendly feeling, and prepare the way for it? Is that it? [THE CHAIR:—Yes, sir.] There is a very great difference here. If we recommend this feature of our report to the several judicatories, and ask them to agree upon a Basis of Union in accordance with this, we are doing a very unwise thing, in my judgment, a very unwise thing. But, if we recommend it merely as a temporary matter to prepare the way, we are doing a wise thing; we ought to adopt it. I should like to know if this is the meaning of that paper.

REV. DR. WYLIE:—It is the meaning. We have already passed the articles which were proposed as the basis of Union; we are now considering recommendations to effect and bring about the object of the basis. The simple object of this recommendation is to promote friendly feeling so as to bring us together as soon as possible into one body.

DR. MCLEAN:—Well, with that understanding, sir, I trust we shall see proper to adopt it at once.

REV. DR. WM. DAVIDSON (U. P.):—I have not had an opportunity to speak with all the brethren, but I think I can say in behalf of the delegation that we will all vote for this paper as it now stands amended.

On motion, the amendment "in every practicable way" was laid upon the table.

It was taken up again, however, and the Rev. Wilson Phraner, (O. S.) moved that the amendment "in every practicable way" should come in place of the last clause, "by communion with each other at the Lord's Table, subject, etc.," remarking that out of respect to the feelings of brethren who might have difficulty here, they would do better to avoid a distinct allusion to this matter of intercommunion.

The question being taken, Mr. Phraner's amendment was passed unanimously.

The question recurring upon the paper as amended, the vote was recorded as follows:

OLD SCHOOL—Unanimous in favor.
NEW SCHOOL— " " "
U. P.— " " "
R. P.—Five yeas, one nay.
D. R. and C. P.—Unanimous in favor.

3. That the members of this Convention who may vote for the foregoing basis of Union, to be laid before the churches, shall not thereby be regarded as being committed to advocate its adoption when laid before the branches of the Church respectively, but shall be free to act according to the indications of Providence.

Adopted unanimously by a rising vote.

4. That, in case the above basis of Union should be adopted, a

committee be appointed to lay the action of this Convention before the highest judicatories of the various branches of the Church here represented.

Adopted by a rising unanimous vote.

The vote was now called for and taken, on the adoption of the paper submitted by the Committee, *as a whole*. Rev. Dr. Musgrave urged the recording of the vote, as was customary on such memorable occasions. Time being limited, however, and the hour growing late—10 P. M.—the vote was taken by churches with the following result.

OLD SCHOOL—Unanimous in favor of it.

NEW SCHOOL— " " "

UNITED PRESBYTERIAN—Ten delegates for and one against it.

REFORMED PRESBYTERIAN—Five for and four against it.

REFORMED PROTESTANT DUTCH—Unanimous in favor of it.

CUMBERLAND PRESBYTERIAN—Declined voting.

The Paper was declared by the President adopted by the *Churches* voting, *unanimously*, and is as follows:—

BASIS OF UNION.

I. An acknowledgment of the Old and New Testaments to be the inspired Word of God, and the only infallible rule of faith and practice.

II. That in the United Church, the Westminster Confession of Faith shall be received and adopted, as containing the system of Doctrine taught in the Holy Scriptures; it being understood that this Confession is received in its proper historical, that is, the Calvinistic or Reformed sense.

Whilst the Committee recommend the foregoing basis of doctrine, they wish to be understood as recognizing the orthodoxy of the Larger and Shorter Catechisms; of the Heidelberg Catechism; and of the canons of the Synod of Dort.

III. That the United Church shall receive and adopt the Presbyterian form of Church Government.

IV. The Book of Psalms, which is of Divine inspiration, is well adapted to the state of the Church in all ages and circumstances, and should be used in the worship of God. Therefore, we recommend that a new and faithful version of the Psalms be provided as soon as practicable. But inasmuch as various collections of Psalmody are used in the different Churches, a change in this respect shall not be required.

RECOMMENDATIONS.

1. That we unite in requesting our respective Churches in their supreme Judicatories, to appoint a Committee of five each, which shall constitute a Joint Committee, whose duty it shall be to meet, at a time and place to be agreed upon, and proceed, with all convenient dispatch, in an attempt to form a Basis of Union, according to the principles of this report: which Basis they shall submit to the Churches for their consideration and adoption; it being understood that this is not designed to

interfere with the pending negotiations for union between two of the larger bodies represented in this Convention.

2. As there is so much agreement among the Churches here represented in all essential matters of faith, discipline, and order, it is recommended that friendly and fraternal intercourse be cultivated by interchange of pulpits, by fellowship with one another in social meetings, and in every other practicable way.

3. That the members of the Convention who may vote for the foregoing Basis of Union, to be laid before the Churches, shall not thereby be regarded as being committed to advocate its adoption when laid before the branches of the Church to which they respectively belong; but shall be free to act according to the indications of Providence at the time.

4. That in case the above Basis of Union be adopted, a committee be appointed to lay it before the highest Judicatories of the various branches of the Church, here represented.

The announcement of the result was received with clapping of hands and joyful applause, on the ceasing of which,

The President said:

"The Lord hath done great things for us, whereof we are glad!" How can we better express our feelings than by prayer? I would ask the Rev. Mr. Bell of Iowa, the oldest member of the House, I believe, to lead us in prayer.

A brief prayer of thanksgiving, and of entreaty for the further light and direction of the Divine Spirit was offered, when a member struck up the hymn

"All hail the power of Jesus' name,"

two stanzas of which were sung to the tune "Coronation," by the convention, standing.

Rev. Dr. Spear (O.S.,) then said:—I wish to represent a body of men whose voices have not been heard distinctly here yet—the Foreign Missionaries. I would propose, that inasmuch as this movement originated in the contact of Christianity with heathenism in California, in 1853 and 1856, and then renewed in the North-west, and made the basis of action of the General Assembly, and as the question has essentially one origin, the Missionary element, I would move as follows:

That, this Convention of several parts of the Presbyterian body in the United States of America, in concluding so auspiciously the work assigned to it, of preparing the way for what we trust may be complete organic union, do solemnly return thanks to God, the Father, the Son, and the Holy Ghost, for the manifest answer to the prayers of ourselves and those whom we represent, in granting the sincere spirit of affection and forbearance, strong conviction as to truth and duty, and a prevalent zeal for the honor of His name and the salvation of souls. 2. That this Convention recognizes in the fact, that this great and blessed movement is the outgrowth of missionary efforts, at home and abroad, a new evidence of the Divine favor towards us, and His defence of the Church in every age of Christianity.

Rev A. G. Wallace (U. P.), Chairman of Business Committee, proposed, on his own responsibility, (he did not offer it as a report of the Committee, since they did not have a formal meeting) the following:

Resolved, That in case the highest judicatories of the several Churches should deem it expedient to hold another National Presbyterian Convention, we propose Xenia, Ohio, as the place, and the first Wednesday of November, 1868, as the time of meeting, and request the pastors to act as a Committee of Arrangements.

2. That the basis of representation be two delegates from each Presbytery, and all the Churches be urged to adhere to this strictly.

3. That in said Convention, as in this, all votes, on every question affecting the principles and practice of any Church, shall be taken by each Church separately, and the vote of each shall be regarded as a unit.

4. That the first Sabbath of May, 1868, be recommended as a day of humiliation, in view of the divisions of the Church, and prayer for a righteous and happy union.

A brother objected to making the Sabbath day, which is a great festival day in the Church, a season of humiliation. The last Wednesday in October was proposed and accepted; and thus amended, the resolutions were adopted.

ELDER, A. E. CHAMBERLAIN:—I was instructed to present the following:

Resolved, That, in the judgment of this Convention, much could be accomplished by holding Conventions for prayer and conference by the branches of the Presbyterian Church represented here, with largely increased representation from each of the branches, during the month of January next; that they be held at Pittsburgh, Cleveland, Washington, Dayton and St. Louis, and such other places as may be agreed upon; and that ministers and elders of the Presbyterian family in said cities be requested to make necessary arrangements and issue calls for such meetings.

Unanimously adopted.

THE PRESIDENT announced that His Excellency, Governor Geary, had sent his congratulations to the Convention, regretting that engagements he could not control, prevented his being with them that evening; but that his excellent and worthy friend, ex-Governor Pollock, was with them. Governor Pollock was invited to a seat upon the platform.

REV. WILLIAM DAVIDSON, D.D., United Presbyterian, Chairman of the Committee to prepare an Address to the Churches on the subject of Union, reported and read the *Address*, as follows:

ADDRESS.

The Presbyterian National Convention, assembled November 8th, in the city of Philadelphia, sends to the ministers, elders, and people represented in this body, cordial Christian salutations.

Fathers and Brethren:—In accordance with our appointment by you we are convened in this place, for prayer and conference, in reference to the terms upon which the respective Churches might be united. And now that we have agreed upon a Basis of Union, which we herewith sub-

10

mit for your candid and prayerful consideration, allow us, ere we separate, and return to our homes, from a work which has been to us a labor of love and sacred joy, to address to you a few words.

The Basis we submit has been adopted, after careful and prayerful consideration. We do not propose it as perfect, or as an ultimatum. Possibly you may desire to modify it. If so, it is in your power. We submit it, that you may give it your serious and earnest attention. Not the wisdom of our action, but the unspeakable importance of the subject, impels us to ask this at your hands; and we trust the infinite wisdom and grace of God may guide you to just conclusions.

"*The unspeakable importance of the subject,*" we say; and, brethren, is it not so? Is it not the revealed will of God that His Church should have corporate union and communion on a Scriptural Basis? Can we be Presbyterians at all, and deny or doubt this? Did not the Divine Saviour of men, in His last great intercessory prayer on earth, and even when already entering upon His unutterable agony, pray for such a measure of spiritual oneness as would necessarily involve the corporate union of all the churches living in the same place? And does not the same great doctrine of corporate ecclesiastical union appear, again and again, inculcated with great fervor, in the lives and writings of His Apostles, and elsewhere in the Holy Scriptures? Do not divisions and schisms in the Church, engendering, intensifying, and perpetuating discord and strife among brethren, grieve the Holy Spirit of God, who is the Spirit of peace, and unity, and love? And are they not pleasing to the spirit and prince of darkness, their author and fomenter? Do not the instincts of every regenerated soul revolt at these spectacles of division and strife among brethren; and this because they have most surely "been taught of God to love one another?"

Undoubtedly, there is a great and constantly increasing desire for union among the Christians of this land at this time, and especially among Presbyterians. We thankfully hail this as an auspicious sign of the times, and believe that the mighty and merciful hand of God has produced it. We believe that it is a fruit of His good Spirit in the hearts of His children, and that it should be religiously cherished.

Nor has this desire for union come too soon. Great dangers threaten us, and great fields invite us. It is full time we should make an honest and earnest effort to unite the forces which division weakens; to husband and turn to the best account the resources which our discords squander, and to go forth, with united heart and hand, to the immense, the glorious task before us. Is it not so? What is the work to be done? First, we must meet the organized opposition of the foes of God and His cause. Ungodliness, Sabbath-breaking, profanity, intemperance, vice, and crime, do every where abound and increase. Romanism, already a formidable power, and daily increasing, is boastful and hopeful of accomplishing, at no distant day, the subversion and extinction of our Protestant Christianity. Heresy, in many forms, environs us. Infidelity is spread abroad throughout the nation, and threatens to become a moral epidemic throughout Christendom. With all these we must grapple at once, and either overcome them, or be overcome by them.

And all this is but the beginning of our task. An immense Home Mission field—the greatest God ever gave to the Church of any nation

—demands our care. Already four millions of blacks, and a like number of ignorant and neglected whites, stretch out imploring hands from the sunny south, and call to us for help. Equal millions in the cities and rural districts of the North, and in the far West are in equal need. Vast bodies of our population, in all quarters of the land, are living beyond the pale of adequate Christian instruction and influence.

Meanwhile, our population is increasing with unexampled rapidity. In a third of a century we shall be one hundred millions of people in this land. In a century, should all things continue favorable to the increase of population, we will be four hundred millions of people, and the child is now born who will live to see this teeming population. For the evangelization of this great people, in this short period, the Church must make provision, or prove recreant to her trust.

Nor is this all. "The field is the world." For centuries the Church has prayed the reigning Head that His "Gospel might have free course" among the nations. At length He has heard her prayer, and in our day has thrown open the gates of the nations, and bidden her go in and possess the land. The Chinese wall has fallen; Greece again rings the Macedonian cry, "Come over and help us;" and Ethiopia is stretching out her hands to God.

Dear brethren, what a vast and glorious work is before us. And then, if you will only use them aright, what vast resources of every kind has God given us. They are sufficient. They are abundant. We are well able to possess the land if we will only unite our strength, husband our resources, and, in God's name, go forth to the toils, and tears, and triumphs of the great work before us. But if we continue to bite and devour one another, we shall be consumed one of another. TEKEL will be written upon us. The enemy will, for the time, triumph. Our failure to do our duty will probably bring untold miseries upon this land, and upon all the earth. Additional generations of this world's population, by thousands of millions, will continue to go down to a dark, a burning, and an everlasting hell; and in the great and dreadful day will lift up their hands in witness against us, and with tongues of torment will say, "You did it."

Ought we not, then, in all humility, earnestness, and prayer, to make the effort for union, and see if it cannot be attained on a Scriptural basis? Perfect uniformity in *all* things pertaining to doctrine, discipline, and worship, may not be attainable; but ought we not, in view of all these things, to ask ourselves, "Is perfect uniformity on points of minor importance necessary?" Is it indeed so, that charity, and forbearance, and long-suffering, and brotherly kindness have ceased to be Christian graces in the Church of God? And if not, is it not, in the awful urgency and solemnity of the present crisis, our duty to inquire how far we may forbear with one another; how far we can conscientiously concede to one another; how far we can, without sin, yield to one another's views and predilections? And this all the more, in view of our substantial agreement in doctrine, worship and order.

Brethren, we invite you to persevere in the work, now so happily begun, of seeking the peace and the prosperity of Zion. By all that is sacred in the revealed will and authority of God—by all that is solemn in the dying prayer of Jesus—by all that is sweet, edifying, and sacred in the communion of saints—by all that is alarming in the threatening aspect of the organized hosts of darkness, as they muster and marshal their battalions in eager array on every side—by all that is dreadful in the calamities that threaten our land, and by all that is frightful in the sight of a world of perishing souls—by all the vast opportunities which are before us in the home and foreign fields, for successful missionary effort—by the past glories of the Presbyterian name, glories now obscured by our unblessed divisions, but which we fondly hope we shall see shine forth once more in full-orbed splendor before we die—by all that is near, and dear, and sacred to the Christian heart, for time and for eternity, we ask, we beg, we implore you, to make unceasing effort, and offer unceasing prayer, until the scattered tribes of our Presbyterian Israel shall be gathered into one.

The address was received with applause.

A. E. Chamberlain (O. S.):—Moved its adoption.

The Rev. Dr. D. X. Junkin (O. S.):—Moved that wherever the word "corporate" occurs it should be substituted by the word "closer," which would answer every purpose. His objection was that it is applied to our Saviour's intercessory prayer and represents Him as praying for a corporate union of the church similar to that which is between the Father and the Son.

Dr. Davidson explained that He prays for such a measure of spiritual unity as involves corporate unity.

On motion the amendment was laid on the table.

The address was thereupon adopted unanimously.

The President:—God grant that that address may go forth in the same spirit in which it is written, and be accompanied by the Divine Spirit to all hearts!

A Delegate's resolutions were here brought up, but were withdrawn by the mover, at the general desire of the Convention, the objection being urged that the idea of union in the Presbyterian Church could not be traced to any one department or section of her work, but had its origin at different times, and in thousands of hearts in different localities, at home and abroad.

The President here read a letter from the eminent missionary, Alexander Duff, D.D., as follows:

The Grange, Edinburgh,
October 23d, 1867.

My Very Dear Friend:—After an absence of three months in the South I have just returned to Edinburgh; and among a pile of letters and documents I found yours of the 7th. For some time to come every moment will be fully occupied, and I indeed may say, occupied beyond my strength, as my state of health remains much as it was. On this account I am grieved to think that I cannot properly write to you such a letter as I would on the subject of your National Convention of the Presbyterian Church on the subject of Union.

I do rejoice that such a meeting is to be held; if it be only for prayer —prayer for the effusion of the Holy Spirit.

From what I know of human nature with its hereditary prejudices, I have long been satisfied that it is not by arguments, however clear, or human eloquence however electrical at the time, that real Christian Union will spring whether among individuals or churches.

Real union must spring from souls under the mighty influence of divine grace; just as naturally as water flows from a perennial fountain. Look at the result of the Pentecostal effusion! So long as the disciples, though consisting of men from distant and different regions of the earth, many local prejudices clinging to them, continued under the full influence of that out-pouring, they continued of one heart and one mind—and for a time even of one purse.

But I cannot dwell on the subject farther than to say, Look for union, not so much to the force of logic as to the power of prayer, with its resulting influences of grace. If men be full of faith and the Holy Ghost they can no longer keep asunder from each other, but will be drawn instinctively and resistlessly towards each other as surely as particles of matter are drawn together by the attraction of affinity, or suns and planets by the attraction of gravitation. I regret extremely that I cannot go into the subject at all at present. Though not with you in person, I shall be with you in spirit and in prayer. Do, if possible, by God's blessing, set an example which may raise the churches in this land to follow it.

Yours very affectionately,

(Signed) ALEXANDER DUFF.

To Geo. H. Stuart, Philadelphia.

The President also announced that he had received a letter from the Rev. David Herron, a missionary of the Saharanpur Presbytery in India, who had desired to be present; from which the following is an extract:—

"St. Catharines, C. W.
"November 4th, 1867.

"I am truly sorry that I shall not be able to be present at the Convention to meet on Wednesday, but my heart and prayers are with you. May He, whose last prayer on earth was—that all His people might be one—be with you, and may every member of the Convention have the same mind that was in Him. You know my views on this subject. I believe that the world will not be led to believe in Christ, till his disciples are visibly united in love and effort. Is not this a plain inference from his own words, 'That they also may be one in us, *that the world may believe that Thou hast sent me?*'

"I shall go back to the heathen with new hope for the success of our labors from this Convention. The work that you are commencing must *go on.* The commands of Christ, the instincts of the spiritual life, the awakened feelings of Christian brotherhood, and the necessities of the work of Christ in the world, all imperatively demand it. This work must *succeed.* The prayer of Christ secures its success. 'Him the Father heareth always.' Christ's prayers are predictions, uttered in the most solemn and affecting manner—coming as it were, from the heart of God with earnest longing for their accomplishment.

"May God bless you all.

"Yours in the bonds of the Gospel,

"DAVID HERRON."

The President also announced letters from the Rev. Drs. Howard, O. S., Cuyler, N. S., and others, expressing warm interest in the Convention and bidding it God speed in its work and labor of love.

Rev. Dr. Breed extended an invitation to such members of the Convention as designed remaining over the Sabbath to meet in his church, (the West Spruce Street) at 3½ o'clock in the afternoon, for a season of communion with one another, and prayer for the descent of the Spirit of God upon them and upon the churches which they represented.

Rev. S. C. Logan (O. S.):—I have an item of news. Since this Convention met, I have received a letter from a Presbytery just organized in Central Georgia by colored Presbyterians, called the John Knox Presbytery. They put forth a manifesto in which they ask to be recognized as a part of the Presbyterian family. They beg to be remembered by God's Presbyterian people. They have thirteen churches, and five ministers ordained.

Rev. Mr. Chamberlain, of Brazil:—I wish to call the attention of Presbyterian brethren to the fact that a Presbytery exists in Brazil, in South America, and that we believe that Brazil belongs to Presbyterians by pre-emption. We bought it with blood more than 300 years ago. The first Protestant mission in this Western Hemisphere was begun in Brazil, in Rio Janeiro, the present capital. That mission was extinguished in blood. The head of the Colony sent forth by Coligni, Huguenots, betrayed the Colonists into the hands of the Portuguese and Roman Catholics, and all the ministers who had gone forth from Geneva, ordained ministers to preach the Gospel to the natives, the aborigines of the country, were permitted the alternative of embarking in an unseaworthy vessel, or recanting their faith. Those who chose to remain, or refused to recant, perished. There the first blood of martyrs for the faith was shed on this Western Hemisphere, and God has recognized this fact in the history of modern missions. His covenant stands forever. From the time that the Old School Presbyterian Church entered that land—other churches have entered and retired from it—to this hour, we have had nothing but encouragement. The only discouragement we have had, has been in the fact that the Church at home has not been ready to come up to the mark which God has placed for us in Brazil. We hold that it is not only ours by pre-emption, but that it is ours by the Providence of God in regard to our mission, and ours also by the Providence of God in giving that country a form of Government which is Presbyterian and Republican, although it is nominally called an Empire; for you know the representative system is in the whole Empire, and the principle of parity is perhaps as clear to the Brazilian as to the American. We have there a wide and hopeful field of labor. There are now three Churches and three Presbyteries in the Empire, and we are desirous of welcoming to our bounds brethren of all these denominations.

Rev. S. C. Logan (O. S.) offered the following, which was adopted:

Resolved, That the President of the Convention be authorized to furnish to the secretaries the names of gentlemen composing the committees to report to the highest judicatories of the different branches of the Church represented in the Convention, the proceedings of this body.

The following are the names so furnished:

To report to the

OLD SCHOOL GENERAL ASSEMBLY, TO MEET IN ALBANY, N. Y., MAY 21st, 1868.

Rev. S. W. Fisher, D.D.—N. S.
" J. Y. Scouller, D.D.—U. P.
" John McMillan,—R. P.
O. E. Wood, Esq.,—N. S.
Wm. Getty, Esq.,—U. P.

NEW SCHOOL GENERAL ASSEMBLY, TO MEET IN HARRISBURG, PA., MAY 21st, 1868.

Rev. G. W. Musgrave, D.D.—O. S.
" William Davidson, D.D.—U. P.
" W. S. Bratton,—R. P.
Hon. Chas. D. Drake,—O. S.
James McMillan, Esq.,—R. P.

UNITED PRESBYTERIAN GENERAL ASSEMBLY, TO MEET IN ARGYLE, N. Y., MAY 27th, 1868.

Rev. J. F. Stearns, D.D.—N. S.
" M. S. Goodale, D.D.—O. S.
" T. W. J. Wylie, D.D.—R. P.
Robert Carter, Esq.—O. S.
Edward Miller, Esq.—N. S.

GENERAL SYNOD REFORMED PRESBYTERIAN CHURCH, TO MEET IN PITTSBURGH, PA., MAY 20th, 1868.

Rev. George Marshall, D.D.—O. S.
" C. P. Wing, D.D.—N. S.
" A. G. Wallace,—U. P.
Hon. H. W. Williams, LL.D.—N. S.
" Wm. M. Francis,—O. S.

Rev J. H. Suydam, Reformed Dutch, offered a preamble and resolution, which were adopted, as follows:—

In view of the fact that the Reformed Protestant Dutch Church is represented in this Convention by only one Classis, *viz:* that of Philadelphia,

Resolved, That the reference of the Basis of Union adopted by this Convention to the several Synods of said Church, be left entirely to this Classis.

So that, in the appointment of the above Committees, the Reformed Dutch Church was omitted.

On motion of Rev. D. V. McLean, D.D., it was ordered that the Secretaries be instructed to deposit the original minutes of this Convention with The Presbyterian Historical Society, located at Philadelphia. It has now in its possession, the Doctor explained, a vast treasury of the early documentary history of the Presbyterian Church, and is endeavoring to get a documentary history of all its branches. The General Assembly of the Old School Church has deposited a large portion of its most valuable publications there.

Rev. A. G. Wallace, from the Permanent Business Committee, reported the following resolutions, which were adopted.

1. That the thanks of this Convention are hereby returned to the Trustees of the First Reformed Presbyterian Congregation, for the use of their commodious Church edifice for the services of the body.

2. That the warm and earnest thanks of the Convention are due and are hereby given to the citizens and families of Philadelphia, for their large-hearted hospitality to us during our sessions; and that we will return to our homes with a grateful sense of the Christian love which welcomed our assembling, and blessed our sojourn among them.*

3. Especially that we bear away with us a thankful and happy remembrance of the exceedingly pleasant and liberal *Banquet* provided by the Committee of Arrangements, in the Sabbath-school room on the evening of Thursday, the 7th inst.

4. That the thanks of the Committee be tendered to the Committee of Arrangements for their wise and efficient plans in regard to the meeting of this body; To Elder Wm. Getty, Chairman of the Committee on Entertainment, for his laborious and successful efforts to provide for our comfort; To the Rail Road Companies for their generous liberality in conveying members to and from the Convention on reduced or half fares; to the reporters of the press for their full and faithful reports of our proceedings; and to our indefatigable secretaries for the faithful performance of the arduous duties assigned them.

---

* The following Resolution was subsequently adopted by the Committee of Arrangements.
Resolved, That the thanks of this Committee be tendered to the Proprietors of the Girard House and Merchants' Hotel, for their generous entertainment, free of charge, of Delegates of the Convention.

Resolved, Also, that the secretaries be directed to publish the minutes and proceedings of the Convention in pamphlet form, and to forward a copy to the address of each Delegate.

REV. DR. T. W. J. WYLIE, said:—I think we have overlooked the circumstance that we have present with us, one whom we all honor, esteem, and love as a Christian Statesman—I mean Ex-Gov. Pollock, and I move that he be invited to take a seat as an Honorary member of this Presbyterian National Union Convention.

Carried unanimously.

REV. DR. CHAS. C. BEATTY moved that Gov. Pollock be invited to take the Chair, pro tem.

GEO. H. STUART, President, said:—"I shall be happy to give way to Gov. Pollock at all times," and surrendered the chair to the Ex-Governor, who took it amid applause.

REV. DR. BEATTY, seconded by REV. B. W. CHIDLAW, said:—I desire to submit to you the following motion: "Resolved, that the thanks of this National Presbyterian Convention be given to GEORGE H. STUART, our worthy and excellent President, for the impartiality and ability with which he has presided over its meetings and deliberations, and that our temporary President now express to him these thanks.

EX-GOV. POLLOCK:—Gentlemen of the Convention, you have heard the resolution; are you ready for the question?

The vote was taken standing, and was unanimous.

GOV. POLLOCK, then resumed, addressing Mr. Stuart thus:—My honored friend, by the terms of the resolution just passed with a unanimity complimentary to the Convention as well as to the object of the resolution, the pleasant duty has been devolved upon me to present to you as the organ of the Convention their thanks for the manner in which you have presided over its deliberations. It affords me very great pleasure thus to communicate the fact that they have appreciated and have recognized in your conduct as their presiding officer, an ability equal to the occasion, and an ability not only equal to the occasion but worthy of the Convention and the object that called them together. I congratulate you, sir, an old, esteemed and honored friend, one who with me has borne the banner of the Reformed Presbyterian Church, one who side by side with other noble spirits has fought many a battle for the truth, and who in the hour of our country's danger and darkness, when the rush and whirl, and storm of war was heard everywhere throughout our land mingling with the groans of the dying and the sighs of the bereaved, have stood where duty called, and where patriotism demanded you to go. I congratulate you, sir, that you have been called on an occasion like this to preside over a Convention gathered not merely to deliberate over matters relating to the interest of our common country, but of a kingdom more glorious than Earth's Empire, and in relation to a Prince whose title is King of Kings, and Lord of Lords. You have been honored. The position is one of dignity, one of grace, and one destined to be historical.

And this Convention—what shall I say of it? Called at an hour when the Providence of God has spoken union with an emphasis, and power that no heart can fail to understand; in an hour when we can hear and feel in the mighty rush of events that to be apart is to violate the rule of Him who has said that He is One—to violate the great thought of the hour. For it is union here, union there, union all around.

Why should this great Presbyterian family be divided? Why should the moral power of our Church be dissipated and wasted? God calls. Everything that is precious in the soul demands union; and in the eloquent language of the Address presented to-night, every consideration drawn from heaven, earth and hell prompts to this onward movement.

Oh, what an hour has this Convention made and marked in the world's history? To-day I witnessed upon this platform a scene that must have filled all heaven with joy—Union—in the full spirit of the gospel of peace—Union in the fulness of the love of Christ. Oh, brethren, I wanted to linger in such an atmosphere, to sit and sing, and enjoy such a foretaste of heaven.

To be brief, my friends, there is a power, there is an attractiveness in the Cross of Christ that makes union not only possible, but disunion impossible; and you have been near that cross, and oh, let me say to you fellow-Christians to-night that the nearer we get to that cross, the more fully within its blaze, the more surrounded by its glory, the less shall we see of self, the less shall we realize of prejudice, the less shall we be disposed to be away from it, and from one another. Precious is that blood. Oh! it has fallen upon many a heart; it has warmed and comforted it; heart has flowed to heart, and in that union of heart sanctified and consecrated by the Spirit of God, you have done the work for him. Yes! *work* for Jesus. That is the power, that is the secret, that is the motive of all this meeting, and of all this union.

God grant that when you shall have adjourned from this meeting; when I and all that are before me shall have passed away from earth—that we may meet in that General Assembly and Church of the first-born, where there is no disunion. No voice of discord is ever heard around the throne; all is union there. Let us begin it here, and continue it there in songs of ceaseless praise!

After the applause which greeted this warm utterance, MR. STUART said:

I have no words, brethren, to convey to you my feelings. The hour is late, and even if I would, I ought not to detain you with words of mine. And there are times, brethren, when we cannot utter the feelings of the heart.

I deserve no thanks from you. I have endeavored to serve you. So far as I knew my duty I tried to do it. I have endeavored, from first to last, to know no man nor denomination in this Convention, but to act as under the eye of the great Head of the Church, and with the thought ever present with me, that I, with you, should have to render my account at the day of final judgment.

We have been seated together for three days on a mount of communion. The sixth, the seventh, and the eighth days of November, 1867, who of us shall ever forget? We shall never all meet again on earth; and if we do not all live to be seated together at the same communion-table, in the same organic Church on earth, blessed be God! there is the hope that every one of us shall meet in the General Assembly and Church of the First-born on high.

I have felt, since I have been brought to know what it is to have Christ for my Saviour, a burning desire to see all the Churches who hold the great fundamental doctrines of the cross of Christ, ONE; and, as preparatory to that, that we, as Presbyterians, should commence the work among ourselves. I am sometimes, brethren, borne down and appalled when I read the records of three of your Assemblies, and discover by your last reports that you have *fourteen hundred* ministers of Christ without a charge, and *eleven hundred and sixty-six* churches without a pastor to go in and out before them, to break to them doctrinally and sacramentally the bread of eternal life. Fourteen hundred ministers of Christ without a charge in the nineteenth century, on the continent of America! Fourteen hundred *Presbyterian* ministers! And why? Because on some minor points—although as three Churches, or four of us, at least, we have already adopted 5133 theological propositions (as embodied in our standards), there are yet some questions that keep us apart! O, brethren! we have got to meet this question of union. With these eleven hundred vacant churches, with these four millions of freedmen, with these thousands and millions of dying men to-day without a knowledge of Jesus Christ, shall we be longer estranged and separate in our work? Yes, my brother of the Reformed Dutch Church, my brother of the United Presbyterian Church, my brothers of the Old School and New School Churches, and my brethren beloved of the Reformed Presbyterian Church, and my brother of the Cumberland Church, this question you and I have to meet at the great day, when the books shall be opened. Shall we, then, stand over questions like these, when souls are passing on to the judgment-seat, without a knowledge of Jesus? Within sound of our voices to-night, in this our beloved Philadelphia, there are thousands who have never been brought to know Christ. Oh! let us arise, and under the Great King and Head of the Church go forth as one United Presbyterian National Church, to take America for King Jesus! [Applause]. May God bless you!

The reading of the minutes of the evening was dispensed with owing to the lateness of the hour, and on motion they were left to the President and Secretaries to examine and prepare for publication.

The 133d Psalm was then sung, beginning

"Behold how good a thing it is,
And how becoming well,
Together such as brethren are
In unity to dwell."

THE REV. JONATHAN EDWARDS, D.D., (O. S.) was then called upon to offer the concluding prayer:

Unto Thee, O Lord, do we lift up our soul! Unto Thee do we give thanks at the remembrance of Thy holiness, at the evidence of Thy presence and Thy covenant faithfulness, at the precious test and experience of Thy grace. Bless the Lord, O our soul, and all that is within us bless His holy name! Our soul doth magnify the Lord; our spirit hath rejoiced in God our Saviour; truly our eyes have seen Thy salvation! Thou hast done great things for us, whereof we are glad; and we bless Thee for all the joy of salvation, the upholding of Thy free Spirit, the fellowship of the saints, and the good hope through grace which shall not make ashamed. And now, to Thee we refer our counsel and aim and work, our resolves, and purposes, and plans. O! our God, we humbly trust that we have aimed at the fulfilling of Thy will, the obeying of the leadings of Thy Providence, the fulfilling and carrying out of Thy purposes concerning us and concerning Thy visible Church. With much unworthiness and weakness, with views all too low, motives all too mixed and unworthy, we have aimed, we have discussed, we have decided, and our work is before Thee. Let it find grace in Thy sight; and let us be mercifully accepted in these our plans, the thoughts of our heart, the wisdom of our speech and the unity of our conclusions. May it please Thee to overrule all for good, to accept and to employ for the furtherance of the great end of the actual and visible unity of Thy Church these schemes and resolves of ours. And, O Lord, increase within us Thy work of grace! Give us deeper, richer, more diversified experiences of Thy grace and salvation! Of penitence, and faith, and hope toward God, through our Lord Jesus Christ! And give us ministerial piety, personal consecration, zealous intelligence, patient persistence, and burning desire to save souls and hold forth the word of life and to preach Christ to a dying, a lost, a ruined world! And Oh, may Thy kingdom come! Thy kingdom of grace into our hearts, and into the hearts of all men, and may Thy kingdom of glory be hastened! Even come! So come speedily, blessed Lord Jesus! And when Thou comest to make up Thy jewels, let us be found at Thy right hand, the purchase of Thy dying love, the objects of Thy living care and intercession, the monuments of Thine eternal purpose, Thine all-accomplishing, victorious grace. And at Thy feet we will cast our crowns and before Thy throne we will praise Thy name for all the joy and the blessedness of Thy great salvation! And to the Father, the Son, and the Holy Ghost, the three-one God, and our God, shall be the glory equal, undivided and everlasting! Amen!

The President, Mr. Stuart, then read from the Word of God Rev. v. 11, 12, 13, the following passage:

"And I beheld, and I heard the voice of many angels round about the throne, and the beasts and the elders: and the number of them was ten thousand times ten thousand, and thousands of thousands; saying with a loud voice, Worthy is the Lamb that was slain to receive power, and riches, and wisdom, and strength, and honor, and glory, and blessing. And every creature which is in heaven, and on the earth, and under the earth, and such as are in the sea, and all that are in them, heard I saying, Blessing, and honor, and glory, and power, be unto him that sitteth upon the throne, and unto the Lamb for ever and ever!"—Amen!

The benediction was pronounced by the Rev. C. P. Wing, D.D., N. S., and the Convention declared adjourned *sine die*.

Geo. H. Stuart, *President*.

G. D. Archibald,
R. D. Harper,
Wm. T. Eva, } *Secretaries*.

APPENDIX.

I.—CORRESPONDING MEMBERS.

Old School Presbyterian Church.

NAME.	PRESBYTERY.	STATE.
Rev. A. B. Cross,	Baltimore,	
" Alfred Nevin, D.D.,	Philadelphia,	
" D. M. Kinney, D.D.,	Pittsburgh,	
" John Hall, D.D.,	New York,	
" D. W. Moore,	Newcastle,	
Rev. Prentiss de Veuve,	Philadelphia,	
Geo. W. Burroughs,	Nassau,	
Rev. Robert Wilson,	West Jersey,	
" P. H. Studdiford,	Raritan,	
J. H. Anderson,	"	
A. V. C. Schenck,	Carlisle,	
Rev. Charles Ford,	West Jersey,	
Robert Wilson,	"	
Rev. Alfred Paull,		
" John Erving,	Central Philadelphia,	
" W. D. McKinley,	" "	
" D. A. Cunningham,	" "	
" R. W. Henry,	" "	
" Wm. Radcliffe,	Philadelphia,	
" S. S. Orris,	Huntingdon,	
" Jas. Glendinning,	St. Clairsville,	
" Wm. McElwee,	Philadelphia,	
" J. W. E. Ker,	Northumberland,	
" A. M. Jelly,	Central Philadelphia,	
" R. Proudfit,	New York,	
" J. B. Davis,	Philadelphia,	
" S. A. Gayley,	Maryland,	
" R. M. Patterson,	Philadelphia,	
" Nathan'l C. West,	Brooklyn.	

Corresponding Members, N. S.

NAME.	PRESBYTERY.	STATE.
Rev. Robert Adair,		
Elder S. F. Bodine,	Philadelphia,	
Rev. Albert Barnes,	"	
" Chas. Brown,	"	
" E. B. Bruen,	"	
" Andrew Culver,	"	
" Chas. F. Diver,	"	
" D. H. Emerson,	Wilmington,	Del.
" Wm. Hutton,	Philadelphia,	
" Jno. W. Mears, D.D.,	"	
" John McLeod,	"	
" Daniel March, D.D.,	"	
" J. Y. Mitchell,	"	
" L. Pratt,	"	
" Geo. Van Deurs,	"	
" Geo. W. Wiswell, D.D.,	"	

Corresponding Members, U. P.

NAME.	PRESBYTERY.	STATE.
Rev. Francis Church,	Philadelphia,	
" J. T. Cooper, D.D.,	"	
" James Crowe,	"	
" James Price,	"	
" J. M. Hutchinson,	"	
" W. C. Jackson,	Cedarville,	Ohio.
" Lafayette Marks,	Philadelphia,	
" H. M. Torrence,	"	
" W. J. Wallace,	Newville,	Pa.
" J. T. Wilson,	Brooklyn,	N. Y.

Corresponding Members, R. P.

Rev. Jno. Douglass, D.D.,	Pittsburgh,	Pa.
" A. G. McAuley,	Philadelphia,	"
" Geo. Scott, D.D.,	Pittsburgh,	"
" David Steele,	Philadelphia,	"
" Wm. Sterritt, D D.,	"	"
" Wm. Wilson, D.D., LL.D.	Cincinnati,	Ohio.
" A. G. Wylie,	Duanesburg,	N. Y.

Synod of Canada.

" C. Chiniquy,	Synod of Canada.	Canada.

II.—ADDRESS

In behalf of the Presbyterian National Union Convention, to the Meeting of Clergy and Laity of the Protestant Episcopal Church. By Henry B. Smith, D.D.

FATHERS AND BRETHREN:—We are deputed by the Presbyterian Union Convention, to convey to you our Christian salutations, and to express our Christian fellowship. We heard last evening that prayer had been offered by you in behalf of the great object which brought our Convention together; our prayers were also offered for you; and this Committee was appointed to reciprocate in person your fraternal sympathies. We rejoice in the opportunity thus given, and in the cordiality with which we have been welcomed. We differ, indeed, in some points of external order; but are we not as one in the common faith, in the essentials of Christianity? Have we not all one Lord, one faith, and one baptism?

We desire to express the honor we gladly render to your Church, for its noble services in the cause of our common Christianity, and against our common foes. Many of the reverend names dear to you are also household names in our communion. Much of your noble Christian literature is at home with us, as the works of our divines are also read by you. With all our minor differences on articles not essential and necessary, there is for both of us a broad, common ground, and a broad and common work. Here, your success is ours also, and our success is yours also.

And there are especially two foes against which we must make common cause—superstition and infidelity, Romanism and rationalism, an excessive ritualism on the one hand, and the growing power of materialism and pantheism on the other hand; for both of these undermine the basis of our common Christian faith. For what you have done in this behalf, for your faithful adherence to the essential principles of our Protestant Christianity, and especially for your constant protest against all that would tend to bring us again under the influence of Romanism, into spiritual subjection to a foreign potentate, we desire to express our most cordial sympathy, and to bid you God speed in this work.

And our prayer is, that God would guide and bless you, and give to your Church continual and increased prosperity; and that we may be helpers of one another in every gracious word and deed, provoking one another only to love and good works.

III.—THE FAREWELL MEETING FOR CONFERENCE AND PRAYER.

According to the resolution adopted, after the adjournment of its business sessions, the Convention held a closing meeting for devotional purposes in the West Spruce Street Presbyterian Church, corner of Spruce and Seventeenth Streets, on Sabbath afternoon, the 10th of Nov. At this meeting, which was very largely attended, the same heavenly spirit prevailed, that had characterized the previous sessions of the body, and the scene of that memorable Friday morning was almost reproduced. At half after three the President of the Convention took the chair. The Scripture account of the meeting of Jacob and Esau, in Gen. 33, was read. Rev. Dr. Musgrave led in prayer, and throughout the afternoon there was uncommon fervency in prayer and praise and an earnest and fraternal spirit in the addresses. Such was the eagerness to take part in the services that very often two or three addressed the chair at once.

The first speaker was a father in Israel who said that he represented in himself most of the denominations gathered in the Convention. By his father's side he belonged to one, by his mother's to another; in his youth he was connected with another, and now he was a member of still another, and his heart yearned with affectionate desire to see them all gathered into one ecclesiastical fold. A young brother related his experience in a western town where a few small fragments of several denominations had been for a long time like sheep without a shepherd. By the blessing of God in pouring out His Spirit upon them, they were all gathered in one happy and now prosperous family around one communion table.

The Rev. Mr. Phraner referred in touching terms to the scenes through which the Convention had been brought, and said that while we might never see *all* Christian denominations gathered into one on earth, we should see it at least in heaven.

Dr. Breed dissented from Mr. Phraner's views as to the future union of all denominations here on earth. The Church is one. The truth is one. The Holy Spirit who gave the truth to the Church dwelt in the Church to enlighten it in the knowledge of the truth, and when that one church under the teaching of that one Spirit came to see that one body of truth as it is, they could not choose but be one. Seeing alike they must say the same thing and all act alike.

Rev. Mr. Duffield said that he had often heard of a golden wedding, but he had never until recently known what it was. But he had found out. They had one at his father's house where, children and grand-children all assembled, the patriarch of the flock read from the word of God, and they joined in worship, praise and prayer. After we reached our home again, my little boy said: "Father, this don't seem like home?" "Why, how is that, my son? Your mother is here and I am here, and this is our home." "Well father, anyhow it don't seem like home." Well, to tell the truth, I felt so myself, though I did not like to confess it, and I began to realize that my family was only a minute fraction of the whole. And so going from this Convention I feel that my Church is only a fragment of the great Presbyterian family.

Mr. Chidlaw made one of his heart-stirring addresses. A little child on going home said, "Mother it was a good meeting, and I liked all the speakers, but I liked that man that throwed his hands about best of all." He said, "When I came to this Convention, I felt as I did once with the soldiers down in Tennessee. We were a small squad and the scouts came in with the word that the rebels were upon us; we had a long way to go and a deep swift stream to cross, and how could we cross that stream? But before we reached its margin word met us that a ferry boat was in waiting. I tell you our hearts bounded with joy at the tidings." Well, when on my way to this meeting, I saw a deep swift terrible river before us, and I sighed, "how *shall* we get over." But the moment Robert Carter's prayer was ended, I saw the ferry boat! And then at the conclusion of this brother's speech, saying this he came up to the platform and took Dr. Musgrave's hand shaking it earnestly, "I found myself on the ferry boat, and thank God I have been on it ever since!"

Dr. Musgrave then rose and said: "I had not intended to say one word, but now I cannot refrain from making a confession. Before the Convention met I had very little hope of any practical good from it. But at the close of Robert Carter's prayer I found myself filled with joy and hope, and from that moment I have been one of the happiest men in the world, and believe we now see the way clear toward a glorious union in our Presbyterian Zion."

The meeting continued nearly two hours, and at the close every one felt in his soul, "Surely the Lord was in this place." The meeting closed with the doxology, "Praise God from whom all blessings flow" and the apostolic benediction.

W. P. Breed.

www.ingramcontent.com/pod-product-compliance
Lightning Source LLC
LaVergne TN
LVHW021403110826
845150LV00007B/1769

* 9 7 8 1 4 2 5 5 1 2 1 3 2 *